PANDEMIA
The Pandemic Crisis:
MANAGING DISASTER TRAUMA

James L. Greenstone

Nova Southeastern University

Cover image © Shutterstock, Inc.

Kendall Hunt
publishing company

www.kendallhunt.com
Send all inquiries to:
4050 Westmark Drive
Dubuque, IA 52004-1840

Copyright © 2022 by Kendall Hunt Publishing Company

ISBN 979-8-7657-0571-1

All rights reserved. No part of this publication may be reproduced, stored in a retrieval system, or transmitted, in any form or by any means, electronic, mechanical, photocopying, recording, or otherwise, without the prior written permission of the copyright owner.

Published in the United States of America

Pandemic

"What if you thought of it
as the Jews consider the Sabbath—
the most sacred of times?
Cease from travel.
Cease from buying and selling.
Give up, just for now,
on trying to make the world
different than it is.
Sing. Pray. Touch only those
to whom you commit your life.
Center down.

And when your body has become still,
reach out with your heart.
Know that we are connected
in ways that are terrifying and beautiful.
(You could hardly deny it now.)
Know that our lives
are in one another's hands.
(Surely, that has come clear.)
Do not reach out your hands.
Reach out your heart.
Reach out your words.
Reach out all the tendrils
of compassion that move, invisibly,
where we cannot touch.

Promise this world your love–
for better or for worse,
in sickness and in health,
so long as we all shall live."

–Lynn Ungar 3/11/20

Copyright © 2020 by Lynn Ungar. Reprinted by permission.

Definitions

Pandemia, Pandemy
An epidemic of unusually large proportions, affecting most of the inhabitants of a certain area at the same time. Source: The Free Dictionary

Disaster
A disaster is an emergency wherein the needs of the situation are greater than the resources available to manage them. A disaster may also require altered standards of care for victims of the emergency.

Crisis Intervention
Crisis intervention is the immediate and temporary assistance given to a person, who because of unusual stress renders that person unable to function as he or she normally would, to assist that person in managing the crisis the person is experiencing and to return to his or her usual noncrisis, or precrisis, level of functioning. This must be differentiated from counseling, psychotherapy, or psychoanalysis. Crisis intervention is the psychological equivalent of physical first aid; Emotional First Aid. Those who are experiencing crisis are not "clients," or "patients." They are "victims," or "sufferers." Crisis sufferers are not mentally ill, and all mentally ill persons are not in crisis. Crisis victims can be mentally ill and mentally ill persons can be in crisis.

The fate of the emotionally wounded rests in the hands of the one who does the initial crisis intervention.
—James L. Greenstone

CONTENTS

Foreword vii
Preface ix
Acknowledgments xi
About the Editor xiii

CHAPTER 1: Dealing with the Pandemic Disaster and Resulting Crises 1
    James L. Greenstone

CHAPTER 2: Crisis Intervention/De-Escalation during the Pandemic Disaster 7
    James L. Greenstone

CHAPTER 3: Parents, Kids, and the Pandemic Crisis: Information Designed to Assist Spouses, Parents, and Children in Handling the Pandemic Stress and the Consequences 17
    Sharon C. Leviton

CHAPTER 4: Words Matter in Disaster Response 21
    Sharon C. Leviton

CHAPTER 5: The Orange Bag Denial 29
    James L. Greenstone

CHAPTER 6: The Crisis of the Pandemic: Panic vs. Preparedness 35
    Bethany Shaw and James L. Greenstone

CHAPTER 7: The COVID-19 Crisis and Law Enforcement 51
Officer Weldon Walles

CHAPTER 8: Suicide and Disaster Response 61
James L. Greenstone

CHAPTER 9: Crisis in Families and with Children 69
Sharon C. Leviton

CHAPTER 10: Disaster Public Policy and Law 99
James L. Greenstone

CHAPTER 11: Disaster Conflict Management 193
James L. Greenstone and Sharon C. Leviton

CHAPTER 12: Eating under Stress and Trauma: Its Need at Post-Stress Meetings 223
James L. Greenstone

Concluding Remarks 229
About the Authors 231

FOREWORD

In March 2020, we awoke to what felt like being in a foreign, unknown space. Overnight, the usual became unusual. Longstanding routines were replaced by the need for new scheduling. The mundane became swallowed up by the call for emergency planning. How were we to cope with, live with, and challenge the beast that invaded our space and our lives.

Everyone has been touched in some way by this virus. The word "everyone" means every person, man, woman, child, baby, regardless of race, religion, gender, color, occupation, or station in life. How people have chosen to deal with the pandemic is not static. Individuals and families have chosen their own path for coping. The strength and the fortitude of our neighbors is stellar. The teachers, the nurses, doctors, caregivers, and unsung heroes of all persuasions have displayed a resiliency during this terrible time.

There are those who do not follow advised protocols. There are those who do not respect the well-being of their neighbors and their community. "Me first" is their motto.

We must be a community and act like a community if we want to survive.

Sharon C. Leviton

Contributed by Sharon Leviton. © Kendall Hunt Publishing Company.

PREFACE

This book is about Disaster. This book is about crisis intervention; about conflict and about relevant law.

It is easy and the usual case to study past disasters. Problems and procedures can be examined, discussed, second-guessed, and plans be made. Here we are living through and in the middle of a disaster that has millions of people involved and involved over a considerable period of time. We experience and live it every day and at the same time study and try to benefit from what we have learned. As time passes, change occurs. Some of it is inconvenient. Some of it affects us to our roots. And some of it bodes both good and bad for the aftereffects that will remain when the disaster subsides, and the crises are managed. What will be the positive that may come from this direct and global experience? What will change forever in our world and specifically in the society in which we live? What both positive and negative aspects of this disaster will affect the new, and younger Generation-C, Gen-C? Will we learn that year-round preparation for disaster and crisis situations must be a part of all of our lives or will we merely deny the possibilities and resort to hoarding and panic buying and similar behaviors when the next disaster occurs? Will altered standards of medical and psychological care be more to the forefront of our study and examination than ever before so that we will already know how to handle these severe emergencies when adequate equipment and care may not be readily available to all who need it? We must take this seriously. We must not take the usual positions that say, "Nothing is going to happen," or "If it does happen, it won't happen to me," or "If it does happen to me, it won't be that bad," or "If it happens and it really is that bad, then there is nothing that I can do about it anyway." Preparation requires acceptance that something very bad could happen that must have an effective response in order to survive it. Not an easy stance for most of us.

Let us all resolve to learn and to benefit from what has been experienced by all of us and to be better prepared to handle whatever comes and to have whatever we need to survive it. The material herein is designed to help toward these ends.

James L. Greenstone

ACKNOWLEDGMENTS

Edward S. Rosenbluh, PhD

W. Rodney Fowler, EdD, PhD

ABOUT THE EDITOR

JAMES L. GREENSTONE

EdD, JD, LPC, LMFT, F.A.A.E.T.S., CDM, EMT, Master Peace Officer, Professor

EDUCATION

- EdD, University of North Texas
- JD, Northwestern California University, School of Law
- MS, North Texas State University
- BA, University of Oklahoma
- BSL, Northwestern California University, School of Law
- AAS., El Centro College, Criminal Justice.
- Internship in Clinical Psychology, The Devereux Foundation
- Graduate, Program of Instruction for Lawyers, Harvard University, School of Law

EXPERIENCE

Dr. Greenstone has been in private practice for over 55 years and has taught for 8 years in the Disaster and Emergency Management Program at Nova Southeastern University, Kiran C. Patel College of Osteopathic Medicine. He is a Supervisory Mental Health Specialist with the Disaster Medical Assistance Team, National Disaster Medical System, United States Department of Health and Human Services. Dr. Greenstone served as the Director of Psychological Services for the Fort Worth, Texas Police Department and has been a licensed and commissioned Peace Officer for over 40 years. He recently retired as a Colonel with the Texas Medical Brigade, Texas Military Forces. Dr. Greenstone has extensive publications and multiple disaster deployments. He was selected as Professor of the Year in 2019.

Courses Taught by Dr. Greenstone in the Master of Science in Disaster and Emergency Management (MSDEM) Program
- DEM 6440 Conflict in Times of Disaster
- DEM 6120 Psychosocial Dimensions of Disaster
- DEM 6410 Emergency Preparedness Public Policy and Law

Dealing with the Pandemic Disaster and Resulting Crises

James L. Greenstone, Ed.D., J.D., DABECI

> *You First*
> *Take care of yourself first, then take care of the others around you. If you have what you need, you will be better able to provide for what your loved ones and others need. Encourage those around you to do the same. Take responsibility for yourself.*

What can you do to manage during these difficult times?

1. Make Yourself a Routine and Keep It.
   - Just because you are at home or not where you are accustomed to being, does not mean you cannot have a routine. Routines promote time management and can help to lower anxiety and worry.
2. Exercise at your own pace.
   - Staying physically active will help decrease depression and anxiety.
   - Find a routine for you that matches your needs, abilities, and physical condition.
3. Invest in online Mental Health apps such as Moodpath, Daylio Journal, Youper . . . and so on. Check out an app's authenticity before using. Trust then verify.
4. Spend time doing an activity you love.

rogistok/Shutterstock.com

5. Stay involved in your community.
   - Utilize video chat and some texting. Oovoo, Skype, Facetime, Zoom, and other apps can be used for this.
6. Discuss uncomfortable or unusual feelings that you might have with a peer counselor or mental health professional.
7. Be observant. Notice changes in those closest to you. Notice those with whom you work and about whom you care. If you notice a change in attitude, behavior, feelings, any changes at all regardless of how minor, quietly inquire and be willing to listen. If you are approached for similar reasons, avoid being defensive and realize that they must care about you. Otherwise they would not have bothered. You cannot be everyone's shrink. But you can show that you care and allow them to respond if they would like to. Sometimes this helps more than you may think. And, this is especially true in these times and afterwards. Personal detection of small issues, yours and others, while they are small may help to prevent these same issues from escalating.

On the job:
1. Prepare, prepare, prepare. Uncertain times require preparation before, during, and after the crisis.
2. Start preparing for the next crisis now.
3. Thoroughly understand the policies promulgated by your company, department, or organization. Follow them.
4. Practice social distancing and limit direct contact as possible. Use the 6-foot rule whenever possible.
5. Obtain and properly use authorized personal protective equipment.
6. Use good hygiene techniques for yourself and encourage them for others on the job and even others with whom you may come into contact.
7. Take care of yourself first and foremost. If you get sick, get medical attention. No martyrs needed here.
8. Pay attention to the others with whom you work. Be sensitive to their needs and accept their sensitivity to yours.
9. If you need to have someone showing symptoms transported to a medical facility, have specially trained EMS personnel do the assessment and transportation.
10. Always pay attention to what is going on around you in your immediate vicinity in order to avoid additional risks.
11. Be sure to clean and to disinfect your equipment using designated sprays or wipes.
12. Properly dispose of any used personal protective equipment (PPE) utilized.
13. Use designated procedures for laundering clothing. Avoid shaking your clothes.
14. Even though on-the-job risk is considered to be low for COVID-19, follow the guidelines provided by the Centers for Disease Control (CDC).
15. Begin assembling personal and professional gear that you might need for response to future disaster and crisis situations. Preparation should be an ongoing process rather than playing "catch-up" after the disaster occurs.

At home:
1. Make a to-do list for each day. These need to be realistic and attainable goals for the day of work.
2. Time segment projects and tasks. Schedule them and stick to your schedule as much as possible.

3. Take small breaks throughout your day. Do something different during these breaks. The break itself may not be enough. Doing something different during the break can bring the needed relief.
4. Create realistic due dates for yourself and stick to them as much as possible.
5. Get your news from the most reliable sources that are available. Check out at least two sources when trying to glean the facts. Trust, then verify.
6. Do not overwhelm yourself with too much news and reports all the time. Limit your exposure and get on with other things in your life and the life of your family.
7. Take a walk on a regular basis. If you cannot get outside, walk inside. If you can get outside and walk for at least a little while, the benefits will be there.
8. Be careful about excesses of any kind. Too much news, too much TV, too much coffee, and so on, should be avoided. Find other activities that need doing and occupy yourself doing them and try to have fun with them at the same time. What about art, music, writing, and anything else that gives you a sense of satisfaction. When faced with difficulties, it is often hard to justify such behaviors to ourselves. Doing so may help you to be more effective in the other, more tedious things that you have to do.
9. Find a way to talk to other people. Skype, Facebook, facetime, telephone, and the like. Find what works for you. Even casual connections help you to feel involved and vital. You affect others; they will affect you.
10. If you have a little extra time, see about learning a new skill.
11. Under the circumstances, the establishment of new routines may be necessary. Make them realistic and where children are concerned, make them child friendly. Routines should be predictable and structured and as such will help to deal with the uncertainties and even the stress surrounding the current crisis.
12. Sleep on a regular basis and at established times. Turn off the television and other inputs and allow yourself restful sleep on a regular basis.
13. If you have routine trouble getting restful sleep, consult your doctor.
14. Remember that sometimes sleep patterns are disturbed by stress, stressful situations, and changes in routine. As you adjust to both internal and external changes you may find that your sleep pattern will also adjust and become more restful and rejuvenating.
15. Look for ways to do fun things by yourself, with your significant other, and with other family members.

If you have concerns about your animals there are resources available to you. These include:
- CDC: Animals and Coronavirus Disease 2019: https://www.cdc.gov/coronavirus/2019-ncov/prepare/animals.html
- American Veterinary Medical Association: www.avma.org/resources-tools/animal-health-and-welfare/covid-19
- Texas Veterinary Medical Association: https://www.tvma.org/Resources/COVID-19-Resources

CHECK OUT ONLINE AND TELEPHONIC MENTAL HEALTH RESOURCES THAT ARE AVAILABLE THROUGH YOUR LOCAL MENTAL HEALTH ASSOCIATION OR LOCAL PROVIDER.

If you are in crisis or have suicidal thoughts, please call the 24-hour crisis hotline at (817) 335-3022 or 800-273-8255. You can also text "CONNECT" to 741741 anytime to reach trained, caring volunteers at the National Crisis Text Line.

Preparation for this time and the next:
1. Develop a personal and family plan to obtain what you need now and will likely need in the future to survive this disaster situation and those that we all know will occur in the future.
2. Preparation at all levels, food, water, necessities, toiletries, and the like should be an on-going, year-round process in order to avoid the panic buying or hoarding that often occurs during man-made or natural crises.
3. Develop a mindset of survival rather than adopting the attitudes of most that it probably will not happen to me, it will not be that bad, or even if it is that bad, there is nothing that I can do about it anyway. That is simply not true even though this is a prevalent way of thinking.
4. Put together a "go-bag." Some may be available commercially even though people tend not to buy them. So, put together your own. Include those things that you may need for yourself and for those close to you in the event of a disaster. Plan both for incidents that require you to leave your normal residence as well as those that may require you to shelter-in-place. Plan a bag for each member of your family and keep it stocked and up to date. For specific guidance, see Greenstone's *Elements of Disaster Psychology, and Emotional First Aid: A Field Guide to Crisis Intervention and Psychological Survival.* (2015)

Understanding Crisis and Crisis Intervention/Emotional First Aid

The fate of the emotionally wounded rests in the hands of the one who does the initial crisis intervention.

Crisis is in the eye of the beholder. Crisis involves stress; unusual stress that renders the sufferers unable to cope with their life as they usually would. A disaster exists when the resources available to address the emergency are less than those needed to address the needs of the victims and the overall situation. A disaster can be of any size. The issue is whether or not the needs of those affected by the disaster can be met with the resources available at that time. Overwhelmed resources usually equals disaster as differentiated from an emergency in which adequate resources can be utilized to resolve or to manage the needs of those affected. Here, we are about crisis and about the possibility of overwhelmed resources both personal and public. The greater and more personal the perceived threat, the greater is the likelihood for crisis to occur.

The crisis trilogy presents a way of understanding the causation in crisis situations. The trilogy involves events occurring that are (1) sudden in onset, (2) unexpected by the victims or their significant others, and (3) appear to be arbitrary in nature. All three are major sources of unusual stress. Because crisis is in the eye of the beholder, what is unusual stress for one may not be for someone else. Look at the Crisis Cube (Greenstone, 2008, 2015) to help in understanding this concept. Level of functioning overall, presence or absence of functional emotional problems, experience handling stress and similar daily-life behaviors can be a determiner of a person's susceptibility to experiencing crisis in their life at a particular time. No one is immune to crisis. Enough stress at the wrong time and in the particular person at that time can mean crisis even for the strongest of us. This includes responders and crisis interveners as well. Sherif's (1948, 1956) principles described are very helpful in understanding this and in preparing for such eventualities.

Here is some information about COVID-19 from Johns Hopkins Hospital that you may find helpful: https://www.clpsychiatry.org/wp-content/uploads/Handwashing-advice-from-Johns-Hopkins.pdf.

REFERENCES AND HELPFUL INFORMATION

Centers for Disease Control and Prevention. (2020a, March 10). Interim Guidance for Emergency Medical Services (EMS) Systems and 911 Public Safety Answering Points (PSAPs) for COVID-19 in the United States. https://www.cdc.gov/coronavirus/2019-ncov/hcp/guidance-for-ems.html

Centers for Disease Control and Prevention. (2020b, March 14). What Law Enforcement Personnel Need to Know about Coronavirus Disease 2019 (COVID-19). https://www.cdc.gov/coronavirus/2019-ncov/community/guidance-law-enforcement.html

Greenstone, J. L. (2008). *The elements of disaster psychology: Managing psychosocial trauma—An integrated approach to force protection and acute care.* Charles C. Thomas.

Greenstone, J. L. (2010, Winter). Disaster non-preparedness: The orange bag denial. *International Journal of Emergency Mental Health, Invited Essay, 12*(1), 1–3.

Greenstone, J. L. (2015). *Emotional first aid: Field guide to crisis intervention and psychological survival.* Whole Person Associates.

Greenstone, J. L. (2019). Crisis management: Responding effectively to traumatic crises. *International Journal of Psychology & Behavior Analysis, 5*, 159. doi:https://doi.org/10.15344/2455-3867/2019/159

Sherif, M., & Sherif, C. (1948,1956). *An outline of social psychology.* Harper and Row.

Other material in this report is from the Mental Health Association. Helpful information has been gleaned from various sources in order to provide the best possible during these times of crisis. Every attempt will be made to cite external information given. Other contributors of information contained herein include Carrie Steiner, PsyD., First Responders Wellness Center in Chicago; Johns Hopkins Hospital; American Academy of Experts in Traumatic Stress; *David Belmonte, Content developer for Lexipol; Suzanne Bertisch, M.D., M.P.H.; James Bohnsack, M.D.*

Chapter Takeaways

Personal Notes

Crisis Intervention/De-Escalation during the Pandemic Disaster

James L. Greenstone, Ed.D., J.D., DABECI

What should be the first resort when handling a disaster crisis? Crisis Intervention or De-Escalation.

When a crisis occurs in a person's life it usually occurs suddenly, unexpectedly, and arbitrarily. Such an occurrence tends to raise experienced stress to levels that exceed those in normal, noncrisis times in the individual's life. When this happens, the individual may have difficulty leading his life and making decisions in the way that he normally does. This individual is not as much out-of-control as out-of-structure. And, not mentally ill either. All of us rely on structure in our lives. When that structure is significantly changed, that individual will experience a crisis in life that will not be reconciled until the experienced structure is regained. Since the individual will have some difficulty in regaining this structure alone, the immediate and skillful intervention of a skilled crisis intervener, law enforcement or civilian, could mean the difference between that person being able to get on with life constructively as the individual usually would rather than continuing to deteriorate further into the crisis scenario. The results of this continued deterioration can be psychologically debilitating or even deadly. A crisis is time sensitive and self-limiting. Do nothing and the crisis will eventually end. Where it will end poses the real problem in terms of regaining effective functioning. The following Crisis Cube may help to explain this crisis phenomenon. A detailed explanation of the Cube is contained in the references listed below (Greenstone, 2008, 2015; Greenstone & Leviton, 2011).

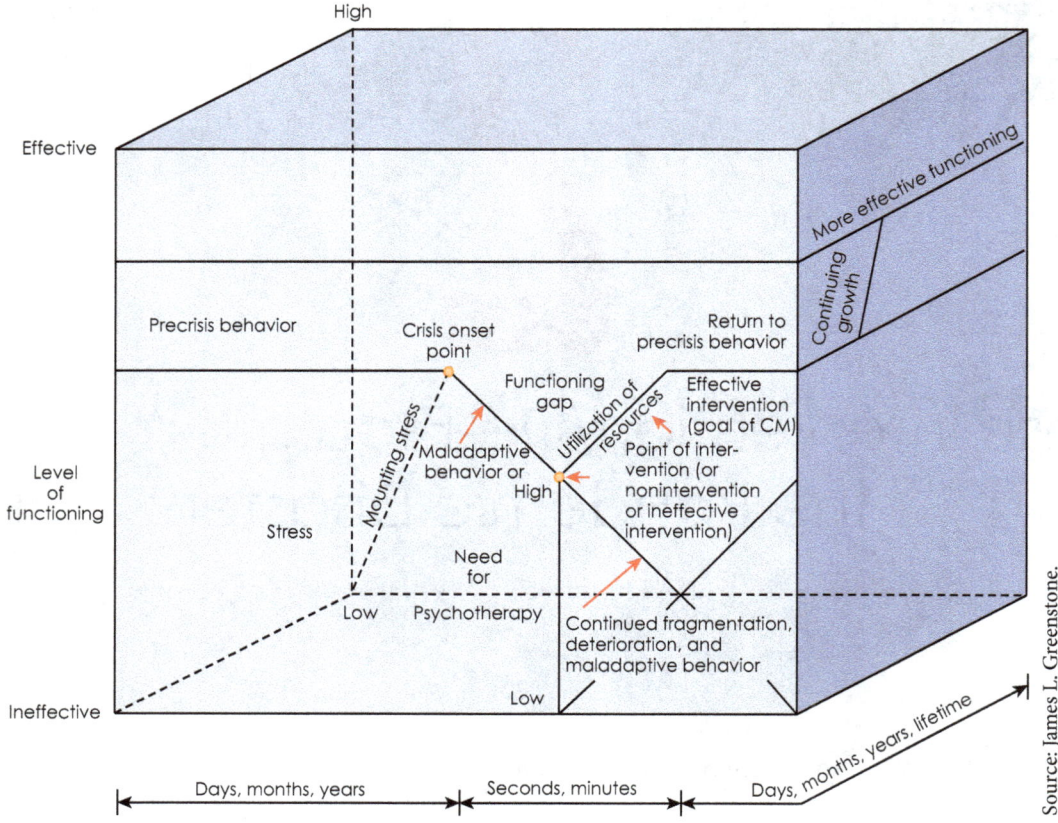

FIGURE 2.1. THE CRISIS CUBE

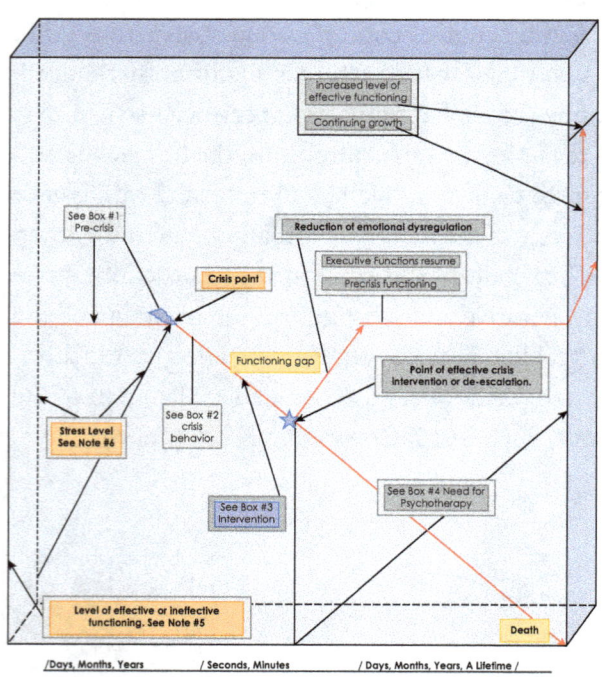

FIGURE 2.2. THE REVISED CRISIS CUBE 2021

Number 1

- Precrisis Behavior (usual behavior)
- Stress increases to overwhelm ability to achieve usual decision-making.
- Executive Functions of the Brain intact to this point. (Prefrontal Cortex)
- Stress remains the issue in creating emotional dysregulation.
- Prefrontal Cortex shuts down limiting executive functions.

Number 2

- Maladaptive Behavior downward spiral begins.
- Emotional Dysregulation continues.
- Amygdala and Limbic System in charge.
- Rational decision-making impaired.

Number 3

- Reasoning not possible.
- Remove victim from crisis or crisis from victim.
- Decisions made for Victim PRN.
- Physical Intervention PRN.
- Let victim settle down.
- Questions that may allow executive functions.
- Return self-control ASAP.
- The quicker the effective intervention, the less likely the need for post crisis psychotherapy.

Note #5: Individual functioning from ineffective to effective.

Note #6: Stress level from low to high.

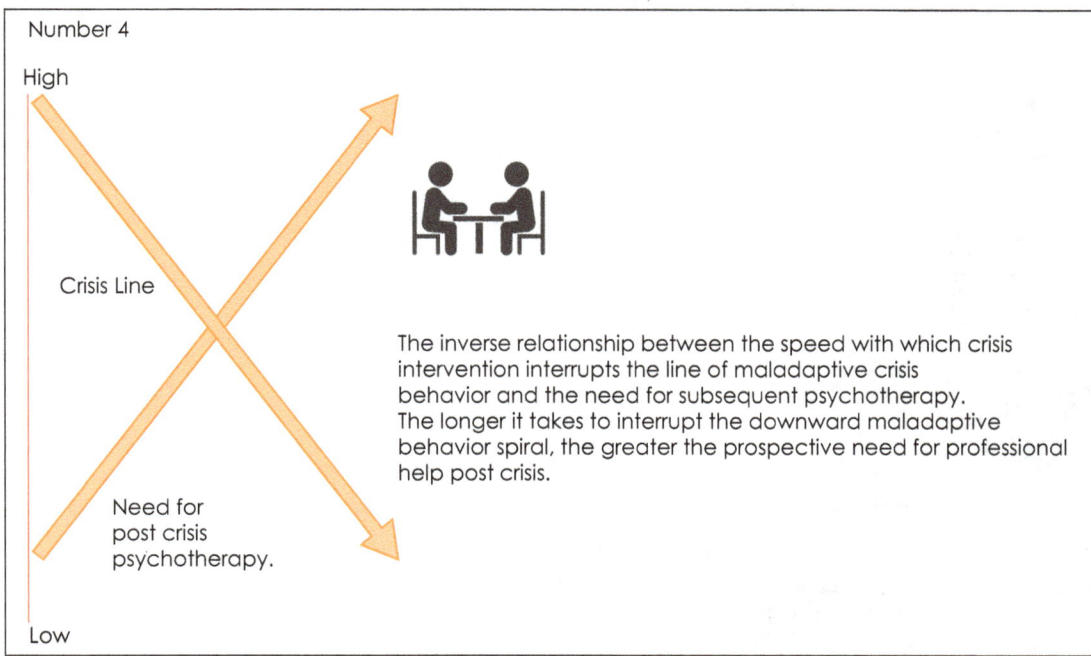

FIGURE 2.2. THE REVISED CRISIS CUBE 2021 (CONT.)

Whatever needs to be done by the trained crisis intervener present during such a situation, they must act immediately, quickly, and decisively. The intervener must seek to control the situation as much as possible until the crisis victim is able to assume that control as the crisis victim usually would. No more, no less. Control can be exhibited by the intervener's willingness to listen to the victim, by helping the individual to move to a safer place as needed, getting the victim to medical assistance if needed, by showing personal confidence that the intervener can and will assist the victim to regain structure in life, and by a willingness to provide thoughtful alternatives to the current behavior of the victim. The intervener is actually acting to some degree instead of the crisis victim but only until that victim can regain self-control. It is important that control of the victim's life be returned to the victim as soon as possible and be done sensitively and consistently. Sometimes questions, requesting permissions, acknowledging strengths, and using good listening skills can bridge this structure-gap in the victim's life.

It is important for the skilled crisis intervener to attempt to find out what is the source of the crisis that the person is experiencing. Sometimes the source will be more obvious to the observant intervener, sometimes not. Observation and a few well-constructed questions combined with a willingness to listen to the responses will often go a long way in this encounter. It is important to understand that the more severe the perceived threat and the greater the danger to the victim, the greater the risk of crisis. The Pandemic—Crisis Continuum below demonstrates how this might occur. It is explained in detail in the references (Greenstone, 2008, 2015; Greenstone & Leviton, 2011).

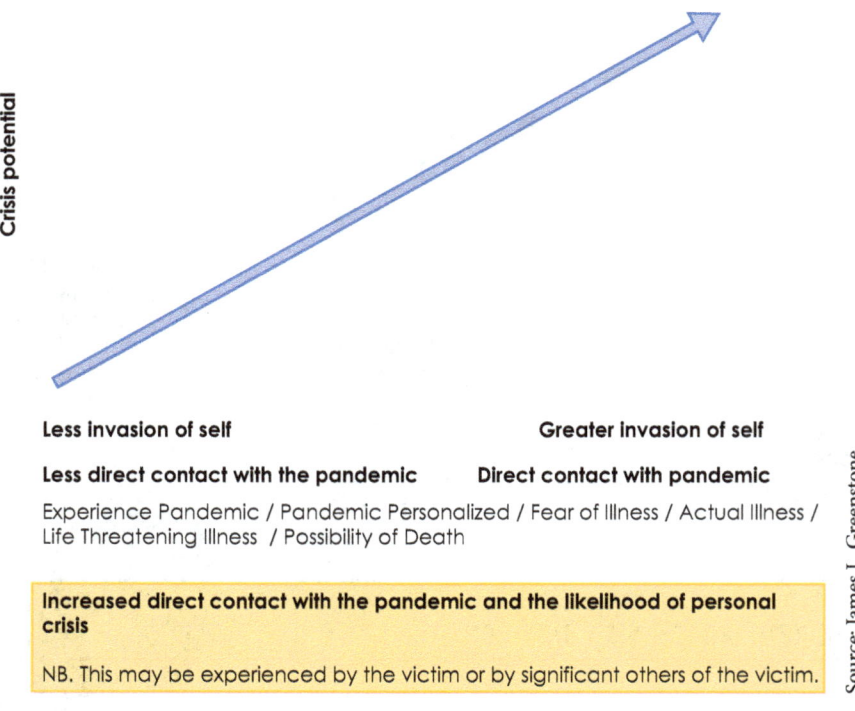

FIGURE 2.3. THE PANDEMIC—CRISIS CONTINUUM

Once some calm and structure has been established or returned to the victim, realistic problem solving can take place. Attempting to reason with a person who is experiencing a crisis may yield little, if any, positive results. If the steps described earlier are followed initially, the likelihood that reasoning and planning will work at this stage will improve dramatically. The intervener has acted immediately, taken control as necessary, been willing to listen without judgment, and has progressively returned control to the victim. Now, it may be possible to get the person additional help as needed, and to include that person in the decision-making process. Always remember, and never forget, that communications between people involves at least two important components. The first component is what the crisis intervener says to the crisis victim. The second is how what was said is understood by the listener. Every attempt should be made to ensure that the message sent is actually the message received. Do not assume anything. Clarify what you said by asking the victim to tell you what was received. Include the crisis victim in the decision-making process as much as possible considering how the victim is faring at that time. Keep the victim involved. By not keeping the victim involved the recovery process tends to enhance the victimhood.

If additional psychological help or psychotherapy is needed and desired by the victim, referrals should be carefully made. The intervener may want to research such sources before suggesting them to the victim. A botched referral can cost both the victim and the intervener an otherwise successful intervention.

Remember the model described earlier: Immediacy, Control, Assessment, Disposition, Referral and Follow-up as needed and as possible. The intervener's concern is with crisis management rather than crisis resolution. They are assisting the sufferer to return to the victim's own level of precrisis functioning.

As may be obvious, utilization of the same model when attempting to assist fellow interveners who are in crisis, this model will work as well. The willingness to help another intervener or responder is important. It is also important to allow another skilled intervener to help you if you may be overwhelmed by your personal or professional situation and are approaching crisis. Think about it. Help each other and help those you serve. It may be that you are the vital link that is needed.

Ask Good and Helpful Questions

- Avoid asking "why" questions.
- Keep your questions present-oriented. "Who," "What," "Where," "When," "How."
- Keep your questions simple.
- Confirm that the sufferer understands your question.
- Avoid complex or multipart questions.
- Ask permission if your actions involve them.
- Do not ask more questions than are necessary.
- Do not assume that silence by the victim means nothing.
- Allow sufficient time for the sufferer to answer the questions asked.
- Ask open-ended questions to gain more information.
  - What happened?
  - Can I talk with you?
  - Will you tell me what is going on?
  - Is there something that I can do to help?
  - How can I assist you?
  - Who can I call to be with you at this time?
  - Where would you like to go?
  - When did this happen to you?
  - Can you tell me a little more?

Responding to the Victim in an Effective Way

Responding to another person's feelings is a delicate process. In gathering information from victims, interveners must handle feelings with care and concern. If the intervener wants the victim to continue to talk about facts pertinent to the problem, the intervener cannot judge, use logic, or attempt to give advice. The individual's feelings must be legitimized. The goal is to increase communication rather than to shut it down.

Crisis Intervention Procedure

What is most often needed in the early stages of the pandemic crisis is crisis management. Not crisis treatment or crisis resolution, but crisis management. This involves such things as, but are not limited to, structure, answers, honesty, direction, and guidance. The model may vary according to style and training, but the goal is the same.

1. Understand and respond to the timeliness of a crisis.
2. Remember that crises are self-limiting.
3. Remember that crises are time limited.
4. Understand that most reactions to a crisis or disaster situation are normal, to be expected, and usual under the circumstances.
5. Know the threats presented by your particular situation.
6. Adjust to the reality that you cannot attend to or preserve every victim.
7. Learn to accept that some victims will die.
8. Encourage self-reliance among victims.
9. Follow the model for crisis intervention of
    Immediacy,
    Control,
    Assessment,
    Disposition,
    Referral, and
    Follow-up.
10. Remember that different people may respond differently to the same situation.
11. Accept your duty to normalize.
12. Educate others so that panic will not ensue.
13. Exude confidence even though you might be scared yourself.
14. Although you will be involved with victims, acknowledge problem ownership of the victim.
15. Avoid overidentification with victims. They need your help, not your pity.
16. Recognize symptoms of psychological stress such as anger, self-blame, isolation, withdrawal, blaming, fear, feeling stunned, variations in mood, feelings of helplessness, the tendency to deny, memory problems, family discord, sadness, and grief.
17. Recognize the physiological symptoms such as limited or no appetite, chest pains, body aches, headaches, gastrointestinal problems, hyperactivity, drug and/or alcohol abuse or misuse, trouble getting to sleep or staying asleep, troubled dreams and nightmares, and low energy levels and fatigue even after rest or sleep.
18. Emphasize the team approach.
19. Force fluids for interveners.
20. Use fluids as indicated for victims.
21. Remember that responses of victims may be mediated by cognitive functioning, physical health, personal relationships, duration and intensity of normal life disruption, personal meaning attached to the

disaster or related events, the usual psychological well-being of the victim precrisis, and by elapsed time since the disaster occurred.
22. Always perform an immediate assessment of victims or sufferers when encountered.
23. Enlist assistance of those able to be of help.
24. Support those who need support.
25. Listen. Listen carefully.
26. Help victims to reconnect with usual and normal support systems.
27. Expect that victims may need help accessing support systems.
28. Be cautious in offering advice to sufferers.
29. Provide the needed psychological structure for a victim.
30. Provide the needed physical structure for a victim.
31. Be reliable in what you say you will do.
32. Return control of the victim's life to the victim as quickly as the victim is able to exercise the control.
33. Do not say that you understand exactly how the victim feels.
34. Remember that your credibility as an intervener is continually being evaluated by the victim.
35. Do not tell victims to stop feeling what they feel.
36. Do not tell victims that they should not feel the way that they feel.
37. Do not tell a victim not to cry. Do not challenge perceptions of the victims. Crisis is always in the eye of the beholder.
38. Never say that you do not think that things are really as bad as the victim says they are.
39. Be careful that your responses to victims do not elicit negative responses or reactions to your intervention. Credibility is at issue.
40. Be respectful of a victim and his or her needs.
41. Intervene within the scope of your competency and resources.
42. Identify those at high risk for immediate referral and treatment.
43. Normalize responses.
44. Empathize with victims.
45. Reduce psychological arousal.
46. Access support for the most distressed victims.
47. Screen for depression and suicide.
48. Ask if the victim has felt depressed: has the victim lost interest in things he or she would normally have interest in; has the victim had thoughts that life was not worth living; and has the victim had recent thoughts about killing himself or herself.
49. Assess suicidal possibilities by focusing on the lethality of the means and the specificity of the plan.
50. Assess for stress disorders by assessing startle responses, emotional numbing, emotional arousal or emotional avoidance, and the persistence of the symptoms.
51. Assess victims for possibilities of alcohol or substance abuse by asking if they felt that they should cut down; have others annoyed them by telling them to cut down on drinking; have they felt guilty about their own drinking; and do they routinely need a drink to start the day in order to overcome a hangover.
52. Those involved may present with many symptoms.
53. Symptoms presented may not be expected.

54. Watch your sufferers for signs of agents to include nausea, muscle aches, respiratory problems, unusual fatigue, and dizziness.
55. Expect many questions about certainty of exposure or degree of exposure.
56. Try to respond to questions about long-term effects in a realistic manner based on what you actually know rather than on unsubstantiated or rumor information.
57. Expect confusion, bewilderment, and the inability to care for self.
58. Expect confusion, anxiety, emotional flailing, and trial-and-error problem-solving behavior.
59. Enlist the aid of victims who you want to help. Not everyone will react to the situation in the same way. Some will want and need to do something helpful. Accept their help as appropriate.

ADDITIONAL RESOURCES

Greenstone, J. L. (2008). *The elements of disaster psychology: Managing psychosocial trauma—An integrated approach to force protection and acute care.* Charles C. Thomas.

Greenstone, J. L. (2015). *Emotional first aid: Field guide to crisis intervention and psychological survival.* Whole Person.

Greenstone, J. L., & Leviton, S. (2011). *Elements of crisis intervention: Crises and how to respond to them* (3rd ed.). Brooks/Cole, Thomson Learning.

Greenstone, J. L. (2019). Crisis management: Responding effectively to traumatic crises. *International Journal of Psychology and Behavioral Analysis, 5*(1), 159–161. doi:https://doi.org/10.15344/2455-3867/2019/159

Chapter Takeaways

Personal Notes

Parents, Kids, and the Pandemic Crisis:
Information Designed to Assist Spouses, Parents, and Children in Handling the Pandemic Stress and the Consequences

Sharon C. Leviton, Ph.D., DABECI

To be used by parents, grandparents, children, spouses, hotline workers, counselors, and peer team members, in an attempt to minimize the psychological trauma resulting from the crisis caused by the pandemic

Every crisis situation involves an element of grief and loss often involves an element of grief. A person grieves over the loss of anything felt to be important in his or her life. If the loss is so great that it totally tears apart the sufferer's well-being, the person will experience crisis. There is no short cut in the grieving process. The sufferer grieves on his or her own internal schedule. There is no such thing as "getting over" this pain, a phrase commonly used to encourage the sufferer. A more realistic goal is to get past it. Managing to get through the pain usually appears as a result of one taking baby steps during the early grieving process.

The world is in the midst of a pandemic crisis. As is usually the case when a crisis of this magnitudes arrives, our children suffer the most. Our children have it worst of all. Generally, they lack even the limited understanding possessed by adults. Their reality is often framed by fantasy, partial truths, and an immature ability to discern what is happening around them.

Contributed by Sharon Leviton. © Kendall Hunt Publishing Company.

For this reason, and many others, this information is provided as a guide. It is a guide for parents, grandparents, children, and the loved ones engaged in an attempt to help themselves and to help each other.

Thirty Steps to Handling the Pandemic and Its Consequences

1. Pull together as a family by establishing a sense of purpose for your family.
2. Allow your feelings to be whatever they are; avoid berating or discounting your feelings or those of your children.
3. Let children talk with you about whatever they need to talk about; their fears, concerns, confusion, anger, sadness, and problems.
4. Talk in words that your child can understand. Avoid euphemisms. Turn off electronic devices as possible.
5. Allow your children to see your grief and be honest with them about your feelings. Avoid as much gore as possible in your expressions.
6. Do not expect your child to resolve your grief.
7. Reassure children that they are safe and will be taken care of.
8. Do not be afraid to say that you do not know the answer to your child's question. Your honesty may make it easier to tolerate the ambiguity in his or her mind.
9. If your kids ask about the possibility of death, tell them that mommy or daddy has a special job to do for their country and that sometimes, under those circumstances, people do die. Reassure them that they will be taken care of and that the parent who is away is doing everything possible to remain safe and to return as soon as possible.
10. If a death occurs, share with the children in terms that they can understand and avoid the tendency to be euphemistic. Straight talk usually works best.
11. Remember that children often take their lead about their own behavior from their parents. They will watch and learn how you handle the unexpected changes to their life, the reality of the pandemic, and injuries or death resulting from it.
12. Children will look to you for structure, guidance, limits, and support. Give it to them.
13. Ask your children what they need from you for you to be helpful to them. Maybe they need a hug, time to talk, play time with you, or straight talk. Different age children will need different things at different times. Adapt to the age and maturity level of your kid.
14. Identify areas of concern in your life over which you have control. Exercise that control.
15. Have realistic expectations of yourself and your children in order to minimize stress.
16. Be realistic about your child's role in the family while a husband or wife is absent. Remember that a five-year-old cannot be the "man of the house" or a "mature young lady." Avoid assigning impossible tasks for children to fulfill.
17. Write letters to the loved ones who are away and encourage children to do the same. Letters should be newsy, informative and tell about home, family happenings, and life cycle events. Parents and older children can write letters. The younger child can draw pictures.

18. Avoid depressive letters as much as possible. Focus on the positive. This will help you focus your life and cheer the reader.
19. Continue projects that you have already begun.
20. Create a routine for yourself and stick with it.
21. Maintain your personal health and hygiene.
22. Stay in touch with your friends. This mutual support is helpful.
23. Set boundaries with your children. Hear their feelings and understand the behavior that might result from feelings. Establish limits to provide stability, structure, and continuity. Do not overdo it either way.
24. Observe changes in your child's behavior, attitudes, and expressions. Pay attention both to verbal and to nonverbal behavior. Be prepared to respond as appropriate.
25. Use support groups as necessary for yourself and for your kids. Participate separately, or together with your children, as appropriate.
26. Get professional help for yourself and/or your children as needed. Sometimes, counseling, in conjunction with support groups, offers maximum benefit.
27. Every day, find something to laugh about. Use laughter as a stress manager and reducer.
28. Walk or exercise regularly and include sufficient rest and relaxation in your schedule.
29. Both for yourself and for your children, maintain the continuity of the familiar. This includes schedules, school attendance, friendships, TV programs, activities, and the like.
30. Listen, hear, and respond. Do not lecture.

Specific Guidelines: What Parents Can Do to Help Their Children Cope with Feelings

- Talk with your child, providing simple, accurate information to questions.
- *Talk with your child about your own feelings.*
- Listen to what your child says and how your child says it. Is there fear, anxiety, insecurity? Your repeating the child's words may be very helpful, such as, "You are afraid that…." or, "You wonder if…." This helps both you and the child to clarify feelings.
- *Reassure your child, "We are together. I care about you. I will take care of you."*
- You might need to repeat information and reassurances many times. Do not stop responding just because you told the child once.
- *Hold your child. Provide comfort. Touching is important for children during these times.*
- Spend extra time putting your child to bed. Talk and offer assurance. Leave the night light on if necessary.
- *Observe your child at play. Listen to what is said and watch how your child plays. Frequently, children express feelings of fear or of anger while playing with dolls, trucks, and friends.*
- Provide play experiences to relieve tension. Work with play dough, paint, play in water, and the like.
- *Allow your child to rely on his/her security blanket or toy, as needed.*
- If you need professional assistance, seek it early to maximize the benefit.

Chapter Takeaways

Personal Notes

Words Matter in Disaster Response

Sharon C. Leviton, Ph.D., DABECI

The responder's function is to serve as crisis intervener/wordsmith in crisis situations. Words matter. The responder chooses and uses words carefully, thoughtfully, and purposefully in order to assist the crisis victim to return to a precrisis level of functioning.

Persons in crisis often experience extreme feelings of fear, anger, grief, hostility, helplessness, hopelessness, and/or alienation from their self-concept, their family, and society. Victims may experience a pervasive sense of anxiety which produce disorganization and chaotic thinking. They may feel overwhelmed and unable to move in any direction. The most compelling description of the crisis state is the feeling of being totally out of structure. The crisis victim will look to the responder to provide structure in a world that seems to be falling apart.

The responder's sensitivity and attention to the victim's immediate needs predict the ability to manage the situation. The emphasis of Crisis Intervention is on immediate response rather than on long- or short-term counseling. The goal of the intervener/responder is to provide "emotional first aid" (E. S. Rosenbluh, personal communication, June 8, 1981) to the person in order to interrupt the downward spiral of maladaptive behavior. The intervener has two major tasks: (a) to reduce emotional trauma and (b) to return the victim to the precrisis level of functioning (Greenstone & Leviton, 1993).

The responder's function is to serve as intervener/wordsmith. Effective responders understand that words have the potential to calm or incite, to empower or diminish, to provide clarity or create confusion, to open up or close down the flow of information, and to enhance or sabotage the process of assisting the victim regain a sense of equilibrium and structure.

Words do matter. A responder who might think, "I will just say that and see what happens," is courting disaster. It is an attitude that breaches the trust and perhaps the safety of a person who is already in a fragile way. The responsible responder chooses and uses words carefully, thoughtfully, and purposefully. What follows are several vignettes. They are included to illustrate effective and noneffective use of words. "R" represents the responder; the other initials are those of the victim.

Vignette #1

M.J.   I'm an old, tired woman. I have outlived my children. I've outlived my usefulness.

R.   What about your friends?

MJ.   I have to go to the graveyard to see them.

R.   I'm sorry for all your losses, Mrs. Jones.

M.J.   I just don't want to do this anymore. Enough is enough.

R.   What is it that you don't want to do?

M.J.   I don't want to bother with life. It's too much trouble. Too much trouble ….

R.   Is there something that you do want to do? Maybe something you haven't been able to do or see in a long time?

M.J.   Well, I always liked card games. I liked the challenge.

R.   Card games. Do you drive, Mrs. Jones?

M.J.   I drive to the grocery store. And the doctor sometimes.

R.   Do you mind if I look at your driver's license?

M.J.   Am I in trouble?

R.   (smiling) No, I'm checking because I care about your safety. By the way, there is a very nice community center at 301 Main Street (reaching into his pocket). This card has their phone number and address. I would like you to call them and ask about their card games. If you don't mind, I will just sit right here while you call. Then you can tell me all about what you find out. We'll talk some more if you'd like.

M.J.   It's been a long, long time since anybody's cared about me.

Vignette #2

R.   Can you tell me what happened in the last 12 hours, Mr. Brown?

B.B.   Yes, I can tell you. I was laid off again.

R.   Is that good or bad for you?

B.B.   Are you crazy? How can it be good? You must be nuts or getting a big share of taxpayers' money, so you don't know about being poor.

R.   Look, man—

B.B.   Don't "look man" me. I got a wife and 2 kids to support. We bought a house so my mother-in-law could live with us. I can't support all those people now.

R.	What are you most concerned about now?
B.B.	I don't have a job. I can't pay my bills. I'm going to lose everything.
R.	I hear your concern. I'm sorry about my poor attempt at humor. It was a joke I once heard. You said you were laid off before. How did you handle things when that happened?
B.B.	The economy was better then. My old company gave us some leads. I didn't have as many bills, so it wasn't so bad. This really scares me. I have never been scared like this before. I don't know what to do and I don't know how to figure it out.
R.	What you have told me is plenty. But is there anything else that maybe you haven't told me.? Any other concern?
B.B.	I … I … I don't even know how to admit this. I am just plain embarrassed. I feel humiliated that I can't support my family. And to have my mother-in-law know I can't support her daughter …. That is probably the worst part of all this.
R.	It sounds like you care a lot about your family and do your best for them. Have you talked with your wife?
B.B.	I haven't even told her.
R.	What do you think will happen when you tell her?
B.B.	(deep breath) You know, probably nothing bad. She's a good person.
R.	Sounds like you both are. How about giving her a chance to show her support. This is a family matter isn't it?
B.B.	I guess I hadn't thought of it like that before.

Vignette #3

R.	This is Lee Smith of XZLY Police Department. Is this Jane Brown?
J.B.	Yes, this is Jane Brown.
R.	Well, Janie girl. I'm calling to help you resolve the problem you're having over there.
J.B.	My name isn't Janie. I'm not anyone's girl. I don't have a problem … click

Vignette #4

R.	You're a lawyer aren't you, Larry?
L.L.	Yes.
R.	How could you get yourself in such a mess?

Vignette #5

R.	You're supposed to be the expert in the family, Joe.
J.	No response.
R.	Even I would have known how to handle that.
J.	No response.

Vignette #6

R. How did you decide to skip school, Bobby?
B. I had to study for an exam. That seemed more important.
R. You skipped school, Bobby. Can you explain your actions?
B. No response.

Vignette #7

R. You had a golden opportunity. What the hell were you thinking about?
T. No response.

Vignette #8

R. You did some mighty stupid things. Just like my husband. What you should have done was…
F. You know, lady I'm feeling enough shame to last me a lifetime. I don't need to listen to you pile more on. You can't help me. Just go away.

While the first two situations were effectively managed, the last several vignettes showed how the responder's effectiveness can be impaired by the use of sarcasm, preaching, shaming and editorializing. These responders will have a difficult time creating trust with the victims. They have compromised the integrity of the intervention process in the service of their own agenda.

Vignette #9

MS. I want visitation with the children more than one weekend a month. Can't she understand how important my children are to me?
R. Seeing your children means a great deal to you.
MS. How can she do that to me! I've raised those kids. I've carpooled every day, paid for their schooling, baby sat with them, cuddled them when they were sick. I'm the one they come to when there's a problem. My little boy needs to have me around.
R. It sounds like you need them, too.
MS. All of a sudden everything is in such a muddle. I may not have been the best husband, but I'm a damn good father. My wife is leaving, I won't get to see my children much. I can't concentrate on my job. … I … I feel terribly alone!! I … I … can't handle this. I feel so cut off and helpless ….
R. I can hear you're in a lot of pain. Have you ever felt like this before?
MS. No, I've always been the "go to" guy. I could handle anything.
R. Maybe now you need a little help. What do you need from me right now?

MS.	Maybe just to listen. Everybody in our family is taking sides. I need someone who is neutral. Someone who isn't in line to take something else from me. Can you just listen and then tell me what you're hearing.
R.	Yes, I can do that.
MS.	I have one quick question.
R.	I'm listening
MS.	Am I going crazy?
R.	You're not crazy and you're not going crazy, Mike. Is it ok if I call you Mike? What you're feeling is pretty normal under the circumstances.
MS.	Hearing that is helpful … Let me figure where to begin …
R.	Take your time. I'll be here.

During the ventilation the responder should do the following:
- be alert to verbal and nonverbal cues being given
- show appropriate concern for the feelings expressed
- listen actively to issues and the attendant feelings
- be empathetic and attentive
- listen to understand the victim's perspective

There are times during an intervention when the responder may not know what to ask or how to ask the victim for information. The following is presented as a resource.
- …I hear your pain/concern/fear/frustration, etc.
- …Help me understand.
- …This is what I am hearing. Is that what you meant to say?
- …Tell me more about that.
- …Could you elaborate on that?
- …No, I don't know exactly how you feel, but I'm trying to understand more about your feelings/concerns/etc.
- …It's important to me because it's obviously important to you.
- …Is there anything else?
- …Have you ever had that feeling before? How did you handle it then? What are you feeling?
- …Would you share what you're thinking?
- …It's important that I understand what you're telling me. Would you clarify for me?
- …Talk to me … (use a soft voice)
- …Where are you now?
- …What if …?
- …Are you aware that every time you …?
- …Have you thought about what might happen if …?
- …Something does not feel right about this. What is really going on? or What is really concerning/scaring/worrying/angering you? (These questions are attempts at tuning in to the person without becoming threatening. The person can always back away, and you can apologize for misreading them).
- …Let's take a look at …

CHAPTER 4: Words Matter in Disaster Response

- …mmm hum, yes
- …When you tried that what happened?
- …Was that helpful?
- …What is the worst thing that could happen?
- …What is the best thing that could happen?
- …When you think about that what do you feel?
- …What will you gain?
- …What will you lose?
- …What need does that serve?
- …Has that worked for you before?
- …Is it working well for you now?
- …What do you need from me right now?
- …How can I be helpful to you now?
- …Of all your concerns what is the most pressing?
- …It sounds like ….
- …Let's take one thing at a time.

What is the crisis? Sometimes well-intentioned responders become so focused on verbal techniques or what this author calls "verbal gadgetry" that they fail to take care of the most basic business. This observation applies to seasoned responders as well as novices. At some point in the intervention it becomes clear that conditions are not improving. The victim is closing down, the responder is becoming frustrated and there is no positive movement.

This situation usually occurs when the responder has failed to get in touch with the basic question: WHAT IS THE CRISIS? What event or series of events occurred in the sufferer's life at this particular time and more critically, what meaning does the person attach to the event? Crisis is in the eyes of the beholder. The way the sufferer currently perceives the world is that person's reality. An intervener cannot be helpful unless both the victim and the intervener are on the same sheet of music (Leviton & Greenstone, 1997).

Please refer to the earlier vignettes. For Mrs. Jones, the crisis was not a wish for death; it was an unfulfilled longing for human contact and involvement. For Mr. Brown, the crisis wasn't the job loss, but the overwhelming sense of humiliation that accompanied the job loss.

Crises occur 24×7. Effective interveners must prepare themselves to respond immediately. They must be ready for whatever confronts them. They may have only a single chance to assist the victim. Words matter!

REFERENCES

Greenstone, J. L., & Leviton, S. C. (1993). *Elements of crisis intervention: Crises and how to respond to them* (2nd ed.). Brooks/Cole.

Leviton, S. C., & Greenstone, J. L. (1997). *Elements of mediation*. Brooks/Cole.

Chapter Takeaways

Personal Notes

The Orange Bag Denial

James L. Greenstone, Ed.D., J.D., DABECI

If denial exists anywhere, it exists here. The seemingly unconscious process of refusing those implements of survival which might be needed during a disaster scenario, because acceptance also means acceptance of the likelihood of a disaster occurring, is the focus here. Disasters do and will occur. Refusal of the implements of survival denies that reality. Acceptance confirms it. Perhaps acknowledgment of this process will impact the individual's frame of reference or psychological structuring, and thereby affect observed behavior (Sherif & Sherif, 1956).

The Issue

Perhaps the reason that persons refuse to prepare for the onset of a disaster relates to the new psychological term recently coined, "Orange Bag Denial" (Greenstone, 2009). Man-made and natural disasters will occur. One has only to look around to confirm this reality.

Many will remember a few years ago when, in a prominent way, a product came on the market that promised to provide sufficient supplies to help an individual to survive the first 72 hours of a disaster, man-made or natural. These provisions were carefully provided in an orange canvas backpack that sold for about $30 to $35. In the opinion of this author, the supplies provided would have probably cost more than the $35 price tag if one were to purchase them separately. In addition to the flashlight, batteries, water, food, tools, and the like, the size of the backpack allowed for personal gear such as extra clothing and other supplies. Altogether the pack was still light enough for even the slightest individual who does not like to carry anything on her back, to carry the bag and to move around with ease.

The Search

Being a preparer, this writer and preparer has long had a personal "go bag" ready for the various circumstances in which he might find himself (Greenstone, 2008). Even so, this new orange bag was of some interest. So, as one might expect, it was quickly determined that they were readily available at most Super "XXX" Stores in the area. "XXX" is not the real name of the store. What was found there was surprising and yet not completely unexpected.

An individual search of the store was begun. This was probably because of an aversion to asking for directions. Anyway, the bags were nowhere to be found even though advertised. Finally, several employees were approached for directions to the bags. They were found standing together obviously discussing profit and loss statements. They were not knowledgeable about the bags and could not recall seeing them on the store shelves. The manager was summoned. He knew about the bags. He explained that they had been removed from the shelves because they were not selling. That was the next inkling that something was afoot. Further, he explained that he was about to return the bags to the supplier but that many of the bags were still in the store stock room.

In the stock room, the bin was full of these orange emergency bags. The manager was queried if the bags were still available for sale. He said that they were and that he would sell them at an incredibly good price for as many of them as were desired. The price was so good, all were purchased. An immediate thought was that they could be given as Christmas or Chanukah gifts. Who knew?

After the bags were purchased and loaded into the car, they were transported to be used as "presents."

The Results

When it was mentioned to a very smart wife and partner that the bags would be given as gifts, she warned against such action. Not fully understanding the issues, this author argued, disagreed, and finally acquiesced. This proved to be the correct choice. The rest was amazing.

There were several family members and fellow preparers with whom this writer was close personally, and to whom the bags might be given. Not so much as a holiday gift, but later because of concern about their readiness if something bad happened.

Most of the few close friends to whom the orange gifts were given were visibly and verbally shocked by this expression of kindness. To the person, their eyes bugged with surprise, they appeared stunned; they asked why such a gift would be given to them. Several were shocked and asked, "Do you know something that I don't?"

Therein was born the concept of the Orange Bag Denial. It occurred to this author that acceptance of the gift would also mean an acceptance of the possibility that a disaster might occur and that the contents of the orange bag might have to be utilized. In the alternative, not to accept the bag, as a few did, was avoidance and a denial of such a possibility. In other words, "If I do not take the bag designed for a disaster, maybe I will be spared the disaster. On the other hand, if I accept the bag, then also I have to accept the fact that a disaster may occur for which I may need these supplies."

Some of the Related Numbers and Findings

There are at least four stages of preparedness denial. According to Eric Holdeman (2008), Director of Emergency Management for King County, the four stages are:
1. It will not happen;
2. If it does happen, it will not happen to me;
3. If it does happen to me, it will not be that bad; and
4. If it happens and it is bad, there is nothing that I can do to stop it anyway.

In an August 2006 poll conducted by Time Magazine, it was reported that most American citizens were not prepared for a disaster and had their "heads in the sand." Half surveyed said that they had experienced a disaster. Only 16% of those said that they were adequately prepared for another disaster. Many justified their poor preparation by indicating that they did not need to prepare because they did not live in areas of high risk for any kind of disaster (Ripley, 2006).

Facts seem to support the assertion that 91% of Americans live in places of significant risk to some type of disaster situation that could dramatically affect their lives. This study was conducted by the Hazards and Vulnerability Research Institute at the University of South Carolina (Ripley, 2006). There seems to be a fine line, according to this quoted article, between optimism and foolishness. In a country whose citizens, many times, distrust its leaders, the vast majority continue to think that in a disaster, our government, local, state and national, will quickly come to our aid as in non-disaster times. The response to Hurricane Katrina was one of the strongest counter-testimonies to this ill-conceived belief.

Conclusion

Maybe all of this is just the hyperactivity of a psychologically oriented mind (Greenstone & Leviton, 2011). Who knows? I have got my bag. Or, maybe we need to get our heads out of our … sand and readjust to the real world need to prepare and to continue to prepare (Greenstone, 2010).

REFERENCES

Greenstone, J. L., & Leviton, S. (2011). *Elements of crisis intervention: Crises and how to respond to them* (3rd ed.). Brooks/Cole, Thomson Learning.

Greenstone, J. L. (2008). *The elements of disaster psychology: Managing psychosocial trauma—An integrated approach to force protection and acute care.* Charles C. Thomas.

Greenstone, J. L. (2009, Fall). Why we do not prepare: Orange bag denial. *Journal of Police Crisis Negotiations: An International Journal, 9*(2), 169–170.

Greenstone, J. L. (2010, Winter). Disaster non-preparedness: The orange bag denial. *International Journal of Emergency Mental Health, Invited Essay, 12*(1), 1–3.

Holdeman, E. (2008). *Disaster denial.* Department of Emergency Management, Cowlitz County.

Ripley, A. (2006, August). Floods, tornadoes, hurricanes, wildfires, earthquakes: Why we don't prepare. *Time Magazine, 168*(8), 10–16.

Sherif, M., & Sherif, C. (1956). *An outline of social psychology.* Harper and Row.

Chapter Takeaways

Personal Notes

The Crisis of the Pandemic: Panic vs. Preparedness

Bethany Shaw, A.A., A.S., B.S., M.S.

James L. Greenstone, Ed.D., J.D., DABECI

Crises like the COVID-19 pandemic occur suddenly, arbitrarily, and unexpectedly. For millions of Americans, stressors such as unemployment, a radical change in their daily routine, and the isolation created by social distancing occurred with little warning. These stressors have adversely affected the mental health of millions of Americans. Through a review of available literature, this paper intends to examine the stressors of the COVID-19 pandemic and to gain a better understanding of how emotional first aid tactics can be used to decrease anxiety, panic, and sustained trauma to the citizens of the United States. In or-

der to make a more resilient society, preparedness efforts and education on emotional first aid techniques must be employed prior to the crisis occurring. Research shows that proactively preparing for the future is paramount to the success and resiliency of our nation.

Introduction

On January 20, 2020, life as we knew it in America was about to drastically change, we just did not know it yet. Suddenly, arbitrarily, and unexpectedly, a crisis began when a man in Washington State returned from Wuhan, China, carrying Novel Coronavirus (Greenstone, 2015, p. 1; Taylor, 2020). A few short weeks

© American Academy of Experts in Traumatic Stress. Reprinted by permission.

later, millions of Americans would be unemployed, hundreds of thousands of children would be home from school, entire cities would be placed in lockdown, and social distancing would become the new catch phrase; the Novel Coronavirus Disease (COVID-19) pandemic was here in America. Hundreds of thousands of Americans would become infected with the virus, and millions more would be scared, fearful, frustrated, anxious, looking for effective coping mechanisms, and worried about their uncertain future. This paper intends to examine the stressors of the COVID-19 pandemic and to gain a better understanding of how emotional first aid tactics can be used to decrease anxiety and sustained trauma to the citizens of the United States and the world.

Background

This paper is relevant to the study of emotional first aid and disaster management as the pandemic is currently spreading at an unprecedented rate. The outbreak is expected to last several months or more, and deaths and the rates of infection are expected to grow exponentially. As of today, March 23, 2020, CNN reports that there are more than 341,000 coronavirus cases globally with nearly 15,000 deaths worldwide (Hollingsworth et al., 2020). According to the Centers for Disease Control and Prevention (CDC) as of March 20, 2020, there were more than 15,000 cases and over 200 deaths in the United States alone. This staggering number leaves many people trying to cope with uncertainty and establish a "new normal" as millions of Americans have been told to shelter-in-place, and to only leave their houses when picking up essentials such as groceries and medication at the pharmacy. Knowing what emotional first aid efforts are most effective during this time will provide lessons which can be taken into the future to better aid those who are feeling overwhelmed in times of crisis.

Overview

A crisis, as defined by Dr. James Greenstone is an event which is "sudden in onset, unexpected by the victim or their significant others, and is arbitrary in nature" (Greenstone, 2015, p. 1). Merriam-Webster defines a crisis as an "emotionally significant event or radical change of status in a person's life" (Merriam-Webster, n.d.). It is clear that the COVID-19 pandemic struck suddenly, is arbitrary in nature, was unexpected by most citizens, and is considered to be an emotionally significant event in people's lives. It is due to this reason that emotional first aid is imperative to help those looking for more effective ways to cope with the reality of what is happening.

As the extreme stress of the COVID-19 crisis is expected to continue over the next several months, decision-making capabilities are likely to become hampered by such stress, ultimately causing a "downward spiral of ineffective maladaptive behavior(s) to individuals" (Greenstone, 2020). This downward spiral may cause irrational fears and behaviors such as panic buying and hoarding of materials, as well as heightened anxiety and depression to many citizens who are now suddenly isolated by "social distancing." "Emotional first aid is designed to interrupt the downward spiral of ineffective maladaptive behavior and return the individuals involved to their level of pre-crisis behavior as soon as possible" (Greenstone, 2020). It is this return to pre-crisis behavior which allows us to return to function as we normally would.

The Crisis Cube pictured below (Figure 6.1) was developed by Dr. James Greenstone and describes how extreme stress can cause an emotional breaking point spiraling someone into crisis. As noted in the cube, once someone reaches the crisis onset point a decline in functioning and an increase for maladaptive behavior occurs. What is imperative in emotional first aid is to return to a state of precrisis behavior as quickly as possible.

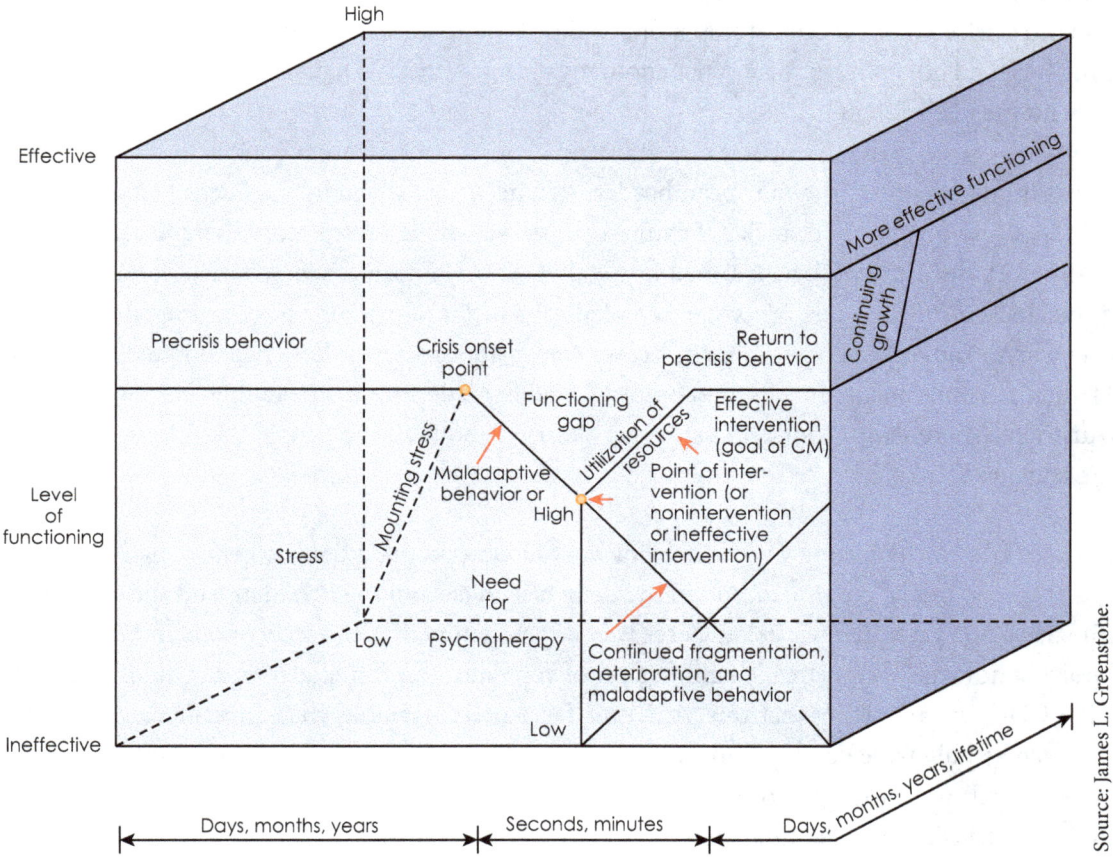

FIGURE 6.1. THE CRISIS CUBE

The Personal Side of Emotional First Aid

Emotional first aid is a "set of life skills used by lay citizens and emergency responders to provide the support a person who is emotionally shocked needs immediately following a crisis event" (What is emotional, n.d.). During the early days of this pandemic, I found that I needed to administer these emotional first aid tactics on myself as I found my world was spiraling out of control. Below is my story and how emotional first aid can be used to help others just like me.

MY STORY

Wife, mother, daughter, sister, friend, graduate student. Happy, bubbly, outgoing. That is how usually I define myself; however, after returning to New Hampshire from a vacation to Nevada on March 8, 2020, I found that my world was about to be flipped upside down. All of the news headlines were suddenly about COVID-19, toilet paper (or the lack thereof), how there is no vaccine available for this virus, that the elderly population are the most at risk, and that personal protective equipment (PPE) and ventilators were already in short supply. CDC reports included not knowing much about the virus, modes of transmission, immunity, and so on which caused me a great deal of anxiety and uncertainty. After all, if we do not know what the virus is comprised of, how can we stop it or avoid it? I found myself asking, am I safe? Am I going to get this? Is my husband going to get this? What about my elderly father? What about my children? The anxiety and worry hit me like a ton of bricks.

I was facing immense stress. The European borders had been shut down by President Donald Trump as of March 13, 2020 and I had a child stuck in Spain. My husband who is a respiratory therapist and the manager of the respiratory department for a 250-bed hospital in New Hampshire's largest city was already working around the clock, 7 days a week. My sister is a medical assistant for a very busy orthopedic office in New York State where "roughly 5% of Coronavirus cases worldwide are" (New York has roughly, 2020), I have an elderly father, an immunocompromised stepmother, and my oldest son and daughter-in-law were vacationing in Australia. There I was. Alone and stressed. Worried about all the people that I know and love. Was everyone going to be ok?

I found myself not concentrating very well, being very anxious, more quick-tempered than usual, and very lonely. As the news media continued, so did the daily briefings from the President and the COVID-19 task force. The news was grimmer every day. Cases were skyrocketing, health care workers in Washington State were reporting how they were already running out of ventilators and simple everyday items like masks and gloves, the CDC was reporting that this virus was far more contagious than initially thought, and other countries such as Italy were having to make choices about who would live or die as hospitals were beyond capacity. My watch was pinging with news alerts, and there was no escape. The radio was talking about it, talk shows on television were talking about it, my friends and family were talking about it, and I was even receiving emails about it. I felt like I was being bombarded by COVID-19. Stores, businesses, and restaurants were being mandated to close, grocery store shelves were becoming bare, schools were closed, millions of Americans were filing for unemployment, and three types of people were beginning to emerge in the population; those who were panicked, those who were prepared, and those who just did not believe that this virus was real.

While I have to admit I am a preparedness freak at heart, I initially panicked. Fortunately, I have been educated in emotional first aid. I reevaluated my "symptoms" of anxiety, lack of concentration, poor sleep, worry, isolation, loneliness, and fear, and started to recognize that I was in crisis. Was I functioning? Sure. But I was not functioning the way I did before this event occurred. I could not focus on my normal daily tasks or things like walking the dog. What I was focused on was worry over coronavirus.

THE "AHA" MOMENT

The "aha" moment of my crisis appeared when I least expected it, but it was helpful and what ultimately led me to my recognition of my symptoms. Now this is going to seem silly in the grand scheme of things, but this is just to give you some indication of where my head was during this time. So, as my son was in Spain with return flights being cancelled, my husband at the hospital, my sister texting from NY with cold symptoms, my daily checks on my father and stepmother, and the eldest returning from his vacation to Australia, the dishwasher broke. After some investigation I discovered the latch was not locking. The handle would not close and the door looked like it was sticking out a bit too far. So, after finding the model number I ordered the part. The part arrived several days later and was in fact the exact same as the part currently on the dishwasher. It too did not latch. It did not fix the door from protruding out so after installation it was uninstalled, placed back in the box, and returned to the company where I purchased it. My husband arrived home after work and did some further investigation only to find that the dishwasher was not broken at all. There was a lid on the top rack which was blocking the door from shutting completely. Yup. That was it. A lid on the top rack of the dishwasher which prevented me from running the dishwasher all week. Now, had I been functioning at a "normal" rate of capacity, I would have quickly seen the lid on the top rack, moved the lid to the lower rack and started the dishwasher. Instead, I could not see beyond my tunnel vision of the dishwasher being broken. I could not see the lid because I was overwhelmed. I could not see the lid because I was emotionally exhausted. I was tired and dumbfounded. It was time to make some changes.

After trying to get some restful sleep, I awoke the next morning determined to get back to "normal." Back to functioning at a normal capacity or "precrisis functioning" (Greenstone, 2015, p. 4). I had to fight the fears of uncertainty, ways to cope with others panic stricken behavior, the new normal of changing routines, and ways to stop worrying about something that is so clearly out of my control (COVID-19). Simply put, I needed to take care of myself. I started "responding to the crisis; not just reacting to it" (Greenstone, 2015, p. 37). I started using FaceTime and Skype to talk to family members so I would feel less alone. I started exercising more, started meditating, and doing deep breathing exercises twice a day. I shut off the television except for the daily presidential updates and have avoided social media. My family and I have started a positivity music challenge every morning so that we start the day off with a positive uplifting song. I have focused on getting back on track with a routine; regardless if it is a new routine—it will become my new normal. I have realistic expectations of what is to come and have returned to my roots of preparing for the future.

As a disaster recovery and emergency management student I have been educated in preparedness and know how to prepare, but even so, I still panicked. I also know that panicking does not make you prepared or competent as it generally leads to poor decision making and frustration (Bergland, 2016). Thankfully, I have used my skills to manage this crisis and you can too. I know that what I was feeling was normal and valid under the circumstances and I know that I cannot solve this crisis, but only continue to manage it. Ultimately, this too shall pass.

Stressors

"COVID-19 (Corona Virus Disease 2019) has significantly resulted in a large number of psychological consequences" (Li et al., 2020). Social distancing has been widely encouraged to all members of the population, which has led some to feel increasingly isolated and anxious (Campbell et al., 2018; Willis, 2020). Business closures have left citizens with limited resources due to layoffs which has caused increased stress as financial burdens rise (Campbell et al., 2018), and social media platforms have aided in disseminating "misinformation about the outbreak," causing an escalation in panic behavior(s) among the public (Depoux et al., 2020). Studies have shown that isolation, increased stress, and loneliness can give rise to substance abuse and/or addiction (Boyle, 2018; Campbell et al., 2020), and "domestic violence experts warn the isolation could be 'devastating' for survivors forced to shelter somewhere unsafe" (Silva, 2020). Millions of children are now forced to worry about where their next meal is coming from as they are no longer receiving free or reduced-price meals at school (Dolan, 2020). Parents are overwhelmed by their new roles as "teachers" and 24/7 caregivers, leaving little time for a break or "alone" time. Health care facilities are "scrambling to increase bed capacity and hire desperately needed nurses and medical personnel on short notice" due to surge concerns (Nguyen et al., 2020), and responders are worried that PPE will not be there when it is needed most; risking their lives and the lives of their families (Vesoulis, 2020). COVID-19 is not only causing psychological consequences, it is a mental health crisis. Without help, more and more people may become affected as the pandemic is expected to continue for months.

How to Practice Emotional First Aid Tactics

As the stressors listed above continue to weigh heavily on millions, emotional first aid tactics are an effective way to decrease anxiety and sustained trauma to American Citizens. Emotional first aid requires that you stay calm, recognize when you are in emotional pain, learn to notice the signs of stress and burnout, be gentle and compassionate with yourself, keep your stress within tolerable limits, practice stress reduction techniques when necessary, find meaning in loss, and above all else put yourself first (Greenstone, 2015, pp. 31–39; Greenstone & Leviton, 2011; Leanza, 2018; Winch, 2014a, 2014b).

Doing those things that may allow one to feel calm is imperative when you begin to feel overwhelmed. To become calm when tense, focus on your breathing (Lindberg, 2018; Pfefferbaum & Shaw, 2013; Wallen, 2019; Winch, 2014a, 2014b). According to Scott Dehorty of Delphi Behavioral Health "breathing is the number one and most effective technique for reducing anger and anxiety quickly" (Lindberg, 2018). It is useful to take deep breaths and imagine all the stress is leaving your body every time you exhale (Wallen, 2019). This simple technique can be done anywhere without bringing attention to yourself and can be very effective at releasing anxiety.

Pay attention to emotional injuries and recognize when you are in emotional pain. Owning your pain, acknowledging how you are feeling, and accepting that you are hurt, sad, or overwhelmed is perfectly acceptable and necessary (Tartakovsky, 2019). Additionally, it is important to note that "psychological wounds often manifest as physical symptoms such as headaches and illnesses" (Winch, 2014a, 2014b). To help yourself, replace your negative thoughts and words with encouraging self-talk; talk to yourself as if you were talking to a good friend who was feeling the same way (Tartakovsky, 2019; Winch, 2015). If a friend came to you with a problem, you would be supportive. Support yourself in the same fashion. Also, acknowledging you are emotionally wounded will allow you to take the time to heal and focus on getting better.

Signs of burnout and stress can be masked as many other things; therefore, it is essential that you pay close attention if any of the following signs and symptoms apply to you. Not sleeping well, not sleeping enough, or having trouble falling asleep; feeling exhausted; having frequent colds or the flu; experiencing marital and/or family conflict; having tunnel vision; experiencing a sense of helplessness and/or fear; being angry, irritable, and/or negative, having a lack of concentration or forgetfulness (Bourg Carter, 2013; Gans, 2020; Greenstone, 2015, p. 34). If you notice any of these signs or symptoms it is important to recognize how they are affecting you, and to take measures to reduce the stress in your life.

Be gentle and compassionate with yourself. "Thoughts like I'm so stupid" or "I just can't get anything right" drag down your self-esteem and make it more difficult to be emotionally resilient. Show yourself some compassion" (Leanza, 2018; Winch, 2014a, 2014b). Ways to show yourself compassion can be as easy as practicing mindfulness, giving yourself permission to make errors, not aiming for perfection, and remembering that you are not alone; there are millions of others who are experiencing what you are experiencing (Abrams, 2017).

Eating healthy nutritious foods, getting enough sleep and exercise, scheduling time for fun, and having realistic expectations of what the future holds can keep your stress within tolerable limits (Greenstone, 2015, p. 35). According to the National Institute of Mental Health, stress affects everyone and can harm your health when not dealt with properly. Long-term stress can "disturb the immune, digestive, cardiovascular, sleep, and other reproductive symptoms and over time, continued strain on your body from stress may contribute to serious health problems, such as heart disease, high blood pressure, diabetes, and other illnesses, including mental health disorders such as depression or anxiety (5 Things you should know, n.d.). It is due to these negative long-term health issues that it is crucial to keep stress within tolerable limits.

Dr. Leviton's *48 Steps to Pro-Active Management for Reducing Stress* is a great resource for learning how to practice stress reduction techniques. Leviton describes the need to be realistic about expectations, the importance of creating a safe environment, the need to be consistent, making sure to plan before taking action, the importance of maintaining a sense of humor in stressful situations, and the need to respond, not react (Greenstone, 2015, pp. 37–39). Other stress reduction techniques are to reduce caffeine and alcohol, keep a journal, and to keep in contact with friends and family (Jennings, 2018).

Find meaning in loss. Motivational speaker and life coach Tony Robbins has a poignant saying; remember that life doesn't happen *to* you, it happens *for* you. "A loss can be anything which is significant to you such as a job or relationship (or the passing of a loved one)" (Winch, 2014a, 2014b). It is important to reframe your thinking about the issue to see what you may have gained while experiencing the loss (Leanza, 2018; Winch, 2014a, 2014b); this is life happening *for* you. For those experiencing the loss of a job from the COVID-19 pandemic, it is important to remember that they have gained time with their children. Or perhaps, that they now have time to read that book that they always wanted to read or address other issues in their lives where they could not before because they were too busy.

Above and beyond anything, in order to be effective, you must put yourself first. You must take care of your own needs and try to return to a state of precrisis mental health. It is not selfish to do so, it is necessary. Reduce stress, anxiety, worry, and fear. It will help in the long run. "Those who effectively and successfully deal with high stress issues and personal problems when they occur, rather than denying or refusing to deal with them, often come through their present crisis in much better shape emotionally than those who do not" (Greenstone, 2015, p. 7).

How Year-Round Preparedness Can Help Reduce Panic Behavior

Panic can be defined as "sudden uncontrollable fear or anxiety, often causing wildly unthinking behavior" (Oxford Dictionary, n.d.). As previously stated, panic tends to lead to irrational behavior and poor decision-making abilities (Bergland, 2016). During times of crisis, it is important to prepare, but not to panic.

The United States Surgeon General Dr. Jerome Adams addressed the nation on March 2, 2020 to say, "caution is appropriate, preparedness is appropriate, panic is not" (Berlinger et al., 2020). Panic buying behaviors "have stripped many US grocery stores of staples ranging from bread and milk to meat and toilet paper" (Bekiempis, 2020), and is generally associated with citizens being unable to tolerate uncertainty (Norberg & Rucker, 2020). Gun and ammunition sales have surged (Coleman, 2020; Gandel, 2020) and online retail giants such as Amazon have been unable to deliver products such as paper goods, hand sanitizer, and cleaning agents. The COVID-19 pandemic has caused many Americans to engage in panic behaviors as the perceived threat(s) of going without and potentially falling ill have caused irrational behaviors.

While research has shown that panic is not a common reaction to disasters (Auf der Heide, 2004; Greenstone, 2008; Gantt & Gantt, n.d.), "panic may be the result of a serious perceived threat combined with limited or no avenues of escape for the victims" (Greenstone, 2008, p. 5). As the COVID-19 pandemic continues to cause upset to normal routines such as work, school, and daily life, many Americans may see no end in sight to this pandemic, their social isolation, and fear they will get sick. This may be perceived by many that the COVID-19 pandemic is a very real threat to their health, well-being, and financial and physical security. As "reality is in the eye of the beholder," if someone thinks that the threat is real, it is real to that person, regardless of whether there is an actual threat or not (Greenstone, 2008, p. 5). Many Americans think that they are going to become infected and die, even though the numerical data states that they will not (Subramaniam, 2020). Additionally, there is a fear that the virus will prompt a recession or depression to our economy (Guzman, 2020). It is these perceived threats which have caused people to exhibit panic behavior as they feel there is no way of escaping the COVID-19 pandemic and the restrictions it has caused on their "normal" day-to-day routines.

Panic and panic buying can be significantly reduced with year-round preparedness efforts. The Federal Emergency Management Agency (FEMA) as well as Ready.gov encourage the American public to slowly and methodically plan and prepare for a disaster. This includes creating a family preparedness plan, having a "go-bag," having a "shelter-in-place" kit, purchasing insurance for natural disasters, and slowly stocking your pantry with nonperishable food items little by little so there will be no need to strip the shelves of supplies when a disaster or emergency strikes (Rowett, 2017). Having 365 days a year to systematically prepare for an event allows everyone ample time to stockpile essentials (even those on a restrictive budget or those who live in remote areas of the country). Maintaining an adequate level of supplies reduces stress once a crisis occurs thus reducing panic behaviors.

Orange Bag Denial

As stated above, it is possible for everyone to systematically and methodically prepare for a disaster of any kind; however, as of 2015, the Federal Emergency Management Agency (FEMA) reported that "nearly sixty percent of American adults have not practiced what to do in a disaster and only thirty-nine percent have developed an emergency plan" (Sixty Percent of Americans, 2015). So why then are so many people not prepared?

People avoid preparing for a disaster for a variety of reasons. Some of these reasons involve fear, biases, risk perception, past experiences, and the lack of financial means to obtain supplies (Meyer & Kunreuther, 2017; Swain, 2017; Wilson et al., 2007). Others assume that if they do not prepare, they will not ever be involved with a disaster situation; thus, if they do not obtain disaster supplies, they will forever be safe (Greenstone, 2010).

Orange Bag Denial is a term coined by Dr. James Greenstone in 2009 which embodies the understanding that those who receive or purchase an "orange bag" (an emergency bag with enough supplies to sustain one person for 72 hours) also have to "accept the possibility that a disaster may occur and that the contents of the orange bag might have to be utilized. In the alternative, not to accept the bag, in essence was avoidance and a denial of such a possibility" (Greenstone, 2010). Greenstone's theory states that when accepting the bag, there is also an acceptance that a disaster may occur where the supplies could have to be used and by not accepting the bag, perhaps the person may be spared the disaster (Greenstone, 2010). The acceptance that a crisis may occur and disrupt normal life is one which many cannot bear and thus the reason so many people are not prepared.

The COVID-19 pandemic has proven to be a disastrous event which many Americans were unprepared or underprepared for due to Orange Bag Denial. This lack of preparation will have an astounding effect on the mental health of millions of Americans. While nothing can be done to retroactively prepare for this crisis, education for future preparedness is imperative.

Recommendations

Learning and prioritizing self-care is imperative to resilient mental health. Many Americans "find it so excruciatingly difficult to put their own needs first, especially when it comes to their families" (Hasseldine, 2016), however, in order to function at the highest level possible, you must take care of yourself. The National Alliance on Mental Illness reports that in order "to be able to care for the people you love, you must first take care of yourself" (Taking Care, n.d.). While the concept sounds simple, it is sometimes difficult to put into practice. It seems that there are always other responsibilities (children, career, parents, errands, bills, etc.) which should be tended to before yourself. You must, however, learn to make yourself a priority in order to practice effective emotional first aid techniques.

Emotional first aid education needs to be more widespread in society. Most everyone will experience at least one crisis in their lifetime (most likely more), and the skills listed above can make for a more resilient society. Resiliency allows us to bounce back from stressors more quickly and allows us to return to "pre-crisis functioning" at a much quicker rate (Ackerman, 2019; Cherry, 2019; Elizabeth, 2020; Greenstone, 2015; Harvard Health Publishing, 2017). Additionally, resiliency "is associated with longevity, lower rates of depression, and greater satisfaction with life" (Harvard Health, 2017).

The importance of preparedness must not be lost on future generations of Americans. Had more people been adequately prepared for the COVID-19 pandemic, less panic buying would have occurred, and more people would have been less stressed—having the peace of mind that they have all they will need to withstand the crisis. Psychologists and psychiatrists need to work together to best determine how to overcome the concepts of Orange Bag Denial. Significant research needs to be completed in this area. Preparedness efforts need to be undertaken at elementary schools so young children can come home excited about preparing and spread the message to their parents and grandparents. Whole communities and all stakeholders need to be involved in preparing, and a more proactive approach (instead of reactive) needs to be undertaken by Americans.

Conclusion

Undeniably, the COVID-19 pandemic is a crisis in the United States. Increased stress due to an uprooted routine, isolation, and uncertainty have caused many Americans emotional turmoil which could be reduced or eliminated by employing emotional first aid techniques. While all crises will end on their own eventually (with or without treatment; Greenstone, 2015, p. 7), to make a more resilient society, great care must be given to the mental health of our people. "Those who effectively and successfully deal with high stress issues and personal problems when they occur, rather than denying or refusing to deal with them, often come through their present crisis in much better shape emotionally than those who do not" (Greenstone, 2015, p. 7). Taking care of yourself first, educating the public on how to return to a level of "precrisis functioning," and proactively preparing for the future are paramount to the success and resiliency of our country. May we heed the lessons learned with the COVID-19 pandemic, prepare better for the future, and be capable of withstanding such disruption to our lives without exhibiting panic behavior(s) in the future.

REFERENCES AND ADDITIONAL READINGS

5 Things You Should Know About Stress. (n.d.). https://www.nimh.nih.gov/health/publications/stress/index.shtml

Abrams, A. (2017, March 3). How to cultivate more self-compassion. https://www.psychologytoday.com/us/blog/nurturing-self-compassion/201703/how-cultivate-more-self-compassion

Ackerman, C. (2019, April 10). What is resilience and why is it important to bounce back? https://positivepsychology.com/what-is-resilience/

Auf der Heide, E. (2004). Common misconceptions about disasters: Panic, the "disaster syndrome," and looting. https://www.atsdar.cdc.gov/emergency_response/common_misconceptions.pdf

Bekiempis, V. (2020, March 23). "Could you buy a little less, please?": Panic-buying disrupts food distribution. https://www.theguardian.com/world/2020/mar/23/us-coronavirus-panic-buying-food

Bergland, C. (2016, March 17). How does anxiety short circuit the decision-making process? https://www.psychologytoday.com/us/blog/the-athletes-way/201603/how-does-anxiety-short-circuit-the-decision-making-process

Berlinger, J., Yeung, J., Renton, A., Hayes, M., Wagner, M., & Vera, A. (2020, March 3). US Surgeon General: "Preparedness is appropriate, panic is not." https://www.cnn.com/asia/live-news/coronavirus-outbreak-03-02-20-intl-hnk/h_6681abbaba923828e94e7e56bbb65b81

Bourg Carter, S. (2013, November 26). The tell-tale signs of burnout … Do you have them? https://www.psychologytoday.com/us/blog/high-octane-women/201311/the-tell-tale-signs-burnout-do-you-have-them

Boyle, M. (2018, June 27). Why addicts are often lonely people. https://psychcentral.com/blog/why-addicts-are-often-lonely-people/

Campbell, A. M., Thomspon, S. L., Harris, T. L., & Wiehe, S. E. (2018). How the coronavirus response is increasing the risk of family violence. Intimate partner violence and pet abuse: Responding law enforcement officer's observations and victims reports from the scene. *Journal of Interpersonal Violence*.

Cases in U.S. (2020, March 31). https://www.cdc.gov/coronavirus/2019-ncov/cases-updates/cases-in-us.html

Cherry, K. (2019, October 21). How resilience helps with the coping of crisis. https://www.verywellmind.com/what-is-resilience-2795059

Coleman, J. (2020, March 31). Gun sales surge as coronavirus grips US. https://thehill.com/policy/finance/487804-gun-sales-surge-as-coronavirus-grips-us

Coronavirus Disease 2019 Stress & Coping. (n.d.). https://www.cdc.gov/coronavirus/2019-ncov/prepare/managing-stress-anxiety.html

Crisis. (n.d.). https://www.merriam-webster.com/dictionary/crisis

Depoux, A., Martin, S., Karafillakis, E., Preet, R., Wilder-Smith, A., & Larson, H. (2020). *The Pandemic of social media panic travels faster than the COVID-19 outbreak*. London School of Hygiene and Tropical Medicine.

Designs, D. W. (n.d.). Common reactions to traumatic events. http://www.whentragedystrikes.org/common_reactions.htm

Disaster Preparedness, Response, and Recovery. (2019, May 15). https://www.samhsa.gov/disaster-preparedness

Dixon, A. (2019, November 19). Survey: A growing percentage of Americans have no emergency savings whatsoever. https://www.bankrate.com/banking/savings/financial-security-june-2019/

Dolan, K. (2020, March 13). Think kids won't suffer from COVID-19? Wrong: It threatens them with more poverty, hunger, homelessness. https://www.marketwatch.com/story/think-kids-wont-suffer-from-covid-19-wrong-it-threatens-them-with-more-poverty-hunger-homelessness-2020-03-13

Elizabeth, A. (2020, March 25). What is resilience and why is it important? https://www.lifehack.org/715558/what-is-resilience-and-how-to-be-resilient

Gandel, S. (2020, March 17). Guns and ammo sales spike in U.S. on coronavirus worries. https://www.cbsnews.com/news/guns-ammunition-sales-coronavirus-concerns/

Gantt, P., & Gantt, R. (2020). Disaster psychology: The myths of panic [PowerPoint slides]. www.scm-safety.com/wp-content/uploads/2016/10/DisasterPsychExpanded-2013.pdf

Greenstone, J. L. (2008). *The elements of disaster psychology: Managing psychosocial trauma: An integrated approach to force protection and acute care.* Charles C. Thomas.

Greenstone, J. (2010). Orange Bag Denial. *International Journal of Emergency Mental Health*, *12*(1), 1–3.

Greenstone, J. L. (2015). *Emotional first aid: A field guide to crisis intervention and psychological survival.* Whole Person.

Greenstone, J. L. (2016, August 1). Orange Bag Denial or they called and I'm not ready. https://wholeperson.com/blog/orange-bag-denial-or-they-called-and-im-not-ready

Greenstone, J. L. (2020). DEM 6120-Psychosocial dimensions of disaster [Online classroom sessions]. Nova Southeastern University.

Greenstone, J. L., & Leviton, S. (2011). *Elements of crisis intervention: Crises and how to respond to them* (3rd ed.). Brooks/Cole, Thomson Learning.

Guzman, J. (2020, March 26). New poll finds majority of Americans fear coronavirus will prompt recession. https://thehill.com/changing-america/well-being/longevity/489713-majority-of-americans-fear-coronavirus-could-prompt

Harvard Health Publishing. (2017, November). Ramp up your resilience! https://www.health.harvard.edu/mind-and-mood/ramp-up-your-resilience

Hasseldine, R. (2016, June 22). Why do women find it so difficult to put themselves first? https://www.huffpost.com/entry/why-do-women-find-it-so-d_b_7621976

Holdeman, E. (2008, October 1). Disaster denial. http://cowlitzcountydem.blogspot.com/2008/10/disaster-denial.html

Hollingsworth, J., Griffiths, J., Renton, A., Wagner, M., Hayes, M., & Woodyatt, A. (2020, March 24). March 23 coronavirus news. https://www.cnn.com/world/live-news/coronavirus-outbreak-03-23-20-intl-hnk/index.html

Jennings, K.-A. (2018, August 28). 16 simple ways to relieve stress and anxiety. https://www.healthline.com/nutrition/16-ways-relieve-stress-anxiety

Leanza, N. (2018, July 8). Emotional first aid. https://psychcentral.com/blog/emotional-first-aid/

Li, S., Wang, Y., Xue, J., Zhao, N., & Zhu, T. (2020, March 19). The impact of COVID-19 epidemic declaration on psychological consequences: A study on active Weibo users. *International Journal of Environmental Research and Public Health*, *17*(2032).

Lindberg, S. (2018, May 1). How to calm down: 15 things to do when you're anxious or angry. https://www.healthline.com/health/how-to-calm-down#1

Meyer, R. J., & Kunreuther, H. (2017). *The ostrich paradox: Why we underprepare for disasters.* Wharton Digital Press.

New York Has Roughly 5% of Coronavirus Cases Worldwide. (2020, March 22). https://www.nytimes.com/2020/03/22/nyregion/coronavirus-new-york-update.html

Nguyen, C., Bott, M., Myers, S., & Carroll, J. (2020, March 24). Bay area could run short on hospital beds amid COVID-19 patient surge. https://www.nbcbayarea.com/news/local/bay-area-could-run-short-on-hospital-beds-amid-covid-19-patient-surge/2260197/

Norberg, M., & Rucker, D. (2020, March 20). Psychology can explain why coronavirus drives us to panic buy. It also provides tips on how to stop. http://theconversation.com/psychology-can-explain-why-coronavirus-drives-us-to-panic-buy-it-also-provides-tips-on-how-to-stop-134032

Panic. (n.d.). https://www.oxfordlearnersdictionaries.com/us/definition/english/panic_1

Pfefferbaum, B., & Shaw, J. (2013, November). Practice parameter on disaster preparedness. *Journal of the American Academy of Child & Adolescent Psychiatry, 52*(11), 1224–1235.

Rowett, M. (2017, September 30). Disasters don't plan ahead, but you can: Year-round emergency preparedness tips. https://states.aarp.org/arkansas/disasters-dont-plan-ahead-but-you-can-year-round-emergency-preparedness-tips

Scott, E. (2020, March 20). How to watch for signs of burnout in your life. https://www.verywellmind.com/stress-and-burnout-symptoms-and-causes-3144516

Shaw, B., & Greenstone, J. L. (2020, Summer–Fall). The crisis of the pandemic: Panic or preparedness. *Journal of the American Academy of Experts in Traumatic Stress, 3,* 6–17.

Silva, D. (2020, March 23). Coronavirus isolation raises concerns for domestic violence survivors, experts say. https://www.nbcnews.com/news/us-news/coronavirus-isolation-raises-concerns-domestic-violence-survivors-experts-say-n1165316

Sixty Percent of Americans Not Practicing for Disaster: FEMA Urges Everyone to Prepare by Participating in National PrepareAthon! Day on April 30. (2015). https://www.fema.gov/news-release/2015/04/28/sixty-percent-americans-not-practicing-disaster-fema-urges-everyone-prepare

Social Isolation Leads to Substance Addiction. (n.d.). https://www.narconon.org/blog/narconon/social-isolation-leads-to-substance-addiction/

Stieg, C. (2020, March 13). When it's all too much, here's how to quell coronavirus anxiety, according to experts. https://www.cnbc.com/2020/03/13/how-to-stay-calm-amid-coronavirus-pandemic-anxiety-relief-tips.html

Subramaniam, A. (2020, March 15). The line between preparedness and panic. https://www.psychologytoday.com/us/blog/parenting-neuroscience-perspective/202003/the-line-between-preparedness-and-panic

Swain, B. (2017, October 9). The psychology of riding it out: Why people don't prepare for hurricanes. https://advanced-hindsight.com/blog/psychology-riding-people-dont-prepare-hurricanes/

Taking Care of Yourself. (n.d.). https://www.nami.org/Find-Support/Family-Members-and-Caregivers/Taking-Care-of-Yourself

Tartakovsky, M. (2019, March 29). What to tell yourself when you're in emotional pain. https://psychcentral.com/blog/what-to-tell-yourself-when-youre-in-emotional-pain/

Taylor, D. B. (2020, February 13). A timeline of the coronavirus pandemic. https://www.nytimes.com/article/coronavirus-timeline.html

Vesoulis, A. (2020, March 24). "I'm mentally and physically exhausted." Healthcare workers battling coronavirus are running out of protective gear. https://time.com/5808992/healthcare-workers-lack-ppe/

Wallen, D. (2019, May 31). How to stay calm and cool when you are extremely stressed. https://www.lifehack.org/articles/lifestyle/8-ways-stay-calm-and-cool-how-more-patient-and-less-stressed.html

What Is Emotional First Aid (EFA)? (n.d.). http://www.whentragedystrikes.org/pdfs/what_is_efa.pdf

Willis, O. (2020, March 22). Coronavirus: Social distancing and isolation can take a toll on your mental health; here's how some people are coping. https://www.abc.net.au/news/health/2020-03-22/mental-health-coronavirus-quarantine-self-isolation/12078550

Wilson, S. A., Temple, B. J., Milliron, M. E., Vazquez, C. D., Packard, M. S., & Rudy, B. (2007, December 31). The lack of disaster preparedness by the public and it's affect on communities. http://ispub.com/IJRDM/7/2/11721

Winch, G. (2014a). *Emotional first aid: Healing rejection, guilt, failure, and other everyday hurts.* Penguin.

Winch, G. (2014b). *Emotional first aid: Practical strategies for treating failure, rejection, guilt, and other everyday psychological injuries.* Hudson Street Press.

Winch, G. (2015, February). How to practice emotional first aid [Video]. *YouTube.* https://www.youtube.com/watch?v=F2hc2FLOdhl

Winch, G. (2018, October). Healing, rejection, guilt, and failure [Video]. *YouTube.* https://www.youtube.com/watch?v=3pYnzLiVefg

Chapter Takeaways

Personal Notes

7

The COVID-19 Crisis and Law Enforcement

Officer Weldon Walles, FWPD Retired

"In order to be a successful peace officer, you must see the disaster in slow motion while you react to it in real time." Weldon Walles

In the United States, small departments outnumber large departments significantly. During a pandemic crisis, small departments can be overwhelmed in terms of personnel strength. If several members of a department contract the COVID-19 virus, whether they become symptomatic or not, this could drastically affect the ability of the department to serve the public. It is important to remember that the law enforcement team consists of everyone who contributes to their mission. This includes communications workers (call takers and dispatchers), jail personnel, vehicle maintenance personnel, technicians, administration, records personnel, and any other members of the team.

Large police departments have more personnel resources giving them the ability to utilize off duty personnel to fill in the gaps. Unfortunately, small departments are the most vulnerable and must have a different plan in place that would mitigate the temporary loss of services. For that reason, the suggestions contained in this chapter can be implemented by any department but are presented as considerations for small departments.

Patrol Division

The most important asset of a police department is the patrol division. Patrol officers are the heart and soul of every police department. They are the ones who make initial contact with the public on almost every call for service. The patrol officer is the one who navigates the neighborhoods and are most familiar to the public in general. They are the ones most often blamed when something goes wrong. They are the first line of defense against crime and the most important goodwill ambassadors that a city has to interact with the public. Almost every officer working in a specialized unit that investigates crimes investigates information related to them by patrol officers, officers who initially responded to a call for service. Nearly all cases prosecuted by the district and county attorneys all begin with an initial investigation by a patrol officer. The patrol division is most often taxed with duties that should be assigned to other divisions in the police department or other departments within the city. Additionally, the patrol officer is the most burdened and the least thanked for their service. Although most officers accept the disappointments associated with their jobs and still do the work many suffer from stress caused by the way the system works under "normal" conditions. This stress can and will affect the officer's personal life and at some point, depending on how they cope with the stress, may affect their immune system. In addition to the everyday stress associated with normal operations, the stress caused by the onset of a pandemic can cause patrol assets to be the most threatened asset of the police department. For these reasons, it is critical for a department that experiences a significant loss of patrol personnel, to have protocols in place to ensure that the basic public safety mission is sustained.

Large Departments

What one considers a large police department is subjective. For purposes discussed here, a large police department is defined as one, with respect to the geographic area and population size, has adequate resources to serve the public during normal conditions in addition to adequate personnel in specialized units that can be reassigned to patrol service during a pandemic crisis.

As mentioned earlier, most large departments already have plans in place to deal with personnel reassignments in times of crisis. Most crisis planned for may involve a minimal number of officers affected in the big scheme of things. However, these plans may not address situations where a large part of the department is not available for service in a single instance. Failure to have an existing plan in place could be catastrophic to the public safety mission. Even though this chapter is geared toward suggestion for small departments, the same concepts can be modified for use in a large one. Additionally, large departments should work with smaller ones in order to support their public safety mission as well. Large departments can participate in modified mutual aid agreements, include small departments in specific training related to the crisis and share any helpful data that will be useful to small departments.

Small Departments

For purposes discussed here, a small police department is defined as one, with respect to the geographic area and population size, that has adequate resources to serve the public during normal conditions but lacks adequate personnel in specialized units that can be reassigned to patrol service during a pandemic crisis. These are typically small municipalities and rural Sheriff Departments. In small departments, the patrol officer may take on the role of first responder in addition to investigator. These officers take reports, file the cases, make arrests, process crime scenes, and present testimony in court. Cross training of personnel in these departments is critical during times of crisis as each officer takes on responsibilities that are normally handled by several officers in larger departments. Many small departments rely on reserve officer programs to supplement their staff. Departments that do not have a reserve officer program should consider the benefits such a program would bring to their department. Additionally, small departments should revise mutual aid agreements if they have not already done so to address the unique challenges presented by a pandemic crisis.

Mutual Aid Agreements

Most police departments will have some type of mutual aid agreement. These agreements may be statewide agreements or local agreements. For the purposes of this discussion, it is not important how the agreements work because it varies from state to state. It is important to know that these agreements exist and are designed to allow cities to assist each other in times of crisis.

One action a large department can take that will provide additional personnel to their own department and to their smaller partners is to have a plan in place to temporarily reassign officers who serve in specialized units to the patrol division. These officers can not only utilize their skills as former patrol officers, but they can also use the skills they have gained from working in a specialized unit.

Reassignment of Specialized Unit Personnel as Mutual Aid Responders

Large departments may have many specialized units such as detectives, traffic, crime scene, Special Weapons and Tactics, to name a few, that can be designated as mutual aid responders when assistance is required in a neighboring jurisdiction. By designating these units as mutual aid responders during a time of pandemic crisis, dispatchers could redirect on-duty personnel in these units to assist neighboring communities without taking from an already taxed patrol division.

Patrol Refresher Training

Although these officers were assigned to the patrol division when they first began their careers, it may be necessary to temporarily assign personnel in these units to patrol refresher training. The duties of a patrol officer are constantly changing along with the technology they use. This training should be implemented prior to any crisis to allow the officer to become familiar with new technology, procedures, and processes that have changed since the officer served in patrol.

Cross Training

CROSS TRAINING OFFICERS IN COMMUNICATIONS

Another idea both large and small departments should consider prior to a pandemic crisis is cross training of police department personnel in areas where cross training is not traditionally done. Officers, especially in small departments should be cross trained in communications. The communications staff is critical to the police department's mission. The COVID-19 virus or any other virus that may come along will not be picky about who it infects. Traditionally, communications operators work in tight, close quarters and are more susceptible to exposure from other workers. Knowing that a pandemic can overwhelm the communications staff is reason enough to initiate cross training of officers that can replace exposed workers in a time of crisis.

CROSS TRAINING OFFICERS IN JAIL SERVICES

Many small departments operate jails. Typically, the personnel working in city jails are trained in every job associated with the operation of the jail. Many of the rules and procedures that the corrections officers follow is not familiar to the police officer who works in the law enforcement side of the police department. For this reason, police officers should be cross trained in basic jail services. As with communications workers, corrections officers work in close proximity to each other and detainees of which they have no reliable data as to the exposure level of the individual prior to his entry into the jail. Therefore, jail personnel are more vulnerable and at a higher risk to exposure to a virus than others in the police department. Police departments may want to consider devising a basic corrections officer academy for police officers to attend. The department may be able to use this training as part of the state continuing training requirements.

Protocol on Calls for Service during a Pandemic

During normal noncrisis times the police department can be overwhelmed with calls for service. Minor calls may have to hold for hours before an officer can be dispatched. When this happens, additional stress is placed upon the communications workers because an impatient public will repeatedly call wanting an officer to respond. A pandemic can stress personnel strength to the point that the police department can be overwhelmed with calls for service. During the time of a pandemic crisis when patrol resources are stretched beyond limits it may be necessary to suspend dispatching calls for service that are minor in nature. Suspending nonemergency calls for service should not be taken lightly. If a department chooses to initiate this policy, the department should appoint one or more police supervisors to oversee the suspension of these calls. Certain criteria should be established in writing that when followed will ensure that the call suspended from police response is one where there is no evidence that the call is made from where an emergency exists. This may limit the stress and liability associated with making these decisions.

Suspension of Arrests Involving Misdemeanor Warrants

Police departments may have to take unusual actions in order to keep their patrol force available to answer calls for service where life or property is in danger. One of the duties of officers who patrol is to arrest persons who have existing warrants. Many times, these warrants are related to traffic violations of the misdemeanor category. Officers may, through routine enforcement or investigation discover that a vehicle being driven in their view has a warrant attached to the registration of the vehicle. Officers routinely discover these warrants and initiate a traffic stop in which the final result is the person being taken into custody and transported to jail. Police departments should consider suspending the arrest of persons who have misdemeanor warrants if it is legal to do so in their jurisdiction. This should be applicable when no other serious crime has been committed. By suspending arrests on misdemeanor warrants patrol officers will not be tied up at the jail processing the arrested person leaving them available for more serious calls. However, a policy should be in place that will allow a supervisor to authorize the arrest on the misdemeanor warrant depending on the facts and circumstances of the encounter.

Suspension of Routine Traffic Enforcement

During a pandemic crisis, the mindset of the patrol officer and supervisor should be one where being available for calls that require an emergency response is the top priority. The less close quarter interaction officers have with the public and each other the more helpful it will be in deterring the spread of a pandemic virus. Therefore, departments may consider suspending routine traffic enforcement by patrol officers. This does not mean that officers should ignore traffic violations. It does mean that officers should not deem their sole objective during any part of the shift to be to apprehend traffic violators.

Create an Anti-Exposure Protocol

During a pandemic crisis the department should create an anti-exposure protocol for its officers to follow. This may include wearing masks, refraining from eating in public places, social distancing, suspending any unnecessary interaction with the public.

Create an Exposure Protocol

Departments should consider creating an exposure protocol and define the instances where an officer should report when he is or believes he is exposed to a pandemic virus. The department can create a simple form for an officer to fill out those details on how the exposure occurred. The information from this form can be placed in a database for future reference. The protocol should also outline when an officer should be tested and criteria for removal from and return to service.

Create an Exposure Database

Departments should consider creating a database that captures information related to officer exposure to a pandemic virus. This database can give real-time information on personnel strength helping administrators make decisions on personnel assignments.

Personnel Strength Database

Prior to a pandemic crisis, departments should give consideration to creating a personnel strength database. This database will utilize information from the exposure database and the skill sets of each officer. By creating this database, administrators can at a glance know which officers are not available for reassignment due to exposure to a pandemic virus. For officers who are available for reassignment, the database can assign codes to each officer that relates his fitness for duty in a particular assignment. These codes may also relate personal health information that can allow administrators to determine if a particular assignment will put the officer at an unnecessary risk due to a particular health condition. For example, an officer may be at work, but maybe undergoing chemotherapy or may have a breathing disorder such as bronchitis or asthma putting him at a greater risk if he contracts the virus.

It is critical to keep personal health information private when dealing with information relating to police department personnel. Some officers may choose not to be vaccinated or their health condition is such that they are not able to be vaccinated. The code system used may be multifaceted. The codes used may indicate multiple sets of information. For example, the code may relate that the officer has been vaccinated, previously had Covid, cross trained in several jobs, and any other information the department deems necessary to provide data useful to administrators in planning a response. By doing this, a planning matrix can be designed to fit personnel into assignments without having to analyze each officer's information separately. Even if a pandemic is not experienced, a database of this type can be utilized when emergencies are experienced during normal police operations. Administrators could set the parameters that would rapidly provide administrators with the names of personnel that would fit the needs of a particular assignment.

EXAMPLE OF DATABASE USE

Examples of Data Codes:
A: Certification as Master Peace Officer Proficiency
B: Certification as Advanced Peace Proficiency
C: Certification as Basic Peace Officer Proficiency
D: Probationary Officer
E: Special Investigator Certification
F: Cross Trained in Communications
G: Cross Trained in Jail Operations
H: Cross Trained in Crime Scene investigation

I: Cross Trained as an Investigator/Detective
V: Vaccinated for Covid-19
Rc: Recovered from Covid virus

This list includes a few of the many areas in which data codes may be utilized. The following table is an example of what the data chart may look like for an officer who has been vaccinated, recovered from the COVID 19-virus, holds a master peace officer certification, and is cross trained in communications, jail operations, and has a special investigator certification.

DATA BASE RESULTS

Name	Rank	Assignment	Availability	Code
John Law	Officer	North Division	Yes	A-E-F-G-V-RC

Once the database is in operation the administration can put the desired criteria for their personnel needs into the database and be provided with the names and availability of personnel who fit the parameters of the search. The administrator can then make choices based on existing personnel rules that govern transfer of personnel.

The patrol division of a police department is the backbone of the police department, especially in times of crisis. At the very least, police administration should strive to make the job of the patrol officer as easy as possible. One way to do that is to make as many officers as possible available to assist patrol in their mission. Traditionally, police departments have reserve or part-time officers who work in patrol. Departments should increase the number of reserve officers in their department to help in times of crisis. This influx of additional personnel will help alleviate the complications experienced during a pandemic. Reserve officers cannot be trained overnight and require additional monetary resources. Administrators who wish to create a sustainable reserve force must include this plan in their budgets in time to implement the plan prior to the next pandemic.

Creating a Reserve Force for Jail and Communications Operations

Departments should consider creating a reserve force for jail and communications personnel. Traditionally, reserve forces in these areas do not exist. As mentioned before, the virus is not picky about the occupation of the person it infects and communications and jail workers are at high risk. It only makes sense to create a reserve force for these two areas of the police service. Departments would have to devise a training program similar to that used in the training for reserve police officers and apply that model to the training of communications and jail personnel.

How the Legislature Can Help

The legislature can help police departments by enacting laws that are specific to pandemics. For example, the legislature can work with the state peace officer certification body to create an exception where, under certain conditions, an honorably retired peace officer who chooses to serve, may be reactivated to service for a specific period during a pandemic.

The legislature could give funding to police departments that operate crime labs in order for them to conduct rapid molecular testing. This would give police departments immediate access to testing of their personnel for the COVID-19 virus.

Conclusion

Patrol officers have the most dangerous and difficult job in the police department. During times of crisis no matter what the crisis may be, the patrol officer is the first to respond, the last to leave, and most often taken for granted. If none of the suggestions presented in this chapter are taken and implemented by police administration, at the very least they should devise a plan that will take into consideration the sacrifices these officers make on a daily basis and implement those plans that will make their job easier and safer.

Chapter Takeaways

Personal Notes

Suicide and Disaster Response

James L. Greenstone, Ed.D., J.D., DABECI

Those who may be contemplating taking their own life are not trying to move toward death itself. They are really trying to move away from the extreme pain and severe conflict that they are currently experiencing. Suicide and suicidal gestures are not really about death at all. This realization not only can reduce the fear that interveners and responders may have about talking to someone threatening suicide but also enable them to be truly sensitive to the real issue at hand at that moment. The skills here are invaluable and must be taught early and emphasized often.

The Ten Steps to Dealing with the Potential Suicide

1. *Act early. If you suspect suicide, act now! Don't wait until it's too late. Make contact early. Do not leave the sufferer alone. Time will not work here for the intervener.
2. Speak of suicide openly. If you can talk openly about it, maybe it will be easier for the sufferer to speak of it. Using the word, "suicide" will not make the person suicidal. Tell the sufferer, "I don't want you to die." Listen carefully to what is said. Reassure and remain calm. The sufferer may think that you are there to accuse them. They may also challenge your sincerity. Let the sufferer talk and let them know that you are trying to understand their hurt.
3. *Never say*, "You don't really want to do that." They really do want to do it.
4. *Never say,* "Why do you want to do that?" They probably do not know "why," and the question will increase their defensiveness. Ask present oriented questions if you need information such as, "*What happened?*"; "*How do you feel?*"; "*What's going on?*"; "*Would you like to talk about it?*"

5. Remember that a suicidal person will have trouble focusing on the future and that, *"Things will get better."* Keep your focus on the present and what can be done to assist them now.
6. Never challenge the sufferer to, *"Go ahead and do it."* You may be giving him or her permission to do the act that you will regret for the rest of your life. If there are weapons present, try to remove them, or to convince the subject that putting down the weapon will make things safer for you and the subject. Do not focus too much on the weapon. You can successfully intervene in this situation even if there is a weapon present. Regardless, always protect yourself when weapons, or other potential dangers, are present.
7. Be careful of whom you call to talk, or whom you allow to talk, with the victim. They may be part of the problem. E.g. Family members, minister, doctor. The best person to handle a suicidal individual is a trained intervener or responder.
8. Remember: Suicide has nothing to do with death. Suicide has to do with conflict in a person's life between the sufferer and at least one other person or institution, either present or absent in their life at the moment. Death may be only the unfortunate by-product of the suicidal gesture.
9. If you believe that the person is suicidal, do not leave them alone. If physically with the person, stay with him or her or get someone else to stay if you must leave. If on the phone, stay on the phone with them to the degree that you can. If you must get off the phone, or if the subject gets off the phone, make contact again without unnecessary delay.
10. Rule of Thumb: Check out the "specificity of the suicidal plan," and the "lethality of the suicidal means." The more specific the plan and the more lethal the means, the greater the risk of suicide. Ask the sufferer what he or she intends to do and how. There may come a time during a suicide intervention when you believe that the subject is about to act on their suicide plan. At such a time, a tactical, or combined intervention, resolution may be necessary. Always have such a plan in place for such an eventuality.*

The Lethality Scale

	0 points	1 point	2 points	3 points	4 points	Total
Age Male	0-12 yrs.		13-44 yrs.	45-64 yrs.	65 and Up	
Age Female	0-12 yrs.	13-44 yrs.	45 and Up			
Personal Resources Available	Good	Fair		Poor		
Current Stress	Low		Medium		High	
Marital Status	Married with Children	Married without Children		Widowed or Single	Divorced	
Current Psychological Functioning	Stable			Unstable		
Other problems or symptoms	Absent			Present		

Communication Channels	Open			Blocked		
Physical Condition	Good	Fair			Poor	
Suicide by Close Family Member	No		Yes			
Depressed or Agitated Currently	No				Yes	
Prior Suicidal Behavior by Subject	No		Yes			
Reactions by Significant Others to the Needs of the Subject	Helpful			Not Helpful		
Current Financial Stress	Absent		Present			
Suicidal Plan of the Subject	Has None	Plan with Few Details	Subject has Selected the Means for Suicide		Subject has a Highly Specific Plan for Suicide	
Occupation of Subject	Non-Helping Profession or Other Occupation	M.D., Dentist, Attorney, or Helping Professional	Psychiatrist, Police Officer, or Unemployed			
Residence	Rural	Suburban	Urban			
Living Arrangements	Lives with Others				Lives Alone	
Time of the Year this Incident is Occurring		Spring				
Day of the Week this Incident Occurring		Sunday or Wednesday	Monday			
Recent Occurrence of Serious Arguments with Spouse or Significant Other	No	Yes				
Recently, the Subject's Significant Other Was:		The Focus of a Disappointment	Lost to the Subject in Some Significant Way			
					TOTAL POINTS	

CHAPTER 8: Suicide and Disaster Response

The "Rule of Thumb" referred to can be of help in a field situation when a quick assessment of suicidality is needed. However, the Lethality Scale can provide additional and considerably more detailed information for making this evaluation. It takes time to utilize the Lethality Scale correctly. It can also be utilized throughout the incident as more information about the subject or victims becomes available. As the accuracy of the information utilized increases, the usefulness of the Scale also increases.

FIGURE 8.1. THE LETHALITY SCALE OF THE AMERICAN ACADEMY OF CRISIS INTERVENERS

Name of Subject:

Date and Time Scale Completed:

Name of Negotiator Completing this Scale:

Criteria

Minimal Risk (0-15 points) _____

Comments and Action Notes:

Low Risk (16-30 points) _____

Medium Risk (31-46 points) _____

High Risk (47-60 points) _____

Directions for Use: Circle response in appropriate row and column. Place points from top of column in the far-right column. Sum all scores under Total Points and match with total Criteria at bottom of page. Scale can be run multiple times on same subject as more information becomes available.

Source: Dr. Edward S. Rosenbluh

Suicide by Cop

This is a very dangerous situation in which the suicidal victim may use the police to accomplish the suicidal act.

You may be talking to a potential "suicide by cop" victim if he or she:
- Demands he be killed by you or by the police department.
- Sets deadlines for his or her own death.
- Requests additional weapons.
- Has just killed a "significant other" in their life. E.g. Spouse, parent or a young child.
- Provides you with a "verbal will."
- Has an elaborate plan for his death.

Note: This person represents a significant threat to hostages, themselves, and to negotiators and other law enforcement officers and responders. This individual may take an officer's life in order to cause a deadly response by the police. He may kill a negotiator or intervener who has elected to go face to face.

Adolescent Suicide

Adolescent Suicide and Negotiating with the Young Suicidal Actor must be considered carefully. The teenage years are a period of turmoil for just about everyone experiencing them. Many changes are taking place both emotionally and physically and new social roles are being learned. Sometimes solutions to problems are not readily available to the teen and the result can be loneliness. The more that interveners and responders understand about the unique nature of teen suicidal actors, the better prepared they will be to intervene effectively.

All of us speculate about how our life will be and what we should do to make it so. With teens, it can be particularly difficult to understand all that is going on around them. Family problems, divorce, embarrassment and even poor grades in school can exacerbate a sense of great concern about one's life and the reasons to continue or to end it. Teens may have some difficulty recognizing the bigger picture that just as things change, so do feelings and inner turmoil. It may become too much to handle for the young mind and depression can result. Such depression increases the risk of suicidal behavior. There may be a need for support during these times and such support might come from a parent, a good friend, or a mental health professional. However, recognition of the problem by those closest to the teen is the first step in the process toward better mental help at these times. Denial will not make the problem go away. Undoubtedly, it will make the problem worse as the loneliness and the feelings of not being understood increase. To the contrary, with effective help, most can recover from the depression fairly quickly.

WHAT TO LOOK FOR

Mood swings are normal. A lot of swings in mood often accompany teen years. Everyone feels sad at times. Feeling sad is not out of focus here. A depressed mood that continues for two weeks or more could be a significant sign that deserves our attention. Listen to what teens say. Watch what teens do. Help could be needed if you hear: "I am sleeping much later than I used to." Or, "I'm not sleeping well and I wake up early in the morning." "I am beginning to take a lot of naps," could be cause for some concern. Changes in appetite and unplanned weight gains or losses are additional clues. Remember that you do not have to be a psychologist to pay attention to the signs of suicide in teenagers or to take appropriate action when needed.

What to listen for:
- "I feel restless."
- "I have withdrawn from friends and family."
- "I can't concentrate very well."
- "I've lost interest or pleasure in my usual activities."

- "I feel guilty," or "I feel hopeless and helpless."
- "I used to be outgoing. Now I seem to be withdrawing."
- "I have sudden mood changes."
- "I really feel that life is not worth living anymore."

MORE CLUES

- *It seems to be that young people who have attempted suicide in the past are at greater risk.
- Those who talk about suicide may actually do it. It is a myth to think otherwise.
- Feelings of loneliness, hopelessness and rejection are characteristics of those teens who may consider killing themselves.
- Some teens who abuse alcohol or drugs are more likely to consider, attempt or succeed at suicide than are non-abusers.
- Teens who may be planning to kill themselves may give away personal possessions, discard things that are usually meaningful to them, or begin cleaning their own room.
- The teen may suddenly become cheerful, or even appear upbeat, after a bout with depression. The sudden change may foretell that they have made the decision to end their own life. Do not put off getting help in these circumstances.
- Remember that one of the most dangerous times occur when severe loss of any kind has been experienced or personal humiliation has been felt.*

Content between asterisks from *Elements of Crisis Intervention: Crises and How to Respond to Them*, 3rd edition, by James L. Greenstone and Sharon C. Leviton, 2011. Cengage Learning Inc. Reproduced by permission. www.cengage.com/permissions

Some findings may help understand these situations.
1. Those who talk of helplessness and hopelessness may be at great risk.
2. Talking about suicide will not prevent it from happening as some believe.
3. Depression and the ultimate risk of suicide may have biological as well as psychological causes.
4. A family history of suicide may be a significant risk factor in predicting suicidal behavior in teens.
5. The suicide rate for teens is about the same as the national average. Although not as high as the media would have us believe, suicide among teenagers is a serious health problem.
6. Males seem to commit suicide more than females. Females attempt suicide more often, however.

The American Psychiatric Association and The American Psychological Association provide much insight into teen suicide and suicide intervention. Many times, persons who are depressed, or depressed and suicidal, will find it hard to talk to anyone about what they feel. Feelings of worthlessness and hopelessness may contribute to this unwillingness to reach out to others. They may even deny their own emotions or think that talking to someone will only burden the listener. Remember, they may truly believe that no one cares anyway. Some may feel that someone will make fun of them.

Although much of the reluctance to reach out and express themselves may be justified by previous encounters, such can make the problems worse. We know that most of those who may contemplate suicide will leave some clues. Also, we know that in many cases the teen who is suicidal has spoken with, or at least tried to speak with, someone about what the teen is experiencing. If the teen alludes to the subject of suicide or brings it up directly, take it seriously and take some time to talk about it. The difference that this small act of talking and listening can make could be inestimable.

Reassure the troubled teen that he or she has those around them that are ready and willing to help. Do not be afraid to listen to the teen and to try to understand the dilemma of wanting to live on the one hand and die on the other. It is part of the experience. Sometimes it is hard to let someone else know that there is a need to talk about something as serious as our emotions.

There is a tendency when talking with a person who is suicidal to preach or to lecture about why the teen should not kill himself or herself. Further, it will not be very helpful to point out to the teen all of the reasons for staying alive or the things for which the teen has to live. Instead, listen and reassure. I repeat for emphasis, **listen and reassure!** Depression and suicidal tendencies can be treated successfully. Tell the teen that also, but only after you have listened a lot and reassured as needed. We know that depressive disorders respond well to psychotherapy and to medication. Antidepressants can act within two to three weeks and are often used in addition to psychotherapy.

Chapter Takeaways

Personal Notes

Crisis in Families and with Children

Sharon C. Leviton, Ph.D., DABECI

Crisis and the management of crises have become front and center in our daily lives. Increasingly, the news media, the blogs, the discussions at the dinner table and conversations online focus on the crisis of the day. There is a ripple effect of anxiety, concern, sadness, and grief that we share to a greater or lesser degree. We hear the voices of the victims and today's technology allows us to see their hurt up close regardless of the geographical distance that separates us.

At any given time 24/7, an individual responder, a team of responders, or multiple teams may be responding and they are providing emotional first aid in crisis situations.

Well trained responders learn early in their careers that having an established procedure to follow is vital to enhancing their effectiveness. A crisis intervention is a logical and orderly process. Step by step the responder assists the victim in moving from a state of disequilibrium to at least their precrisis level of functioning.

The time to develop a procedure is before attempting to respond. Every action and every interaction must be thoughtful, measured, and purposeful. This is not a time to say, "I will try this out and see what happens." Such a haphazard approach would court disaster for the victim and the responder. Be aware, be prepared, train, train, train.

Contributed by Sharon Leviton. © Kendall Hunt Publishing Company. Content between single asterisks throughout the chapter is from *Elements of Crisis Intervention: Crises and How to Respond to Them*, 3rd edition, by James L. Greenstone and Sharon C. Leviton, 2011. Cengage Learning Inc. Reproduced by permission. www.cengage.com/permissions

What Is a Crisis?

A crisis occurs when unusual stress temporarily renders an individual unable to direct his or her life effectively. As the stress mounts and the usual coping mechanisms provide neither relief nor remedy, the person often experiences extreme feelings of grief, hostility, helplessness, hopelessness, and alienation from self, family, and society. Stress can be a reaction to a single event or to several events occurring simultaneously or serially.

Over their lifetime, people develop assumptions and points of view which color and determine their behavior. They act daily in accordance with these concepts and deeply held beliefs. This may be why what seems crisis producing to one person may be quite ordinary to another. The need to identify the victim's perception of the crisis event is a key element in effective crisis management. The way the crisis victim currently perceives the world is the victim's reality.

Family Crisis

*Excessive stress and tension, usually resulting from multiple or significant changes in a person's life, are often the basis of most crisis situations. Because family members do not operate in a vacuum, one person's crisis often becomes a crisis for the family. Major sources of personal crises include illness, financial problems, business problems, job promotions/demotions/or loss, problems with one's children, layoffs, maintenance of a current career or entrance into a new one, adoption or birth of children, abortion, pending marriage, separation and divorce, blending of stepfamilies, severe injuries, deaths in the family, health care issues, eldercare issues, gender issues, safety and protection issues, housing issues, education issues, intimacy, relationship issues, ineffective parenting, child neglect and abuse.

Most crises have a primary victim, but they also touch those who are affected through the primary victim. These secondary victims are usually significant others of the person experiencing the crisis. In rapes, suicide, battering, incest, drug abuse, family disputes, natural disasters, war, death, and illness, the intensity of the trauma, the emotional upheaval, and the difficulty in adjustment relating to the event can be as severe for the significant others as for the primary victim. Secondary victims often experience their own crisis as they try to fit what has happened into life as they see it. For example, a rape victim's parents, spouse, or boyfriend, or the children who witnessed the rape might experience their own crisis with an intensity equal to that of the primary victim. Guidelines and procedures for crisis situations with primary victims must be applied in a similar manner to significant others. Unfortunately, a responder often overlooks this task particularly where children are involved. The well-meaning responder might feel pressed for time, might not ask whether children are in the house, might not gain permission to speak with the children, or might not be aware of the importance of meeting with the children. Children's reality is frequently formed by fantasy, partial truths, and an immature ability to discern what is happening around them. They need their own reliable source to listen and to respond effectively to their feelings and concerns.

The group of significant others has been broadened increasingly to include co-workers, schoolmates, teammates, and many others who collectively or individually are impacted by a crisis situation in their setting. When bad things such as shootings, hostage situations, suicides, injuries, deaths, accidents, and disasters of other types happen in a workplace, a school, a hospital, or a courthouse, the emotional fall out spreads beyond that of the primary victim's family. Suddenly and unexpectedly, co-workers and fellow students who survive must face their own vulnerability and their personal concerns that the tragedy has triggered. In a matter of minutes their environment has undergone a change. They could have been the primary victim of the shooter, or the hostage taker or of a careless driver. Their life could have ended in a mine shaft accident. The situation becomes personal. Increasingly, crisis response teams are brought into these situations to provide emotional first aid as needed.

1. Pull together as a family by establishing a sense of purpose.
2. Allow your feelings to be whatever they are; avoid berating yourself for discounting your feelings or those of your children.
3. Let your children talk with you about their fears, concerns, confusion, anger, sadness, and problems.
4. Talk in words your children can understand. Avoid euphemisms.
5. Allow your children to see your grief and be honest with them about your feelings. Avoid as much gore as possible in your expressions.
6. Don't expect your children to resolve your grief.
7. Reassure your children that they are safe and will be taken care of.
8. Don't be afraid to say that you do not know the answers to your children's questions. Your honesty may make it easier for them to tolerate the ambiguity in their own minds.
9. If a death occurs, share with your children in terms that they can understand.
10. Remember that children often take their lead for their own behavior from their parents. Children will watch and learn how you handle crises.
11. Children will look to you for structure, guidance, limits and support. Give these things to them.
12. Ask your children what they need from you. Maybe they need a hug, time to talk, play time with you, or straight talk. Children of different ages will need different things at different times. Adapt your actions to your children's ages and levels of maturity.
13. Identify areas of concern in your life over which you have control, and exercise that control.
14. Have realistic expectations of yourself and your children to minimize stress.
15. Be realistic about each child's role in the family.
16. Continue projects that you have begun.
17. Create a routine for yourself and stick to it.
18. Maintain your personal health and hygiene.
19. Plan outings and activities with friends. This mutual support can be helpful.
20. Set boundaries with your children. Hear their feelings, and understand the behavior that might result from these feelings. Establish limits to provide stability, structure, and continuity. Don't overdo it by being too strict or too lenient.
21. Observe changes in your children's behavior, attitudes, and expressions. Pay attention to both verbal and non verbal behavior. Be prepared to respond as appropriate.

22. Use support groups as necessary for your children and for yourself. Participate separately or together with your children, as appropriate.
23. Obtain professional help for yourself and your children as needed. Sometimes counseling in conjunction with support groups offers maximum benefit.
24. Find something to laugh about each day. Use laughter to assist in managing stress.
25. Walk or exercise regularly and include sufficient rest and relaxation in your schedule.
26. Both for yourself and for your children, maintain the continuity of the familiar. This includes schedules, school attendance, friendships, TV programs, and regular activities.
27. Listen.
28. Hear.
29. Respond.
30. Model.
31. Don't lecture.

HOW PARENTS CAN HELP THEIR CHILDREN COPE WITH CRISIS-RELATED FEELINGS

1. Talk with your child; provide simple, accurate answers to questions.
2. Talk with your child about your own feelings.
3. Listen to what your child says and how he/she says it. Does the child display fear, anxiety, or insecurity? Repeating your child's words can be very helpful. Use phrases such as "You are afraid that..." or "You wonder if ...". This helps both you and your child clarify feelings.
4. Reassure your child. For example, tell him/her, "We are together. I love you and I will take care of you."
5. You may need to repeat information and reassurances to your child many times. Do not stop responding just because you told your child something once.
6. Hold your child. Provide comfort. Touching is important for children during crises.
7. Spend extra time putting your child to bed; talk and offer reassurance. Leave a night-light on if necessary.
8. Observe your child at play. Listen to what your child says, and watch how he/she plays. Frequently children express feelings of fear or anger while playing with dolls, toy trucks, or friends.
9. Provide play experiences to relieve tension. Work with Play-Doh, paint pictures, play in water, or some favorite activity. If children show a need to hit or kick, give them something safe such as a pillow or a ball.
10. If your child has an especially meaningful toy or blanket, allow him/her to rely on it somewhat more than usual.
11. If you need professional assistance, seek it early to maximize the benefits.

Crisis, Stress, and Holiday Celebrations

Holidays, birthdays, and anniversaries all come sooner than we expect. For many people, the prospect of the holidays and of family celebrations is filled with anguish and anxiety. And when these holidays and celebrations take place without that special loved one, they are much harder to get through. Holidays can be accompanied by the emotional battering of anticipatory stress followed by post holiday blues. It can take weeks to recover from the agony of unfilled expectations, the debt resulting from overspending to create the "perfect holiday," and the disappointment of rediscovering that family conflicts and losses remain unresolved despite the promises of holiday music and commercial messages.

Therapists know that holidays are times when patients and clients often turn away from the hard work they have been doing with their counselors and rely on the season, the holiday, or the celebration to do it for them. Loan officers know they will be deluged with requests from people who will "buy now and worry later."

During holiday seasons, loneliness, depression, alienation, stress, exacerbated personal problems and situations, financial problems, disappointment, dissatisfaction, lack of fulfillment, unrealized hopes, aging, loss, fear, gain, anxiety, terror, guilt and unresolved worry plague many of us. Present perhaps all year long, tensions increase with the expectation that somehow, in some way, the holiday will make it "all better." The season itself does little or nothing to solve the problems in our lives. Yet many of us annually perpetuate the fantasy that this year it will be different. The responsibility for creating emotional comfort rests with the individual, not the season. Changing our belief from "the holiday will make it better" to "I will make it better" is the first major step in managing holiday stress and preventing post-holiday letdown.

TEACHABLE MOMENT

The responsibility for creating emotional comfort rests with the individual, not the season or the holiday.

TWENTY STEPS FOR AVOIDING HOLIDAY CRISIS

1. Be realistic in your expectations about holidays and celebrations. Keep the euphemisms about the holiday in balance, and accept things as they are at the moment. Remember that acceptance does not necessarily mean agreement.
2. Remember, it is not what the holiday does for us, but what we do with the holiday that makes the difference. Use these events to build family unity, strengthen the bonds between family members, and remember loved ones who are far away.
3. Recognize that you are responsible for your life and that nothing and no one can be responsible for you. Saying to yourself, "If only Bob were here everything would be OK," merely sidesteps your getting on with your life as necessary.
4. Live year-round, and especially at this season, by the present realities, not by your fantasy of how you want things to be.
5. Look to yourself as the source of your well-being and happiness.
6. Spend realistically. Give realistically. Going into debt will not create a "perfect" holiday or celebration.
7. Put gift giving and tasks in perspective.
8. Recognize your grown children as adults.
9. If necessary, remind your parents that you are an adult.

10. Clarify family expectations long before the holiday season or celebration. Communicate feelings, exchange ideas, discuss arrangements, and check schedules; include all family members as appropriate. Avoid assumptions.
11. If you are planning a visit with your parents, make your expectations clear. Alert your parents about arrangements you might be considering. Avoid assumptions about babysitting, sleeping arrangements, transportation, and so on. "Home for the holidays" can be either a nightmare or a lovely experience. Consideration, fairness, clarity, careful planning, and shared feelings help determine a visit's success.
12. Invite your parents to your home for the holiday.
13. Acknowledge and allow for the feelings you experience. What you feel is very real. Allow yourself to miss loved ones who are away, and allow your children to express their feelings.
14. Remember it is all right to let your children see your feelings; it may help them learn more about handling theirs.
15. Share the work of holiday events. Assuming all the responsibility often results in victimhood.
16. Stick to regular diet and sleep routines as much as possible.
17. Manage your time. Learn to say no when saying yes would be unrealistic.
18. To avoid letdown, plan some interesting activities for after the holidays.
19. If you are in counseling, stay in counseling during the holiday season.
20. Learn to appreciate who and what you have rather than wishing you had someone or something else.
21. Enjoy this particular time of the year, and this particular time of your life. It will never happen again.

Reactions of Children to Crisis

The adult members of the family came home after the funeral. Judy, aged six, ran to her mother and hugged her. Judy asked a few questions about the funeral ceremony but as usual got no satisfying answers. Her mother tearfully replied, "Grandma is in heaven now. Go see if Amy can play with you this afternoon."

Judy had had a special relationship with her grandmother. Mrs. Brown lived with the Smiths until she required institutional care. Judy never really understood why her grandmother had been sent away. In fact, there were a lot of things Judy wondered and worried about. Why couldn't she visit her grandmother after she became ill? What did Grandma look like when she was sick? How would she find out the end of the stories Grandma told her? How will she be able to share secrets with Grandma now? Her biggest concern was what did she do bad to make Grandma leave her? Now that Grandma's gone to heaven, who will answer her questions?

Judy didn't want to play. She was afraid to disturb her mother. She felt lonely, stuck and desperately in need to talk with Grandma.

Childhood crisis might be more difficult to assess than adult crisis. Children have a limited fund of experience with which to handle crisis, limited cognitive structure, limited training, and usually an immature emotional base. Perhaps even more important is the fact that very young children have not yet developed a sense of cause and effect nor a sense of time. Therefore, whatever pain occurs seems to go on forever. As the child becomes older and struggles with their identify, independence, psychological changes, peer pressures, and cultural and parental demands the potential for heightened stress increases. Often, as occurred with Judy, the child's need for help goes unrecognized, ignored or belittled. Often as also occurred with Judy, the child is told to go out and play; to be a big boy or a big girl; to be the man of the house now that Daddy is gone as a result of divorce, military service, job transfer, or illness. The child is to be seen but not heard.

Often, on an act of protectiveness, parents exclude children from discussions of crises. Questions may be answered evasively or not at all, as in the case of Judy. Protectiveness carried to extremes, may result in the child's having little ability to communicate concerns, to have questions answered, or to establish the cognitive and emotional channels necessary for their own adaption to change and loss.'

The responder can help the child deal with concerns such as:
- Threat to nurturance.
- Changing patterns of expression of feelings.
- Disrupted patterns of communication.
- Changes in lifestyle because of finances.
- Disrupted scheduling.
- Necessity of assuming responsibilities beyond their abilities.
- Perception of loss.
- The need to grieve.

Difficulties with schoolwork and peer relationships; excessive withdrawal; repeated angry outbursts; and involvement in repetitive, ritualistic, symbolic acts may reflect the stresses experienced by the child. These difficulties can be managed through skillful intervention.

As an example, in intervening with Judy, the little girl in the case described above, the following procedure might have been used by her mother:
1. Legitimize her feelings. Judy clearly expressed her need to be heard and her frustration at being discounted. She felt abandoned by her grandmother who died recently, yet possibly responsible for her leaving them through some unknown behavior on Judy's part. She grieved over unfinished business with her grandmother. There was no chance to hear the end of the stories and share secrets. An effective intervener would listen to the child and acknowledge her feelings with honesty and caring.
2. Provide Judy information according to her emotional and cognitive capacity. Perhaps the mother could explain, "Grandma did not dessert you; and we did not send her away. Sometimes people need care that they can best get in a hospital or a special nursing home. Mommy and Daddy loved Grandma as you do, and we wanted her to have the best care possible. We picked a very special place that we thought she would like. Grandma loved you very much. She enjoyed telling you those stories. Soon you will be able to read them yourself. That might be a special way of spending some pretend time with Grandma."
3. Assure her that Grandma is no longer suffering pain or discomfort. "I saw Grandma after she died. She looked comfortable and not in pain." It is not necessary at this time to go into a long, detailed descrip-

tion. Judy merely needs some reassurance about what dead people and her Grandmother in particular look like.

4. Offer to take Judy to the gravesite. Allow it to be her choice to accept or reject the offer. Going there will provide her with an opportunity for visiting with Grandma and seeing the site. Let her dictate whether she wants Mother to stand beside her or would prefer a few moments of privacy with her grandmother. Afterward, ask if she has any other questions or wants to share any ideas or feelings. Judy might just jump in the car and suggest getting an ice-cream cone. The relief of seeing that everything is in order is an important part of the adaptation process.
5. Provide her the nurturing that she asked for. Return her hug and hold her. Let her know by your touch that you are not pushing her away.
6. If necessary, explain that you are tired now and would like some time alone. At this point, Judy can probably accept your need to move to some other activity. Her immediate needs have been met.

GENERAL REACTIONS OF CHILDREN TO CRISIS

Although many feelings and reactions are shared by people of all ages in response to the direct or indirect effects of crisis, meeting the needs of children requires special attention.

Typical reactions of children, regardless of age, include the following:
- Fears stemming from the crisis extending to their home or neighborhood.
- Loss of interest in school.
- Regressive behavior.
- Sleep disturbances and night terrors.
- Fears of events that may be associated with the crisis situation, such as airplane sounds or loud noises, replays on TV of the incident.

REACTIONS OF SPECIFIC AGE GROUPS

Children of different age groups tend to react in unique ways to the stress caused by crises and their consequences. The following typical reactions to stress are summarized for each age group and are followed by suggested responses.

Preschool (Ages 1-5)

Typical reactions to stress include the following:
- Thumb-sucking.
- Bed-wetting.
- Fear of the dark or of animals.
- Clinging to parents.
- Night terrors.
- Loss of bladder or bowel control or constipation.

- Speech difficulties.
- Loss of or increase in appetite.
- Fear of being left alone.
- Immobility.

Children in this age group are particularly vulnerable to disruption of their previously secure world. Because they lack the verbal and conceptual skills necessary to cope effectively with sudden stress by themselves, they look to family members for comfort. These children are often strongly affected by the reactions of parents and other family members.

Abandonment is a major fear in this age group. Children who have lost family members (or even pets or toys) because of circumstances either related or unrelated to the crisis will need special reassurance.

We recommend the following responses to help children integrate their experiences and reestablish a sense of security and mastery.
- Encourage expression through play reenactment where appropriate.
- Provide verbal reassurance and physical comforting.
- Give the child frequent attention.
- Encourage the child's expression of feelings and concerns regarding the loss, temporary or permanent, of family members, pets, toys, or friends.
- Provide comforting bedtime routines.
- Allow the child to sleep in the same room with the parent. Make it clear to the child that this is only for a limited period.

Early Childhood (Ages 5-11)

Common reactions to stress in this age group include the following:
- Irritability.
- Whining.
- Clinging.
- Aggressive behavior at home or at school.
- Overt competition with younger siblings for parent's attention.
- Night terrors, nightmares, or fear of darkness.
- School avoidance.
- Loss of interest and poor concentration in school.
- Fear of personal harm.
- Confusion.
- Fear of abandonment.
- Generalized anxiety.

Fear of loss is particularly difficult for these children to handle, and regressive behavior is most typical of this age group.

We recommend the following responses:
- Patience and tolerance.
- Play sessions with adults and peers where affective reactions can be openly discussed.
- Discussions with adults and peers about frightening anxiety-producing aspects of events and about appropriate behavior to manage the child's concerns and the stress.
- Relaxation of expectations at school or at home. It should be made clear to the child that this relaxation is temporary and that the normal routine will be resumed after a suitable period.
- Opportunities for structured, but not unusually demanding, chores and responsibilities at home.
- Maintenance of a familiar routine as much as possible and as soon as possible.

Preadolescent (Ages 11-14)

The following are common reactions to stress for this age group:
- Sleep disturbances.
- Appetite disturbance.
- Rebellion in the home.
- Refusal to do chores.
- School problems, such as fighting, withdrawal, loss of interest, and attention-seeking behavior.
- Physical problems, such as headaches, vague aches and pains, skin eruptions, bowel problems, and psychosomatic complaints.
- Loss of interest in peer social activities.
- Fear of personal harm; fear of impending loss of family members, friends or home.
- Anger.
- Denial.
- Generalized anxiety.

Peer reactions are especially significant in pre-adolescence. These children need to feel that their fears are both appropriate and shared by others. Reponses should be aimed at assessing tensions, anxieties, and possible guilt feelings.

We recommend the following responses:
- Group activities geared toward the resumption of routines.
- Involvement with same age group activity.
- Group discussions geared toward examining feelings about the crisis and appropriate behavior to manage the concerns and the stress.
- Structured, but undemanding, responsibilities.
- Temporarily relaxed expectations of performance at school and at home.
- Additional individual attention and consideration.

Adolescents (Ages 14-18)

Common reactions in this age group include the following:
- Psychosomatic symptoms, such as rashes, bowel problems, and asthma.
- Headaches and tension.
- Appetite and sleep disturbances.
- Hypochondriasis.
- Amenorrhea or dysmenorrhea.
- Agitation or decrease in energy level.
- Apathy.
- Decline in interest in the opposite sex.
- Irresponsible behavior, delinquent behavior, or both.
- Decline in emancipatory struggles over parental control.
- Poor concentration.
- Guilt.
- Fear of loss.
- Anger at the perceived unfairness of a crisis occurring in their lives.
- Tendency to blame others for negative events that befall them.

Most of the activities and interests of adolescents are focused in their own age-group peers. Adolescents tend to be especially distressed by the disruption of their peer-group activities and by their lack of access to full adult responsibilities in community efforts.

We recommend the following responses:
- Encourage participation in the community and in individual responses.
- Encourage discussion of feelings, concerns, and shared information with peers and extra family significant others.
- Temporarily reduce expectations for specific levels of both school and general performance, depending on individual reactions.
- Encourage, but do not insist upon, discussions of crisis-induced fears within the family setting.

When to Refer Children to Mental Health Professionals

A wide range of normal reactions surround crisis. Usually the reactions can be dealt with by support at home and at school, but this is not always the case. Sometimes the responder needs to recommend professional help. In making such a referral, it is important to stress that it is not a sign of the parents' failure if they find that they cannot help their child by themselves. It is also important to note that early action will help the child return to normal functioning and avoid more severe problems later.

Students who have lost family members or friends, either temporarily or permanently, or feel that they were in extreme danger are at special risk. Those who have been involved in individual or family crises in addition to the crisis they are currently experiencing might have more difficulty dealing with the additional stress. Counseling may be recommended as a preventive measure when these circumstances are known to exist.

Referral is recommended when symptoms that are considered normal reactions persist for several months or disrupt the student's social, mental, or physical functioning.

REFERRAL FOR PRESCHOOL AND ELEMENTARY SCHOOL CHILDREN

Consider referring the family for professional help if the children react in these ways:
- Seem excessively withdrawn.
- Do not respond to special attention and attempts to draw them out.

REFERRAL FOR JUNIOR AND SENIOR HIGH SCHOOL CHILDREN

Consider referral to a mental health professional if students react in the following ways:
- Are disoriented; for example, are unable to give their own name and address or the date.
- Complain of significant memory gaps.
- Are despondent and show agitation, restlessness, and pacing.
- Are severely depressed and withdrawn.
- Mutilate themselves.
- Use drugs or alcohol excessively.
- Are unable to care for themselves in such areas as eating, drinking, bathing, and dressing.
- Repeat ritualistic acts.
- Experience hallucinations, such as hearing voices or seeing visions.
- State that their body feels "unreal" and express the concern that they are "going crazy."
- Are excessively preoccupied with one idea or thought.
- Have the delusion that someone or something is out to get them and their family.
- Are afraid that they will commit suicide or kill another person.
- Are unable to make simple decisions or carry out everyday functions.
- Show extremely pressured speech or talk overflow.
- Exhibit chronic disruptive behavior.
- Make self-destructive decisions.

Grief, Loss and Change: Identifying the Grief Factor in Crisis Situations

Every crisis situation involves an element of grief. Crisis involves loss, and loss often results in grief. A person grieves over the loss of anything felt to be important in his or her life. If the loss is so great that it totally tears apart the victim's sense of wellbeing, the person will experience crisis. If the loss is felt to be minor, the grieving process might be completed quickly with the person using his or her usual coping mechanisms.

It is important for the responder to understand that four elements determine the effect of grief on an individual. These are the intensity of the emotions experienced as a result of the loss, the personal value attached to the loss, the perceived long-term effects the loss will have on the person's life, and the person's resiliency to adapt to change.

As in every crisis situation, the significance of the loss is determined by the victim. Crisis is always in the eyes of the beholder. The way the victim currently perceives the world is the victim's reality. The responder must recognize this principle in order to be effective and thus, helpful to the victim.*

Mistaken Assumption: "I Know Exactly How You Feel." Even under the best conditions, this is doubtful. If you say you know and you really do not, your credibility is destroyed. If you make such a statement to a victim, be prepared to back it up with accurate information about the victim's feelings. Making assumptions about the victim's feelings too early in the intervention can prove disastrous. Victims of a crisis often want to talk to someone, but they will not talk indiscriminately. Being in crisis does not preclude testing the sincerity of those who say they want to help. The victim can challenge your assumptions by saying, "OK, how do I feel?" or "How can you know how I feel? We just met!" The unprepared responder might have to do some fast backpedaling. Begin with an apology: "I am sorry. I can't know exactly what you're feeling unless you tell me. Would you share..." or "How did that make you feel when...".

Effective responders understand that words have the potential to calm or incite, to empower or diminish, to provide clarity or create confusion, to open up or close down the flow of information, and to enhance or sabotage the process of assisting the victim regain a sense of equilibrium and structure.

Mistaken Assumption: Listening to and Acknowledging Feelings Implies That I Agree with the Victim and the Victim's Behavior

With a person in crisis it is possible to listen and respond to feelings even though you do not agree with the person's actions.

*Consider the following statements made by crisis victims to the responder:
- "We moved into a brand-new beautiful home last month."
- "My daughter got married last week to a fine young man."
- "Well, I finally retired last week."
- "My company was downsized. I lost my job."
- "My wallet was stolen."
- "My husband was granted sole custody of our kids."
- "My wife died recently."
- "My house was broken into."
- "I can't find the paper napkin." The victim is 4 years old.

- "I found out yesterday that I have breast cancer."
- "My bird died this morning."
- "My husband's military unit is probably going to deploy soon."
- "I used to love my husband."

The first 3 situations might seem to evoke positive reactions. The final 10 situations might seem to evoke sad reactions. All the statements are repeated below. This time, under each individual statement is an additional statement that identifies the crisis. This information was provided to the responder during the assessment phase of the intervention.

- "We moved into a brand-new beautiful home last month."
  Crisis: I did not want to change my life. I did not want to leave my friends, my neighbors, my garden that I spent 8 years developing. I feel like a trapped stranger and I want to go back to my real home. Now! I have never felt like this. My husband and daughter are upset with my attitude. I am sad. Everyone is arguing and angry.
- "My daughter got married last week to a fine young man."
  Crisis: I dreaded this day since the engagement was announced. Now the day has come. My little girl has left the nest. The family unit is disrupted, and I can't stand it. I'd like to kill that guy.
- "Well, I finally retired last week."
  Crisis: I worked at that company for 40 years. I was top dog there. Now I'm just another nobody. Help me!
- "My company was downsized. I lost my job."
  Crisis: What am I going to do? Maybe my wife could go to work. In my culture, it is not accepted for the woman to work and certainly not to earn more than the man. I will lose respect. I am so torn up...
- "My wallet was stolen."
  Crisis: No, I wasn't physically harmed. What I cherished most was taken from me. I can't replace some special family pictures that I always keep with me.
- "My husband was granted sole custody of our kids."
  Crisis: My kids are going to think I did not fight hard enough to keep them. They are going to think I don't love them. That kills me. I won't get over that loss. What would you do, George?
- "My wife died recently."
  Crisis: I am so lonely. I'm so lost. Nothing helps.
- "My house was broken into."
  Crisis: I feel violated and very vulnerable. I'm going to get justice and you are going to help me.
- "I can't find the paper napkin." The victim is 4 years old.
  Crisis: My daddy drew my picture on it before the car killed him.
- "I found out yesterday that I have breast cancer."
  Crisis: They are going to operate. I'm losing part of my body. I'm in shock.
- "My bird died this morning."
  Crisis: It's not really the bird. He was kind of a nuisance. It's that I cannot handle another death, another loss, another change. You are the only one I can talk to, officer.
- "My husband's military unit is probably going to deploy soon."
  Crisis: I already have all these terrible fears about what is going to happen to him and to us. I have nightmares.

- "I used to love my husband."
  Crisis: My husband refuses to discuss his physical condition with me. The condition was diagnosed 2 years ago. He's in and out of the hospital. He's totally self absorbed and gets angry when I try to talk to him or help him. I feel like Alice in Wonderland. Everything is off balance. My kids want to leave home.

The above 13 situations vary in facts, but the responses of the victims reflect similar feelings of sadness/fear/anxiety/disbelief/helplessness/guilt/longing/disruption/loneliness/isolation that often accompanies loss and/or change. The grief is experienced at a personal level.

The link between a victim's grief and an incident such as a death, dying, illness, accidents or disasters presents few difficulties for the responder. As a society, we understand these situations and we grieve when these events occur. Difficult to deal with is the weight that society places on marriage, a pregnancy, moving into a new home, a promotion, and retirement. The universal expectation is that these events will be the highlights of one's life. Often well-meaning friends, relatives, and associates add to the unrealistic hype. Responders must avoid this trap. They must be observant, they must listen, they must not assume anything, and they must separate their own experiences, needs, beliefs, and feelings from those of the victim when they attempt to mitigate the crisis.

All communications contain three messages: a content message, a feeling message; and a meaning message. Had the responder in the first three crisis situations not been alert, they might have heard the content message and assumed this was not a crisis situation. He might have congratulated the lady on her band-new beautiful home; wished the second lady well on her daughter's marriage to a fine man; and congratulated the gentleman on his recent retirement. The responder would have failed to hear the feelings and concerns that were simmering below the surface. The result: this would have closed down the communications and exacerbated the crisis.

1. Encourage and allow sufferers to express emotions without your judging them.
   Mr. Jones: I retired a month ago after 35 years at the same company.
   R: I see such sadness in your eyes.
   Mr. Jones: I can't stop crying. It's like my whole world just stopped…I feel so ashamed because everyone keeps telling me how lucky I am now that I can do anything that I want. I want to go back to being somebody. I want to feel important and alive! I'm just waiting to die, now.
2. Let sufferers take the time necessary to express feelings before addressing options.
   R: Mr. Smith, you said that no one understands what you are going through.
   Mr. Smith: I've been offered a partnership within an aggressive well established firm.
   R: What does that offer mean to you?
   Mr. Smith: A lot more pain. You see, I'll have to move to the West coast.
   R: And what does that mean?
   Mr. Smith: I just went through a bad divorce…I lost my wife, the house, a lot of things important to me. My parents live here now. This move means giving up more things and more people…Financially I can't afford not to go…but I can't give up anything more…
   R: I hear how hard this decision is for you. There are lots of feelings about moving and giving things up that are important to you. How can I be of help to you?

3. Assure sufferers that their emotions are normal and acceptable.
   Mrs. Brown: My husband died six weeks ago. I don't think I want to go on any more either.
   R: I'm sorry for your pain, Mrs. Brown. What do you need right now?
   Mrs. Brown: You're the only one who has asked me that. Everyone else is so busy telling me what I should do and what I should feel. I have had to be brave so I wouldn't hurt anyone's feelings or worry my children. I'm about to crack up!
   R: It's hard to keep up appearances.
   Mrs. Brown: Please, just let me be me for a little while. Just let me be me.
   R: Take your time. I'm here.
4. Assure sufferers that they can live through a lonely, painful experience.
   R: I hear the pain. I don't know exactly what you are experiencing, but I know you are hurting a great deal. I know you can get through this. It is OK to take baby steps.
5. Let sufferers talk about feelings of guilt that might be associated with the crisis. Accept the validity of the guilt feelings just as you do the validity of other feelings expressed.
   R: Is there another piece that I am missing?
   Jack: Well...this is hard. I've known about the lump for a few months. I didn't say anything to my mom because I was scared.
   R: Tell me what you planned to do.
   Jack: Well, I pretended it would just go away. I hid the letter that came from the doctor. I just denied it was a problem. I guess I'm lucky that my mom finally found out.
6. Allow sufferers to express anger and resentment about the loss. Assure them that these feelings are normal.
7. Remain caring, interested and nonjudgmental.
8. Reach out to victims in appropriate ways.
9. Reach out physically only with permission.

What Victims Might Experience during the Grief Process

- Feeling off balance.
- Dizziness.
- Feeling uncoordinated.
- Erratic appetite.
- Disturbed sleep patterns.
- Feeling drugged without having taken drugs or medication.
- Feeling "out of sync" with one's own body.
- Irritability.
- Anger.
- Feeling disconnected from family, friends, and associates.
- Feeling disoriented.
- Rage from deep within one's own body.
- Feeling as if one is "falling apart" physically and emotionally.
- Feeling out of control.

- Deep sadness.
- Hopelessness.
- Feeling unwilling and/or incapable of making decisions.
- Feeling that nothing has meaning and nothing matters.
- Feeling frozen in time and space.
- Feeling that all activity, no matter how limited much effort is too.
- Confusion.
- Embarrassment about feelings.
- Guilt.
- An overwhelming sense of panic that nothing will ever feel right again.
- Feeling of spinning around but getting nowhere.
- Resentment that the loss has occurred.
- Relief that the ordeal leading to the final loss is over, and then guilt at feeling relieved.
- Feeling empty.
- Feeling numb.
- Feeling pushed down, buried, and very small.
- Turmoil associated with new or competing emotions.
- Ambivalence.
- Euphoria one moment and depression the next.

Self-Intervention for Victims

Responders should help the victims do the following:
1. Avoid major changes that will require being uprooted physically or emotionally from loved ones, support systems, and that which is familiar and safe.
2. Put major decisions on hold.
3. Rely on the security of the familiar.
4. Set realistic expectations concerning work, home, chores, family obligations, and all other areas of life.
5. Seek out those people who are helpful and comforting and avoid, where possible those who exacerbate the person's discomfort. Being well-intentioned does not necessarily translate into helpful behavior.
6. Recognize that the death of a significant other creates a sense of helplessness in survivors. Sufferers should identify those areas of life over which they have control and exercise that control immediately.
7. Maintain a daily routine. Persons suffering from grief should get up, get dressed, get out, and get moving every morning. This help gives the victim a sense of purpose and direction.
8. Care for themselves as follows:
    a. If work schedules do not permit rest during the day, arrange a routine after or before work to allow for extra rest as needed.
    b. Take appropriate vitamins to supplement the diet and minimize stress.
    c. Exercise daily to relieve tension.
    d. Walk daily and allow the senses of touch, smell, feeling, hearing, and sight to be energizers.

9. Let the process of recovery take as long as it takes.
10. Discover and use personal strengths.

Coping with Separation and the Unknown

Responders should help sufferers do the following:
1. Concentrate on the present.
2. Avoid trying to focus on the distant future.
3. Live for today.
4. Enjoy family and social relationships and allow talk about thoughts and feelings as needed.
5. Finish projects previously started. If none are in progress, start a project and find enjoyment in it. Build for success by setting a reasonable, doable pace.
6. View each day as a victory.
7. Remember that each of us copes in different ways. People should find the best way by listening to their needs.
8. Accept personal responsibility for life as a way of helping oneself.
9. Participate actively in daily routines. Routines help return a sense of structure and purpose.
10. Set realistic goals.
11. Reach out to others and let them know the victim's wants.
12. Accept responsibility for their own attitudes, approaches and frames of reference.
13. Set the tone for others with whom they associate.
14. Work with family, friends, and co-workers to help build and maintain a sense of control, purpose, and hope.
15. Encourage honest, open communications.

A TEACHABLE MOMENT

There is no short cut in the grieving process. The victim grieves on their own internal schedule. There is no such thing as "getting over this pain," a phrase commonly used in an attempt to encourage the victim. A more realistic goal is to get through it. Managing to get through the pain usually happens as a result of one's taking baby steps during the early grieving process. It helps to recognize that the process does not follow a smooth path. A person may be moving forward, and suddenly reverse course when certain memories or feelings intrude. These interruptions may be uncomfortable, but they are normal and will likely happen again. The victim begins to recognize the pitfalls, learns to manage the discomfort, allows for their feelings to be whatever they are, takes care of themselves, and recovers at this own pace. Slowly, slowly one heals. Often the reminder to take baby steps is the most important message that the victim remembers.*

The Crisis Revisited: Coping with the Aftermath

For many, a crisis can stir painful memories of previous crises. The crisis victims are required to deal with feelings that either were never resolved or were thought to have been resolved. The emotional wounds seem fresh. The anniversary date of a crisis can be difficult for some. People often begin to feel a sense of free-floating anxiety several days before the anniversary date. Acknowledge the feelings; talk about your feelings with a trusted significant other; utilize the coping skills acquired from the previous crisis situation. If that is not effective seek help from a professional.

Feelings Associated with Dying

*The discussion in this chapter has been about grief, loss, and change in numerous situations. The focus will now center on several aspects of death and dying. The following are some of the feelings associated with dying.

1. Anxiety.
2. Apathy.
3. Paralyzing uncertainty.
4. Deep sadness.
5. Nameless feelings only as free floating anxiety.
6. Fear of not fulfilling the expectations of those providing care to him or her.
7. Helplessness.
8. Fear of failure.
9. Guilt.
10. Grief.
11. Depression.
12. A feeling of urgency to experience a sense of closure.
13. A sense of separation and disintegration.
14. Loss of control over body and environment.
15. Increasing dependency.
16. Threat of abandonment, isolation, and desertion.
17. Concern that the expression of emotion will result in abandonment by family and medical attendants.
18. Fear that expression of tenderness, love, and intimacy may cause significant others additional grief and anguish.
19. Elation about transition to a "better place" or "going to heaven to be with God or other family members"
20. Relief that suffering will soon end.
21. Despair in response to losses resulting from the illness – loss of vocation, loss of the ability to participate in usual activities, losses sustained through the process of physical deterioration, sense of interpersonal loss, and the loss of body parts or changes in body image related to the illness.
22. Urgency to resolve unfinished business.

23. Frustration that reduced level of physical and emotional energy that will not allow resolution of unfinished business.
24. Concern about talking with the doctor about issues connected with dying. The feelings might be shared more easily with a nurse, a clergyman, or another officer.
25. Hostility toward family and medical staff.
26. Envy and jealousy of healthy peers.
27. Rage.
28. Resentment over not being part of the decision procession.
29. Frustration with those who will not give him or her permission to die.

Intervention Procedure

The following are guidelines for intervening with a dying person who is in crisis:
1. Establish rapport with the dying person. The officer must convey an attitude of understanding and acceptance of the victim.
2. Listen to what the victim is saying. Encourage him or her to state the problem as he perceives it.
3. Find out what the victim is doing to manage the crisis.
4. Often the crisis is the result of the dying person's feelings of impotence, loss of control, and loss of autonomy. Suddenly everyone is arranging his or her life—the family, the doctors and other medical staff, and strangers. The person's feelings of rage, helplessness, and mortality may heighten to crisis proportion.
5. Recognize the dying person's need to be alone or his or her need for the physical presence of an officer only.
6. Be sensitive to both the verbal and non-verbal messages given by the victim.
7. Be alert for signs of serious depression such as loss of appetite, severe problems of sleep, marked withdrawal from any pleasurable activity, loss of all sexual interests, extreme agitation, and suicidal ideation. The degree of depression is likely to vary considerably over the course of the illness and is related to the degree of loss perceived at the moment. It is important that the officer be aware that there are times in the dying process when the person does withdraw into himself or herself to quietly work through the intense feelings related to the loss. At other times a withdrawal is the result of a lack of energy to engage in a relationship.
8. Assist the victim to use his or her remaining resources to maintain meaning in his attempt to cope with his dying.
9. Continue to show respect for the dying person and take seriously his needs and concerns. Allow the person to make a transition from life to death with dignity.

Before attempting to manage the sufferer's grief, the officer must have acknowledged his own feelings concerning dying and death. The fine line between adaption to the grief process and maladaptive behavior seems to result in the failure to work through the grief process. Denial of feelings, inability to verbalize concerns, lack of clarity in formulating plans, and unexpressed fears of isolation contribute to the state of crisis. During the course of working with the dying patient, the officer experiences similar feelings of mortality and grief. Unless the officers can feel comfortable with their own feelings about death or at least feel comfortable feeling uncomfortable, they cannot create a setting conducive to allow the victim to begin the grief work.

The Crisis Revisited: Coping with the Aftermath

For many, a crisis can stir painful memories of previous crises. The crisis victims are required to deal with feelings that either were never resolved or were thought to have been resolved. The emotional wounds seem fresh. The anniversary date of a crisis can be difficult for some. People often begin to feel a sense of free-floating anxiety several days before the anniversary date. Acknowledge the feelings; talk about your feelings with a trusted significant other; utilize the coping skills acquired from the previous crisis situation. If that is not effective seek help from a professional.

Issues of Suicide

John is an 18-year-old high school senior. He lives at home with his parents, two younger brothers, and a dog. Until eights weeks ago, he was an active, energetic, high spirited young man. His grades were in the A/B+ column and he was considered to be an interested and involved student who looked forward to graduation and college life. John and Jenny, his girlfriend since sixth grade, were nearly inseparable. John was quoted as saying that as long as he had "Jenny, football and his Lab retriever, life was great."

Two months ago, Jenny announced her need to back away from her primary relationship with John. Graduation and going away to college would be the "perfect opportunity to move on and grow."

John spent the next two weeks pretending that Jenny would reverse her decision. As reality set in, his behavior reflected the pain and disappointment he felt. All of the joy, the enthusiasm, and the anticipation of graduation dried up. He lacked the energy to bathe, the interest to go to school, and the will to care. His brothers complained that they had to take care of his dog. He kept the curtains in his room closed and the door locked. He ate very little and slept poorly.

John's father declared that this was just a stage that he would pass through soon. His mother cried. They both took comfort in the fact that he was not taking drugs or drinking. His mother finally persuaded him to speak with the school counselor.

When John spoke with the school counselor, she asked him what he was feeling.

John: I feel restless. It's like I'm looking for something but can't seem to find it.
SC: What are you looking for, John?
John: Mostly comfort, I guess. Something to stop the hurt.
SC: What else?
John: I don't want to see anyone; not even friends and family. I guess that's selfish...
SC: That happens when we don't feel well. I'm interested in listening to you.
John: I can't seem to concentrate.
SC: Is there anything that holds your attention?

John: Whether life is worth living.

SC: Do you mean whether your life is worth living?

John: Yes, me my life...

SC: Are you suicidal, John?

John: It has crossed my mind. But, no I'm not.

SC: Have you ever been suicidal?

John: No, I have never had a reason to even consider it before. That's the whole thing here. Can I talk to you about this?

SC: Of course! What you have to say is important to me.

John: OK. My whole future revolved around having a life with Jenny. I thought we would marry, have kids, buy a house – you know, the whole dream. We would grow old together. I had everything I wanted and I was lead to believe that she did, too. We made these plans in sixth grade and never looked back. Right now, I feel betrayed and angry and used and incredibly sad. It's like somebody cut my guts out of me. If I couldn't trust Jenny, then who and what in life can I trust? Can you understand what I'm experiencing?

SC: Yes, and I appreciate you trusting me. I know this is very hurtful. Your feelings are certainly normal given the situation. Is there more that you want to tell me?

John: What do I do now?

SC: What do you want to do, John?

John: I feel some relief. Can I come talk to you again tomorrow?

SC: Yes, I want you to agree that you will not do any harm to yourself without speaking to me first. If you agree please read and sign this agreement.

What to Look For

The intervener should stay alert for what he/she might observe. Mood swings accompany teen years. Everyone feels sad at times. Feeling sad is not the focus here. A depressed mood that continues for two weeks or more could be a significant sign that deserves attention. Listen to what the teen says and watch what he/she does. Help could be needed if you hear: "I am sleeping much later than I used to." Or, "I'm not sleeping well and I wake up early in the morning." "I am beginning to take a lot of naps," could be cause for some concern. Changes in appetite and unplanned weight gains or losses are additional clues.

Listen for:
- "I am very restless."
- "I don't want to see anyone; not even friends and family."
- "I can't seem to concentrate anymore."
- "I've lost interest in everything."
- "I feel guilty," or "I feel hopeless or helpless."
- "I seem to be withdrawing more and more."
- "My mood keeps changing."
- "Life is just not worth living any more."

- "My parents will be really sorry when I'm gone."
- "Bully Billy won't be able to find me where I'm going."*

Threats by Children: When Are They Serious?

**Every year there are tragedies in which children shoot and kill individuals after making threats. When this occurs, everyone asks themselves, "How could this happen?" and "Why didn't we take the threat seriously?"

Most threats made by children or adolescents are not carried out. Many such threats are the child's way of talking big or tough, or getting attention. Sometimes these threats are a reaction to a perceived hurt, rejection, or attack.

WHAT THREATS SHOULD BE TAKEN SERIOUSLY?

Examples of potentially dangerous or emergency situations with a child or adolescent include:
- Threats or warnings about hurting or killing someone.
- Threats or warnings about hurting or killing oneself.
- Threats to run away from home.
- Threats to damage or destroy property.

A person's past behavior, however, is still one of the best predictors of future behavior. For example, a child with a history of violent or assaultive behavior is more likely to carry out his/her threats and be violent.

WHEN IS THERE MORE RISK ASSOCIATED WITH THREATS FROM CHILDREN AND ADOLESCENTS?

The presence of one or more of the following increases the risk of violent or dangerous behavior:
- Past violent or aggressive behavior (including uncontrollable angry outbursts).
- Access to guns or other weapons.
- Bringing a weapon to school.
- Past suicide attempts or threats.
- Family history of violent behavior or suicide attempts.
- Blaming others and/or unwilling to accept responsibility for one's own actions.
- Recent experience of humiliation, shame, loss, or rejection.
- Bullying or intimidating peers or younger children.
- A pattern of threats.
- Being a victim of abuse or neglect (physical, sexual, or emotional).
- Witnessing abuse or violence in the home.
- Themes of death or depression repeatedly evident in conversations, written expressions, reading selections or artwork.

- Preoccupation with themes and acts of violence in TV shows, movies, music, magazines, comics, books, video games, and internet sites.
- Mental illness, such as depression, mania, psychosis, or bipolar disorder.
- Use of alcohol or illicit drugs.
- Disciplinary problems at school or in the community (delinquent behavior).
- Past destruction of property or vandalism.
- Cruelty to animals.
- Firesetting behavior.
- Poor peer relationships and/or social isolation.
- Involvement with cults or gangs.
- Little or no supervision or support from parents or other caring adult.

WHAT SHOULD BE DONE IF PARENTS OR OTHERS ARE CONCERNED?

When a child makes a serious threat it should not be dismissed as just idle talk. Parents, teachers, or other adults should immediately talk with the child. If it is determined that the child is at risk and the child refuses to talk, is argumentative, responds defensively, or continues to express violent or dangerous thoughts or plans, arrangements should be made for an <u>immediate</u> evaluation by a mental health professional with experience evaluating children and adolescents. Evaluation of any serious threat must be done in the context of the individual child's past behavior, personality, and current stressors. In an emergency situation or if the child or family refuses help, it may be necessary to contact local police for assistance or take the child to the nearest emergency room for evaluation. Children who have made serious threats must be carefully supervised while awaiting professional intervention. Immediate evaluation and appropriate ongoing treatment of youngsters who make serious threats can help the troubled child and reduce the risk of tragedy.

Peer Pressure

Peers play a large role in the social and emotional development of children and adolescents. Their influence begins at an early age and increases through the teenage years. It is natural, healthy and important for children to have and rely on friends as they grow and mature.

Peers can be positive and supportive. They can help each other develop new skills, or stimulate interest in books, music or extracurricular activities.

However, peers can also have a negative influence. They can encourage each other to skip classes, steal, cheat, use drugs or alcohol, or become involved in other risky behaviors. The majority of teens with substance abuse problems began using drugs or alcohol as a result of peer pressure.

Kids often give in to peer pressure because they want to fit in. They want to be liked and they worry that they may be left out or made fun of if they don't go along with the group.

The following are some tips to help kids deal with peer pressure:
- Stay away from peers who pressure you to do things that seem wrong or dangerous.
- Learn how to say "no" and practice how to avoid or get out of situations which feel unsafe or uncomfortable.
- Spend time with other kids who resist peer pressure. It helps to have at least one friend who is also willing to say "no."
- If you have problems with peer pressure, talk to a grown up you trust, like a parent, teacher or school counselor.

Parents can also help by recognizing when their child is having a problem with peer pressure. The following are tips for parents to help your child deal with peer pressure:
- Encourage open and honest communications. Let kids know they can come to you if they're feeling pressure to do things that seem wrong or risky.
- Teach your child to be assertive and to resist getting involved in dangerous or inappropriate situations or activities.
- Get to know your child's friends. If issues or problems arise, share your concerns with their parents.
- Help your child develop self-confidence. Kids who feel good about themselves are less vulnerable to peer pressure.
- Develop backup plans to help kids get out of uncomfortable or dangerous situations. For example, let them know you'll always come get them, no questions asked, if they feel worried or unsafe.

If your child has ongoing difficulties with peer pressure, talk to his or her teacher, principal, school counselor or family doctor. If you have questions or concerns about your child's mood, self-esteem or behavior, consider a consultation with a trained and qualified mental health professional.

Identifying Students at Risk for Violent Behavior

The following checklists of "early warning signs" will aid in identifying students who might need intervention. The more items that are checked, the greater the potential is for violent acting-out behavior.

Children and adolescents at risk might:
- Express self-destructive or homicidal ideation.
- Have a history of self-destructive behavior.
- Articulate specific plans to harm self or others.
- Engage in "bullying" other children.
- Have difficulty with impulse control.
- Evidence significant changes in behavior.
- Engage in substance abuse.
- Become involved with gangs.

- Evidence a preoccupation with fighting.
- Have a history of antisocial behavior.
- Evidence a low tolerance for frustration.
- Externalize blame for their difficulties.
- Have harmed small animals.
- Have engaged in fire setting.
- Evidence persistent bed wetting.
- Appear to be or acknowledge feeling depressed.
- Talk about not being around.
- Express feelings of hopelessness.
- Give away possessions.
- Appear withdrawn.
- Evidence significant changes in mood.
- Experience sleep and eating disturbances.
- Have experienced prior trauma or tragedy.
- Have been or are victims of child abuse.
- Have experienced a significant loss.
- Evidence a preoccupation with television programs or movies with violent themes.
- Evidence a preoccupation with guns and other weapons.
- Have access to a firearm.
- Have brought a weapon to school.
- Evidence frequent disciplinary problems.
- Exhibit poor academic performance.
- Have been frequently truant from school.**

Content between double asterisks reprinted with permission from a Practical Guide to Crisis Response in our Schools 1999 by the American Academy of Experts in Traumatic Stress, 368 Veterans Memorial Highway, Commack, New York 11725

*APA Warning Signs:
- Loss of temper on a daily basis.
- Frequent physical fighting.
- Significant vandalism or property damage.
- Increase in risk-taking behavior.
- Detailed plans to commit acts of violence.
- Threatening to hurt others.
- Enjoy hurting animals.
- Carrying a weapon.

The American Academy of Child and Adolescent psychiatry APA & MTV, 1999) has also developed a list of factors that might help identify at-risk children. Although no set of factors is absolute, all behavior has meaning. Understanding that meaning helps teachers and interveners help students.

AACAP Warning Signs:
- Previous aggressive or violent behavior.
- Being the victim of physical abuse, sexual abuse, or both.
- Exposure to violence in the home or in the community.
- Having a parent who is violent.
- Heavy exposure to violence on television or in movies.
- Use of drugs and alcohol.
- Presence of firearms in the home.
- Brain damage from head injury.

Identifying Adults at Risk for Violent Behavior

The following checklist can give important clues to the potential for violent acts by those in whom they are observed. Although there is no single or simplistic answer to the problem, greater awareness of some of the factors involved can help in planning and response to such potential behavior. As the number of factors increase, the likelihood of violence may also increase, even though the type of violent behavior may not be apparent. Observation of only a few factors does not preclude violence. Conversely, multiple factors do not predict with certainty that violence is imminent.

- Historical problems, singular or serial, are severe enough to warrant police intervention.
- The person expresses feelings of powerlessness to effect the outcome of his or her dispute with another.
- The situation experienced by the person is the result of a family dispute or divorce, especially if children are involved.
- There is a history of causing deliberate encounters with the police or confrontations with other authorities relative to a personal case before the court or in relation to orders of the court.
- There is current or historical use of minor children as a tool, pawn, or weapon against the other spouse in a family dispute.
- The conflict experienced involves allegations of child abuse or spouse abuse.
- Where there are allegations of abuse, a complaint has been filed by either or both parties that has been or is about to be presented in court.
- Direct threats have been made from one party against the other or by third parties against either or both parties.
- There is a history of difficult court appearances or ineffective legal battles.
- Persons show an unusual interest in or expenditures of limited personal resources for reforming an inadequate, unfair, unjust judicial, social, professional or employment system. Such interests or expenditures seem disproportionate to other activities in the person's life.
- The person has a history of recent multiple life stressors either directly related or unrelated to the current conflict experienced.
- The person indicates high levels of personal dissatisfaction with his or her life.
- The cultural background of the actor emphasizes a major importance of "loss of face" or of male dominance in relationships.

- The person has a perceived or actual lack of personal support systems. He or she might be seen as a loner or as interested in non-human interactions.
- The person makes verbalizations concerning homicide or suicide.
- The verbalizations concern "setting affairs in order" or sound like the making of a "verbal will."
- The person has a history of impulsive acts.
- Those observing the person have an intuitive feeling that something is about to happen of a violent nature.
- The person has recently purchased a weapon and ammunition absent a historical interest in such items.
- The person has a history of high interest in weapons coupled with substantial recent purchases of weapons and ammunition.
- The person has a history of perceived or actual multiple personal losses.
- The person has a history of multiple life changes within a relatively short time period.
- The person has a diagnosed psychiatric disorder.
- The person shows inappropriately subdued affect or behavior that is an inconsistent reaction to the actual issues at hand.
- The person has a history of violent acts with animals during childhood.
- The person's developmental history indicates a lack of early, constant, and nurturing attachments.
- The person grew up within an impulsive family structure or in an overly controlled family.
- Violence in person's family of orientation is seen as a mode of communication.
- The peer group of the subject endorses violence.
- The person has a history of or current job instability.
- The person has a medical history of central nervous system trauma or current subjective CNS symptoms such as complaints of dizziness, blackouts, amnesia, memory loss, headaches, nausea, episodic rage, or sense of confusion with remorse.
- The person shows objective central nervous system signs.
- The person expresses the need to "get even with them."

Pre-incident Indicators Associated with Spousal/Partner Violence

There are many reliable pre-incident indicators associated with spousal/partner/date/acquaintance violence. The list is not exhaustive and those listed will not all be present in every case. If a situation has several of these signals, there is a reason for concern.

- The woman has intuitive feelings that she is at risk.
- Something that the man said triggers a feeling of fear and discomfort.
- His agenda concerning the relationship is much different than is hers.
- He is verbally abusive.
- He breaks or strikes things in anger. He uses symbolic violence (tearing a wedding photo, marring a face in a photo).
- He resolves conflict with intimidation, bullying, and violence.

- He uses threats and intimidation as instruments of control or abuse. This includes threats to harm physically, to defame, to embarrass, to restrict freedom, to disclose secrets, to cut off support, to abandon, and to commit suicide.
- He has battered in previous relationships.
- He uses alcohol or drugs with adverse effects (hostility, loss of memory, cruelty)
- His history includes police encounters for behavioral offenses including stalking, threats, battery, and assault.
- He uses money to control the activities, purchases, and behavior of his wife/partner.
- He becomes jealous of anyone and anything that takes her time away from the relationship; he keeps her on a "tight leash"; requires her to account for her time; wants access to her calendar and planner.
- He discourages her from visiting and having contact with her family and close friends without him.
- He refuses to accept rejection.
- He expects the relationship to go on forever "no matter what."
- He minimizes incidents of abuse and assigns fault for the incident to her.
- He spends a disproportionate amount of time talking about his wife/partner and derives much of his identify from being her husband/lover.
- He has inappropriately surveilled or followed his wife/partner.
- He believes others are out to get him. He believes that his wife's friends encourage her to leave him.
- He resists change and is described as being inflexible.
- He suffers mood swings or is sullen, angry, or depressed.
- He refers to weapons as instruments of power, control, or revenge.
- He consistently blames others for problems of his own making; he refuses to take responsibility for the results of his actions.
- Weapons are a substantial part of his persona.
- He uses "male privilege" as a justification for his conduct. He makes all the major decisions and sees himself as the master of the house.
- He experienced or witnessed violence as a child.
- His wife/partner/girlfriend fears he will injure or kill her. She may have discussed this with others or may have made plans that are to be carried out in the event of her death.

The last segment was a fast-forward look at what happened when young children cry for attention and help, and the adults do not listen or hear or respond effectively. A crisis is self- limiting. A child in crisis will eventually find a solution to his or her problem, that solution being effective to a more or less degree. Parents who did not learn to cope well raise children who don't learn to cope well. The pattern is continued from generation to generation. Refer to the previous charts for confirmation. A person's past behavior is one of the best predictors of future behavior.*

Crisis is equal opportunity. None of us is immune.

> *"From a cold dollars and cents point of view, it is less expensive to protect and rehabilitate a child than it is to endure the social costs of his or her later deviant behavior."* Vincent J. Fontana, M.D.

Chapter Takeaways

_____
_____
_____
_____
_____
_____
_____

Personal Notes

_____
_____
_____
_____
_____
_____
_____

Disaster Public Policy and Law

James L. Greenstone, Ed.D., J.D., DABECI

Standard of Care under Normal Circumstances versus Sufficiency of Care during Disaster Situations

*This is a topic that is the subject of much controversy and debate in professional circles. The reasons may be obvious to most. Traditionally, health care responders are trained and held to the standard of care of their profession when rendering aid. Nothing less is acceptable. Even the public understands this and demands this high level of care; even under disaster conditions. Medical professionals run scared of litigation and liability exposure.

Disasters pose a counter-testimony to the training that most receive. With overwhelming numbers of victims, and supplies that can never be adequate under such circumstances, the care mandated must be first aimed at those who can benefit the most from it. Additionally, it must reach the greatest numbers possible of such victims. All possible care cannot be rendered for all victims of a disaster. And, certainly it cannot be rendered to those who will not survive even with such care. These are less-than-ideal circumstances and we must be prepared to provide less-than-ideal care when that is necessitated. In so doing, survival potential may be enhanced for those with the greatest opportunity to survive. This is not advocacy for not giving the best care possible to all affected. It is meant to suggest that we must respond realistically to the circumstances under which we may find ourselves working.

1. Usual standard of care may not be possible to achieve within a disaster scenario.
2. Understand the application of sufficient care.
3. Expect the standard to shift from Standard of Care to Sufficiency of Care.
4. Adjust your mind-set to this eventuality.
5. Recognize that people will die.
6. Now, recognize it again; this time at the level of your gut or feelings.
7. Sufficiency of care may need to be the standard of care in a disaster.
8. Expect Sufficiency of Care to be the standard under most disaster situations. If the circumstances are better, great. Just do not expect them to be.
9. Plan for this mentally as well.
10. Plan for the eventuality emotionally as well as intellectually.
11. Discuss the concept with other responders pre-incident.
12. Remind each other during the incident.
13. Provide Standard of Care, when possible.
14. Understand that the Standard of Care may not be possible..
15. Work this out for yourself before being deployed.
16. Allow for your feelings about this and for your resistance to it. None of us are currently trained this way.
17. Discourage self-blame of others.
18. Resist blaming yourself.
19. Seek professional help early to resolve difficult issues, as you need such help.
20. Remember, that in disasters, needs will outweigh resources.
21. Remind yourself that all of your available resources must provide the greatest good for the greatest numbers of people.
22. Recognize that you cannot eliminate all suffering, and that some people will suffer despite your best efforts.
23. Also, remind yourself that critical need resources must be allocated to those having the best chance of benefiting from them.
24. In our best professional judgment, we will often have to make these decisions.
25. Learn how to manage and comfort those who will die.
26. Remember that helping those who are already dying to die with dignity is an important aspect of our care for them.
27. Help the greatest number by providing what you have to offer.
28. Resist the guilt that results from not accepting this.
29. Prepare yourself to surrender the standard when necessary and to provide care that is at least sufficient under the existing circumstances.
30. Allow this to be "okay" under these circumstances.
31. Recognize that it is okay because you are prevented from giving a higher level of care because of the totality of the circumstances, not due to your own lack of knowledge and skill.

32. Avail yourself of the current information on protective laws that shield health professionals from civil and criminal litigation and liability exposure. (See other chapters in this book for assistance)
33. Remember that the goal for each of us is not to "get over" what we feel. That is an impossible task. The realistic goal is to find ways to "get past" what has happened and what we feel, and find ways to get on with life. We try to teach this to victims. We need to learn it to help ourselves.
34. Learn to accept limits. Many will find this very hard. Consider the limits of your circumstances and your personal limitations. The ability to do this may vary from culture to culture. Consider your culture and what it says to you about handling limitations.
35. Expect the moral traces of remorse as you think about your experience. Sometimes it presents as a "twinge" when you remember what happened and what you did or were not able to do.*

Content between asterisks used with permission of Charles C. Thomas, from *The Elements of Disaster Psychology*, by J. L. Greenstone, 2007; permission conveyed through Copyright Clearance Center, Inc.

Legal Guidelines in Disaster Crisis Intervention

Probably the last things disaster crisis interveners want to concern themselves with are the legal ramifications of what they are about to do. However, the importance of this area of responder preparation and training should never be underestimated. In today's world, it has been noted that, "No good deed goes unpunished." A little pessimistic? Perhaps. On the other hand, taking time to protect yourself, your livelihood, and your professional reputation is worth the time spent. If you are aware of the legal underpinnings of your profession and the related ethical guidelines, and you do the things you usually do, you will probably be okay. In the alternative, disaster situations create change in the way we see things and may have to do things. Knowledge of the law and legalities may help you when faced with difficult decisions. Here will be discussed some of the legalities and the structure of the law that surrounds interveners. Taken together, this material is not exhaustive. If you are going to work in this field, take some time to stay aware of new legislation and new laws that may become available. The material herein may be dated by the time you are reading this. Become aware of what is changing, current and relevant.

1. *Always treat people as human beings, not just as cases.
2. Show respect to all with whom you are involved.
3. Intervene within the limits of your background and training. Do not exceed those limits, thereby committing the illegal practice of medicine, law, or psychology.
4. Unless you have a preexisting duty to intervene, consider carefully whether you want to perform an intervention.
5. Once you have begun to intervene, don't stop.
6. Discontinue your intervention only if you are relieved by someone with greater skill than your own.
7. Determine how the Good Samaritan laws relate to the types of intervention in which you may be involved.
8. If in doubt about your legal standing, contact a competent attorney and discuss your concerns.
9. Maintain confidentiality of all information you obtain about a crisis victim. Understand under what special circumstances you may have a duty to warn another person or to otherwise breach intervener-victim confidentiality.

10. Document everything you say and do with a victim. This may assist you later if you or your procedures are challenged.
11. Maintain your competency. Update your training and credentials as required.
12. Whenever possible, obtain the victim's consent before you assist with the crisis. If in doubt, ask!
13. If emergency circumstances do not allow for actual consent by the victim, you may be able to proceed under the concept of implied consent. However, in such circumstances, do only what is absolutely necessary to effectively intervene or rescue.
14. Do not disturb a crime scene. If you cannot avoid doing so, note exact locations of whatever is moved so that later you can give such information to proper authorities.
15. If you must search a victim's personal effects, try to have one or two witnesses present to observe your actions.
16. Know what you are required to report to the authorities. Requirements vary from state to state. (For example, child abuse must be reported in most states.)
17. Know the legal procedures in your jurisdiction for admissions for psychiatric care. Usually admissions are categorized as either voluntary or involuntary.
18. Remember that crisis interveners are not usually immune from observation of motor vehicle laws or from legal responsibility for vehicular accidents or property damage.
19. Respect the victim's right to privacy.
20. If the victim is a minor, obtain the permission of one of the parents before intervening. If this is not possible, you may be able to proceed under the doctrine of implied consent, as you would with an adult.
21. Be honest and open with victims.
22. Always think through what you will do, toward what end you will be doing it, what risks are present, and what safeguards you will apply.
23. Prepare yourself with knowledge of the law as well as of Crisis Intervention skills.
24. Remember that liability can be effected by both acts of commission and acts of omission.
25. Respect a sufferer's right to refuse your intervention.
26. Before entering a crisis victim's domain, dwelling, or office, request that person's permission. Know when the laws of your locality permit you to enter without permission.
27. If you are the director or supervisor of a Crisis Intervention agency, be sure all interveners and hotline workers understand and can apply agency policies and procedures.
28. Within Crisis Intervention agencies, develop specific, understandable policies and procedures that clearly regulate and illustrate how intervention is to be performed.
29. As an agency director or supervisor, adhere to agency policy and insist that interveners do likewise.
30. Incorporate agency policies and legal issues into the training of crisis interveners.*

Content between asterisks from *Elements of Crisis Intervention: Crises and How to Respond to Them*, 3rd edition, by James L. Greenstone and Sharon C. Leviton, 2011. Cengage Learning Inc. Reproduced by permission. www.cengage.com/permissions

LEGAL FRAMEWORK FOR DISASTER RESPONSE

1. The local jurisdiction's power to act come from the Tenth Amendment of the United States. Constitution: "The powers not delegated to the United States by the Constitution, nor prohibited by it to the States, are reserved to the States, respectively, or to the people."

2. In a disaster, legitimately, some civil rights may be subjugated to the public welfare.
3. The "Police Power" during times of disaster may extend to:
   a. Establishing curfews
   b. Ordering evacuations
   c. Closing buildings and businesses
   d. Suspending liquor sales
   e. Suspending firearms sales
   f. Closure of roads
   g. Going into or out of a disaster scene
   h. The use of public and/or private equipment and other items necessary for the disaster response.
4. The mission of the Federal Emergency Management Agency, or another group following FEMA, is, *"To reduce the loss of life and property and to protect our nation's critical infrastructure from all types of hazards through a comprehensive, risk-based, emergency management program of mitigation, preparedness, response and recovery."*
5. The Stafford Act grants to the President of the United States the authority to direct any federal agency to:
   a. Utilize its authorities and resources.
   b. To do this with reimbursement or without reimbursement.
   c. 42 United States Code 5170a(1). Support State and local efforts during times of disaster.
   d. 42 United States Code 5170b(a)(1) and (2). Provide food, medicine, federal equipment, facilities, personnel and other provisions for use or distribution.
   e. 42 United States Code 5170b(a)(3)(B). Direct federal agencies to provide search and rescue assistance, emergency medical care and emergency shelter to disaster victims.
   f. 42 United State Code 5170b(c)(1). State Governors to request that the President of the United States direct the Secretary of Defense to utilize the resources of the Department of Defense to assist in responding to a federal disaster.
6. Health care workers serving as disaster responders during times of local, state and national disasters may face special legal issues that should be recognized and addressed by federally and by the states.
7. Liability exposure by all healthcare workers should be examined and a personal determination made regard willingness to accept this risk. At the end of the day, each professional remains responsible for their own actions. While this is generally accepted during non-disaster times, such exposure may change during unusual circumstances.
8. Sovereign Immunity may offer some protection. This is a doctrine precluding the institution of a suit against the sovereign [government] without its consent. Though commonly believed to be rooted in English law, it is actually rooted in the inherent nature of power and the ability of those who hold power to shield themselves.
9. Federal Preemption. This provides that if the federal government assumes control over a special situation such as a disaster, as a power granted to it by the United States Constitution, the states can do nothing to stand in the way of the federal government or do anything to frustrate its purpose.
10. Good Samaritan Laws and Doctrines. These vary from state to state and in their inclusion of health care responders. Each responder should know the Good Samaritan statutes in their jurisdiction. Although sometimes widely assumed that these particular doctrines will protect disaster responders, this may not

be so and has not been widely tested. Check to be sure. If they work in your jurisdiction when responding to a disaster, the protection will be from civil liability. Criminal liability is not protected.
11. Each intervener should investigate the specific state laws applicable to your particular profession. One profession's rules or applicable laws may not apply to your work. Know before you go.
12. Each should become knowledgeable of federal laws, regulations, House and Senate Bills, etc., designed to assist and to protect disaster responders. Some of these current at the time of this writing are included in Appendix Three of this book.
13. Become aware of the National Emergency Management Assistance Compacts and other similar measures. This Compact addresses use of mutual assistance between states and the liability exposure and responsibility during such instances. These are often referred to as an EMAC and even exist internationally in some cases.

Resources for Further Research

LEGAL RESOURCES

Arizona Revised Statute for Privileged Communications, § 32-2085 (1965). (Privileged Communications)
Buwa v. Smith, 84-1905 NMB (1986). (Duty to Warn)
Canterbury v. Spense, 464 F. 2d. 772 (D.C. Cir. 1972), cert. den. 93 S. Ct. 560 (1972). (Informed Consent)
Cutter v. Brownbridge, Cal. Ct. App., 1st Dist. 330 (1986). (Privileged Communications)
Hales v. Pittman, 118 Ariz. 305, 576 P. 2d. 493 (1978). (Informed Consent)
McDonald v. Clinger, 446 N.Y.S. 2d. 801 (1982). (Confidentiality)
McIntosb v. Milano, 403 A. 2d. 500 (N.J.S.Ct. 1979). (Duty to Warn) New Jersey Revised Statutes, New Jersey Marriage Counseling Act, Annotated § 45: 8B-29 (1969). (Exceptions to Confidentiality)
People v. District Court, City and County of Denver, 719 P. 2d. 722 (Colo. 1986). (Privileged Communications)
Rodriguez v. Jackson, 118 Ariz. 13, 574 P. 2d. 481 (App. 1978). (Informed Consent)
Sard v. Hardy, 291 Md. 432, 379 A. 2d. 1014 (1977). (Informed Consent)
Tarasoff v. Regents of California, 131 Cal. Rptr. 14, 551 P. 2d. 334 (1976). (Duty to Warn)
Whitree v. State of New York, 56 Misc. 2d. 693, 290 N.Y.S. 2s. 486 (1968). (Record Keeping)

ADDITIONAL RESOURCES

Listed below are multiple sources of information useful as you are examining the laws and policies related to disaster response and intervention. While not an exhaustive list, what is here is designed to broaden the scope of your inquiry into this vital area of concern. Those involved in disaster response must be aware of the rules, regulations, policies and laws related to these endeavors.

Sources of information on public policy and law related to disaster response.
1. Google
2. Lawsonline.com

3. LexisNexis
4. Law Library
5. Public Library
6. University Library and Librarians
7. Findlaw.com
8. Legalresearch.com
9. Nolo.com
10. Google Scholar
11. BNA Bloomberg
12. myflorida.com
13. congressional.proquest.com
14. fastcase.com
15. docket.justia.com

SPECIFIC RESOURCES

Greenstone, J. L. (2013). *The elements of disaster psychology: Managing psychosocial trauma—An integrated approach to force protection and acute care.* Charles C. Thomas. **Chapters: 4, 9, 15, 16, 17,18,19, 20, 21, plus page 247 and the Bibliography.**

Greenstone, J. L., & Leviton, S. (2013). *Elements of crisis intervention: Crises and how to respond to them* (3rd ed.). Brooks/Cole, Thomson Learning. **Chapters: 11, 12, plus page 115 and Bibliography.**

Greenstone, J. L. (2015). *Emotional first aid: Field guide to crisis intervention and psychological survival.* Whole Person Associates. (ISBN 978-157025-329-4) **Chapter 10.**

Nicholson, W. C. (2013). *Emergency response and emergency management law.* Charles C. Thomas. (ISBN-13: 978-0398088316, ISBN-10: 0398088314)

Drabek, T. E. (2009). *The human side of disaster.* CRC Press.

Office of the Assistant Secretary for Public Affairs, U.S. Department of Health and Human Services. (2007). *Public health emergency response: A guide for leaders and responders.* http://www.montourema.org/images/freo_508_final.pdf

Greenstone, J. L. (2006, Winter). The Texas Medical Rangers in the military response of the uniformed medical reserve corps to hurricane Katrina and hurricane Rita 2005: The new and tested role of the medical reserve corps in the United States. Monograph, State Defense Forces Publication Center.

Greenstone, J. L. (2010, Winter). Disaster non-preparedness: The orange bag denial. *International Journal of Emergency Mental Health, Invited Essay, 12*(1), 1–3.

Greenstone, J. L. (2011, Spring). Use of interpreters with crisis intervention teams, behavioral health units, and medical strike teams: Responding appropriately and effectively. *International Journal of Emergency Mental Health, 12*(2), 79–82.

Halpern, J. (2006). *Disaster mental health: Theory and practice.* Brooks/Cole.

Ursano, R. J. (2003). *Terrorism and disaster: Individual and community mental health interventions.* Cambridge University Press.

WORDS TO LIVE BY:

- **Don't guess at the law.**
- **Document everything.**
- **Everyone thinks that they know the law.**
- **Assume nothing you cannot defend.**
- **Question everything.**
- **Ignorance of the law is not a defense.**
- **What has and has not been tested.**

RESOURCES ON TERRORISM

- Terrorism: ALIC Reading List, September 2002
- Homeland Security
- U.S. Policies on Terrorism
- September 11, 2001
- Terrorism Studies
- International Terrorism
    - Afghanistan
    - General Bioterrorism Emergency Preparedness/Disaster Response National Archives Security
- Policies Terrorism and Related Topics: An ALIC Reading List
  This reading list highlights the materials in the ALIC holdings related to terrorism. Check the ALIC online catalog for the most recent materials on terrorism.

Homeland Security
- READY.gov
  From the Department of Homeland Security, this page gives you information on how to be prepared for terrorist threats.
- Department of Homeland Security
  The official website of the Department of Homeland Security.
- This Week in Homeland Security
  Updated weekly, this newsletter provides current information on American security issues.
- "Restore the Militia for Homeland Security"
  This article, by John R. Brinkerhoff, a specialist in Homeland Defense, was published in the Journal of Homeland Security, November 2001. The article reflects his opinions and does not reflect the opinions of the National Archives.
- The After shock: A New Business Reality
  This article, published online in September 2001, discusses the effect of the terrorist attacks on business.
- CNN.com's War Against Terror
  In-depth special reports from CNN.com highlight important events in homeland security news.

- Gateway to Homeland Security
  From the Air War College, this site lists an amazing array of links on homeland security and terrorism.
- Terrorism in the U.S.
  FBI reports.

U.S. Policy on Terrorism
- White House Position
  Check here to see the Obama administration's position on homeland security and counter terrorism.
- America's War on Terrorism
  The Federation of American Scientists site provides information and analysis of emerging security policy.
- Countering the Changing Threat of International Terrorism
  This National Commission on Terrorism report reviews American policies on international terrorism.
- Counter-terrorism Training and Resources for Law Enforcement
  This portal website serves as a single point of access to counter-terrorism training opportunities and related materials available across the Federal Government and from private and nonprofit organizations.
- Hearing on FBI Counterterrorism Efforts
  The Washington Post's entire transcript of the Senate's Judiciary Committee hearing on FBI counterterrorism efforts held on June 6, 2002.
- The Inman Report: Report of the Secretary of State's Advisory Panel on Overseas Security
  This report outlines the scope and dimension of U.S. security problems in international business and diplomacy.
- National Strategy for Combating Terrorism
  A report from the White House outlining the national strategy for combating terrorism, which focuses on identifying and defusing threats before they reach America's borders.
- The National Strategy for the Physical Protection of Critical Infrastructures and Key Assets
  This report identifies the goals necessary to protect America's infrastructure and assets vital to America's public health and safety, national security, governance, economy, and public confidence.
- Public Agenda Special Report: Terrorism
  Public Agenda Online report focuses on both public opinion and policy issues relating to terrorism in the United States.
- Terrorism and U.S. Policy
  From the National Security Archive, Volume I of the September 11th Sourcebooks.
- Terrorism Project
  This Center for Defense Information (CDI) site provides insight, in-depth analysis and quick facts about the threat of terrorism.
- Terrorist Attack: September 11, 2001
  The Federal Emergency Management Agency site has information on the New York terrorist attacks.
- Terrorist Group Profiles
  This list of terrorist groups is a product of the Naval Postgraduate School.
- U.S. Counterterrorism Office
  The Counterterrorism Office develops, coordinates, and implements U.S. counterterrorism policy.

- The World Trade Center Attack: Official Documents
  A selective guide to the official government documents related to the terrorist attack on the World Trade Center. Very thorough site covering government agencies' responses, made available by Columbia University Libraries.
- September 11. archive. org
  This site, maintained by the Library of Congress, the Internet Archive, and webArchivist.org, provides an archive for web sites covering September 11 events. According to *Choice*, this site is probably the best place to begin research on this topic.
- Legislation Related to the Attack of September 11, 2001
  This Library of Congress site covers bills, resolutions, and legislation regarding the terrorist attacks.
- Terrorist Attack on the United States
  On Mike Maden's Academic Info page, this site provides resources for information on the September 11, 2001, terrorist attacks.
- September 11th Resources
  This Special Libraries Association (SLA) web site is a collection of excellent resources related to the events of September 11, 2001.
- September 11 Resources
  According to *Choice*, this site is a solid, useful starting point for research regarding most aspects of the attacks and their aftermath.
- September 11 Sourcebooks
  This National Security Archives site provides online readers on terrorism, intelligence, and the next war.
- Resources for September 11, 2001
  This site covers extensively all aspects of the attacks and maintains a separate page of links covering the attacks' aftermath and a page of links that survey public attitudes and statistical information.
- Remembrance Photo Gallery
  This FEMA gallery of photographs serves as a memorial of the events of September 11, 2001.
- 9/11 Commission Report
  The full report has been made available on the GPO website.

Terrorism Studies
- Center for the Study of Bioterrorism & Emerging Infections
  At Saint Louis University School of Public Health. This web site offers extensive information on bioterrorism and current research.
- Potomac Institute for Policy Studies
  The institute provides an academic forum for the study of related policy issues on key science, technology, and national security issues facing our society,.
- Terrorism and Crime Studies
  Federal Research Division at the Library of Congress.
- Terrorism Studies Program
  The Washington Institute for Near East Policy, Washington, DC.

- Trends in Terrorism

  This report was published in *Perspectives*, a Canadian Security Intelligence Service publication, December 1999.

International Terrorism: Afghanistan

- Afghanistan

  The Washington Post's overview of the situation in Afghanistan including overviews on Bin Ladin and the key players in Afghanistan.

- Afghanistan: The Harrison Forman Collection

  This online exhibit documents the life and culture of Afghanistan in the late 1960s, several years before the Soviet Union invaded the country.

- Afghanistan: Land in Crisis

  This new special feature from *National Geographic* collects information on Afghanistan, including articles, maps, lesson plans, current news, and more. Some of the site's notable features include an archived Webcast of an October 22 screening of "National Geographic Explores a Changing World" and panel discussion on the Middle East and Afghanistan; and a bibliography of *National Geographic's* print resources related to the topic. This site includes a regularly updated interactive map of Afghanistan displaying cities and attacks, ethnic groups, drought, and vegetation, and more. Teachers will want to check out the four lesson plans, which are geared to various age groups K-12.

- Afghanistan Resources: Taliban Links

  These resources are updated regularly, and most are annotated.

- The Campaign against International Terrorism: Prospects after the Fall of the Taliban

  "This paper provides an update on the campaign against international terrorism following the fall of the Taliban regime in Afghanistan. It examines the main developments since the end of October 2001, including the ongoing military campaign, the Bonn agreement on a new interim administration for the country, and the humanitarian situation." (National Archives, 2016) The paper then looks at the state of al-Queda three months after the attacks of 11 September and discusses possible options for the next phase in the broader campaign against international terrorism.

- General Resources on Terrorism and Afghanistan

  Library of Congress's listing of websites that provide links to general resources on Terrorism and Afghanistan.

- Institute for Afghan Studies

  This site provides information on Afghan conflict, the economy, foreign affairs, history and much more. Contributions are from recognized Afghan and non-Afghan scholars, think-tanks and experts on Afghan studies about social, economic, political and other issues pertaining to Afghanistan.

- Perry-Castañeda Library Map Collection

  The University of Texas online collection of maps of Afghanistan. Types of maps include country, city, detailed, thematic, historical, war, and refugee maps.

- U.S. Department of State-Background Note: Afghanistan

  A profile of the country of Afghanistan including information about its people, history, government, political conditions, and more.

- The War in Afghanistan
  "A listing of web sites that provide links to resources relating to the War on Terrorism in Afghanistan" (National Archives, 2016) provided by the Library of Congress.

General Terrorism
- Annotated Bibliography of Government Documents Related to the Threat of Terrorism & the Attacks of September 11, 2001
  The documents cited in this bibliography were produced by the United States Government concerning the event of September 11, 2001. The bibliography includes documents produced by Congress, the President, Department of the Army, Department of Defense, State Department, Central Intelligence Agency, Department of Energy, Department of Education, Library of Congress Federal Research Division, Federal Emergency Management Agency, Justice Department, Department of the Interior, U.S. Geological Survey, Coalition Information Centers, Naval War College, U.S. Institute of Peace, General Accounting Office, National Committee on Terrorism, Department of the Navy, U.S. Air Force Academy, and Army War College.
- Countering the Changing Threat of International Terrorism
  This National Commission on Terrorism report reviews American policies on international terrorism.
- 2008 Fact Sheet on Foreign Terrorist Organizations
  Department of State; Distributed by the Bureau of International Information Programs, April 10, 2008.
- The Global Coalition Against Terrorism: Media Fact Sheets
  A Department of State website that focuses on facts & figures, foreign diplomacy, Patriot Day events, and information on Afghanistan.
- Terrorist Data: Washingtonpost.com
  A clickable world map leads to information on names, dates, and locations of terrorist activities.
- Office of the Coordinator for Counterterrorism
  Annual reports from the OCC, including Foreign Terrorist Organizations, Patterns of Global Terrorism, and Significant Incidents of Political Violence Against Americans.
- Travel Warnings
  Travel Warnings are issued when the State Department decides, based on all relevant information, to recommend that Americans avoid travel to a certain country.
- FEMA and the September 11, 2001 Attacks
  Search the full text of the "Review of the General Accounting Office Report on FEMA's Activities after the Terrorist Attacks on September 11, 2001."
- Current Issues: Terrorism
  From the American Embassy in London, this site presents recent topics in terrorism.
- Counter Terrorism
  This site, from the National Security Institute, presents current events and issues relating to the topic.
- DoD USS Cole Commission Report
  Report on commission formed to report on improvements of U.S. policies and practices for deterring, disrupting, and mitigating terrorist attacks on U.S. forces.

- New World Coming: American Security in the 21st Century
  U.S. Commission on National Security in the 21st Century has been charged with examining and assessing post-Cold War defense requirements in the most comprehensive reassessment of U.S. defense policy since 1947.

Bioterrorism

- Bioterrorism Articles
  The American Medical Association maintains a site on bioterrorism.
- Food Biosecurity Resources
  From the Food Science department at Penn State, these government resources offer information on food safety and bioterrorism.
- Terrorism and Security Collection
  The National Academies Press offers the full-text of several publications related to bioterrorism for browsing online.
- Update: Investigation of Bioterrorism-Related Anthrax and Interim Guidelines for Clinical Evaluation of Persons with Possible Anthrax
  The Morbidity and Mortality Weekly Report (MMWR) for November 2, 2001, offers guidelines for the treatment of anthrax.
- Chemical and Biological Warfare Internet Sources
  A list of Internet sources provided by Science Reference Services at the Library of Congress.
- Chemical & Biological Arms Control Program
  This Federation of American Scientists program covers all aspects of biological and chemical weapons and their control.
- Center for Civilian Biodefense Strategies
  The Center, located at Johns Hopkins University's Schools of Public Health and Medicine, aims to "increase national and international awareness of the medical and public health threats posed by biological weapons, thereby augmenting the potential legal, political and moral prohibitions against their use."
- Bioterror
  This PBS site, a companion to the Nova show "Bioterror," gives a history of biowarfare and offers resources for further research.
- Chemical, Biological, Radiological, and Nuclear (CBRN) Terrorism
  This report from *Perspectives*, a Canadian Security Intelligence Service publication, "uses open sources to examine any topic with the potential to cause threats to public safety or national security."
- The Bioterrorism Threat
  A health spotlight special report of PBS's Online Newshour.
- MedlinePlus: Anthrax and Bioterrorism
  This National Library of Medicine site explains anthrax and other biological terrorism threats. Provides definitions, symptoms, and typical treatments for the disease.

CHAPTER 10: Disaster Public Policy and Law

RESOURCES ON EMERGENCY PREPAREDNESS AND DISASTER RESPONSE

- DisasterHelp.gov
  DisasterHelp.gov is designed to assist victims of disasters in locating the resources they need. The goal of the site is to combine the resources of all federal agencies in one central location.
- Centers for Disease Control and Prevention
  Environmental health practitioners aid in the control of chemical releases.
- Cultural Resource Protection and Emergency Preparedness
  Cultural Resource Management, Vol. 24, no. 8, 2001. This issue focuses on disaster preparedness and recovery.
- NARA Disaster Recovery and Vital Records Information
  This site includes NARA's contacts to assist federal agencies in need of support on disaster recovery and vital records.

RESOURCES ON NATIONAL ARCHIVES SECURITY POLICIES

- Access to Archival Materials in the Context of Concern about Terrorism
- New Security Procedures in the Washington, DC, area

LAWS AND POLICIES OF SPECIFIC CONCERN WHEN STARTING YOUR SEARCH

- Constitution of the United States
- Medical Malpractice related to Standards of Care and Altered Standards of Care
- Malpractice in other health provider fields that may be present during a disaster. These may be the same or differ from Medical Malpractice
- Ethical standards v. Legal standards
- Civil and Criminal liability exposure
- State Good Samaritan Laws
- Federal Good Samaritan Laws
- Informed consent
- Confidentiality
- Exceptions to confidentiality
- Implied Consent
- Licensing
- Training and credentials
- Documentation
- Crime Scenes
- Police Powers
- Search and seizure
- Reporting requirements i.e., Child abuse and other
- Mental Health Codes

- Involuntary admissions for psychiatric evaluation and care
- Traffic laws during a disaster
- Privacy rights
- Working with minors
- Refusal of assistance
- Entering a domain or private property
- Conflict of policies
- 10th Amendment of the Constitution of the United States
- Civil rights during a disaster
- Federal Emergency Management Agency
- Mitigation
- Preparedness
- Response
- Recovery
- The Stafford Act
- 42 United States Code 5170a(1)
- 42 United States Code 5170b(a)(1) and (2)
- 42 United States Code 5170b(a)(3)(B)
- 42 United States Code 5170b(c)(1)
- Coverage for health care workers serving as disaster responders and legal issues
- Personal responsibility for the actions of individual health care workers and disaster responders
- Sovereign Immunity
- Federal Preemption
- Case Law
- State Laws
- Federal Laws
- House Bills related
- Senate Bills related
- State Regulations
- Federal Regulations
- National Emergency Management Assistance Compacts
- Public Health Laws and Policies
- Centers for Law and the Public's Health: Georgetown University and Johns Hopkins University
- Emergency System for Advance Registration of Volunteer Health Professionals (ESAR-VHP)
- Official Immunity
- Government Code 421.061 Civil Liability
- Civil Practice and Remedies Code 79.003, Disaster Assistance, Texas
- Health and Safety Code 81.007, Limitation on liability, Texas
- Civil Practice and Remedies Code 74.151, Liability for Emergency Care, Texas
- Civil Practice and Remedies Code 74.152, Unlicensed medical personnel, Texas
- Title 42 United States Code, Chapter 139, Volunteer Protection
- Civil Practice and Remedies Code Chapter 84, Charitable Immunity and Liability Act, Texas

- Title 42 United States Code, Section 233(p) as found in the Homeland Security Act of 2002, Public Law 107-296, Section 304
- Title 42 United States Code 239 added by Public Law 108-20, Smallpox Emergency Personnel Protection Act
- Civil Practice and Remedies Code, Chapter 108, Limitation of Liability for Public Servants, Texas
- Civil Practice and Remedies Code, Chapter 104, State Liability for Conduct of Public Servants, Texas
- Civil Practice and Remedies Code, Chapter 102, Tort Claims Payments by Local Governments, Texas
- Civil Practice and Remedies Code, Chapter 101, Texas Tort Claims Act, Texas
- The Emergency Management Assistance Compact (EMAC) Health and Safety Code 778.001, Article VI
- Volunteer Protection Act of 1997
- Charitable Immunity and Liability Act of 1987, Texas
- Texas House Bill 9 / Critical Infrastructure Protection Council
- Senate Bill 513, Amendment to the Civil Practice and Remedies Code, Texas
- Texas Disaster Act of 1975, Texas Government Code, Chapter 418
- Pandemic and All Hazards Preparedness Act, 2006
- Medical Reserve Corps
- State Military Forces
- Section 458.305(3), Florida Statutes (1999)
- 73 N. Dak. L. Rev. 109, 113 (1997)
- *Jones v. United States*, 249 F2d 864 (7th Cir. 1957)
- *Lidie v. California*, 478 F2d 552 (9th Cir. 1973)
- *United States v. Testan*, 424 U.S. 392 (1976)
- *United States v. Faneca*, 322 F.2d 872
- *Howlett v. Rose*, 496 U.S. 356 (1990)
- *Berkovitz byBerkovitz v. United States*, 108 S. Ct. 1954
- *Berkovitz v. United States*, 486 U.S. 531 (1988)
- *Torres v. United States*, 979 F. Supp. 1054, 1056 (DV.I 1997)
- *United States v. S.A. Empresa de ViacaoAerea Rio Grandense (Varig Airlines)*, 467 U.S. 797 (1984)
- *United States v. Gaubert*, 499 U.S. 315 (1991)
- *New York v. F.E.RC.*, 122 S. Ct. 1012 (2002)
- *Louisiana Public Service Commission v. F.C.C.*, 476 U.S. 355 (1986)
- U.S.C.A. Const. Art. 6, cl. 2
- *Liebeck v. McDonald's Restaurants*, 1995 WL 360309 (D.N.M.1994)
- West's RCWA4.24.300. *Maynard v. Ferno-Washington, Inc.*, 22 F. Supp. 2d 1171 (1998)
- *Rodrigue v. United States*, 968 F. 2d 1430 (1st Cir.1992)
- *United States v. DeVane*, 306 F. 2d 182 (5th Cir. 1992)
- *Santillo v. Chambersburg Engineering Co.*, 603 F. Supp. 211 (E.D. Pa. 1985)
- *Mafrige v. United States*, 893 F. Supp. 691, (S.D. Tex.1995)
- Rest. (2nd) of Torts' 324A. *Dorking Genetics v. United States*, 76 F.3d 1261 (2d Cir. 1996)
- Arizona Revised Statute for Privileged Communications, § 32-2085 (1965). (Privileged Communications)
- *Buwa v. Smith*, 84-1905 NMB (1986). (Duty to Warn)

- *Canterbury v. Spense,* 464 F. 2d 772 (D.C. Cir. 1972), *cert. den.* 93S. Ct. 560 (1972) (Informed Consent)
- *Cutter v. Brownbridge,* Cal. Ct. App., 1st Dist. 330 (1986). (Privileged Communications)
- *Hales v. Pittman,* 118 Ariz. 305, 576 P. 2d. 493 (1978). (Informed Consent)
- *McDonald v. Clinger,* 446 N.Y.S. 2d. 801 (1982). (Confidentiality)
- *McIntosh v. Milano,* 403 A. 2d 500 (N. J. S. Ct. 1979). (Duty to Warn)
- New Jersey Revised Statutes, New Jersey Marriage Counseling Act, Annotated § 45: 8B-29 (1969). (Exceptions to Confidentiality)
- *People v. District Court, City and County of Denver,* 719 P. 2d. 722 (Colo. 1986) (Privileged Communications)
- *Rodriguez v. Jackson,* 118 Ariz. 13, 574 P. 2d. 481 (App. 1978). (Informed Consent)
- *Sard v. Hardy,* 291 Md. 432, 379 A. 2d. 1014 (1977). (Informed Consent)
- *Tarasoff v. Regents of California,* 131 Cal. Rptr. 14, 551 P. 2d. 334 (1976). (Duty to Warn)
- *Whitree v. State of New York,* 56 Misc. 2d. 693, 290 N.Y.S. 2s. 486 (1968). (Record Keeping)

WEBSITE RESOURCES

- www.publichealthlaw.net
- http://www.govtrack.us
- http://www.publichealthlaw.net/Resources/ResourcesPDFs/Checklist%203.pdf
- http://www.publichealthlaw.net/Resources/ResourcesPDFs/Checklist%201.pdf
- http://www.publichealthlaw.net/Resources/ResourcesPDFs/Checklist%202.pdf

SELECTED FEDERAL LEGAL AUTHORITIES PERTINENT TO PUBLIC HEALTH EMERGENCIES

Prepared by the Public Health Law Program
Centers for Disease Control and Prevention

Introduction

In the wake of the 2001 terrorist attacks, the 2003 severe acute respiratory syndrome (SARS) epidemic, Hurricane Katrina in 2005, the influenza A (H1N1) pandemic in 2009, Hurricane Sandy in 2012, and the ongoing concern about future similar events, public health officials have acted to strengthen their jurisdictions' legal preparedness for all types of public health emergencies.

Federal laws and legal authorities address a variety of concerns central to public health emergencies, such as emergency declarations, quarantine and isolation, liability and licensure of workers, and mutual aid, among others. Because these laws involve multiple federal agencies and appear in many official documents, the Centers for Disease Control and Prevention's (CDC) Public Health Law Program prepared the following annotated list of selected, commonly cited federal legal authorities for reference by public health officials, legal counsel, and others.

This compilation is subject to three caveats: (1) it is not intended to be exhaustive of all relevant legal authority; (2) it was compiled in September 2009 and updated in 2014, and reflects the laws current at the time; and (3) only selected portions of the laws relevant to public health emergencies are presented.

Disclaimer

The Public Health Law Program (PHLP) provides technical assistance and public health law resources to advance the use of law as a public health tool. PHLP cannot provide legal advice on any issue and cannot represent any individual or entity in any matter. PHLP recommends seeking the advice of an attorney or other qualified professional with questions regarding the application of law to a specific circumstance. The findings and conclusions in this document are those of the author and do not necessarily represent the official views of the Centers for Disease Control and Prevention.

Topics

General Emergency Legal Authorities
Legal Authorities Specific to Public Health Emergencies
Public Safety and Security
Control of Communicable Diseases
Managing Transportation
Managing Animals, Food, and Other Property
Liability, Workers' Compensation, and Licensure
Personal Health Information and Privacy
Related Federal Guidance

[1] Updated by Gregory Sunshine, J.D., an Oak Ridge Institute for Science and Education legal fellow at CDC's Public Health Law Program. Special thanks to the CDC partners who helped develop this resource.

Please note that some laws listed have broad application and thus may be included under more than one topic area; only the relevant portion of the law is discussed under each topic area. These laws might have other provisions not discussed here.

General Emergency Legal Authorities

<u>Homeland Security Act of 2002</u>
<u>Pub. L. No. 107-296, as amended; 6 U.S.C. §§ 311–321m</u>

The Homeland Security Act merges twenty-two disparate agencies and organizations into the new Department of Homeland Security (DHS), including the Federal Emergency Management Agency (FEMA). The Act charges DHS with securing the nation against terrorist attacks and carrying out the functions of all transferred entities, including acting as a focal point regarding natural and man-made crises and emergency planning. The law establishes the National Homeland Security Council, the Directorate of Border and Transportation Security, the Office for State and Local Government Coordination, and transfers powers from Immigration and Naturalization Service (abolished under 6 U.S.C. § 291(a)).

Post-Katrina Emergency Management Reform Act of 2006 (Post-Katrina Act)
Pub. L. No. 109-295; 6 U.S.C. §§ 701 et. seq.

Enacted as part of the Department of Homeland Security Appropriations Act, 2007, the Post-Katrina Act is intended to address various shortcomings identified in the preparation for and response to Hurricane Katrina. The Act establishes new DHS leadership positions, brings additional functions into FEMA, creates and reallocates functions to other components within DHS, and amends the Homeland Security Act in ways that both directly and indirectly affect the organization and functions of various entities within DHS. The Act enhances FEMA's responsibilities and its autonomy within DHS.

Robert T. Stafford Disaster Relief and Emergency Assistance Act of 1988 (Stafford Act)
Pub. L. No. 93-288, as amended; 42 U.S.C. §§ 5121–5207

The Stafford Act authorizes the President to declare a "major disaster" or "emergency" in response to an event (or threat) that overwhelms state or local governments. Declaration under the Act triggers access to federal technical, financial, logistical, and other assistance to state and local governments. The Act directs FEMA to coordinate administration of disaster relief to the states. The governor of an affected state must first respond to the disaster and execute the state's emergency plan before requesting that the President declare a major disaster or emergency, and the governor must certify that the magnitude of the emergency exceeds the state's capability. As of 2013, tribal leaders can also request a Stafford Act declaration from the President (see Sandy Recovery Improvement Act of 2013 below). The President may declare an emergency without the request of a governor or tribal leader if the emergency involves "federal primary responsibility" (such as an event occurring on federal property, for example the bombing of the Murrah Federal Building in 1995). Title VI of the Act provides for a national system for all-hazards emergency preparedness, with authority located at both the federal and state levels.

Sandy Recovery Improvement Act of 2013
Pub. L. No. 113-2 §§ 1101–1111; 42 U.S.C. §§ 5170, 5191

The Sandy Recovery Improvement Act authorizes the chief executive of a tribal government to directly request disaster or emergency declaration from the President, much as a governor can for a state. Previously, tribal groups were treated like local governments in that they could receive a federal disaster declaration only if the governor of the state in which the tribe was located requested one.

Sections 201 and 301 of the National Emergencies Act
50 U.S.C. §§ 1621, 1631

The National Emergencies Act authorizes the President to declare a "national emergency." The proclamation of a national emergency must be transmitted immediately to Congress and published in the Federal Register. The declaration of emergency (or contemporaneous or subsequent executive orders) must specify the powers or authorities made available by virtue of the declaration. A national emergency can be terminated if the President issues a proclamation or if Congress enacts a joint resolution terminating the emergency. A national emergency will terminate automatically upon the anniversary of the proclamation unless the President renews the proclamation by transmitting notice to Congress and publishing it in the Federal Register.

Pets Evacuation and Transportation Standards (PETS) Act of 2006
Pub. L. No. 109-308; 42 U.S.C. §§ 5170(b), 5196, 5196(b)

The PETS Act amends the Stafford Act to require the Federal Emergency Management Agency (FEMA) Director to ensure that state and local emergency preparedness plans "take into account the needs of individuals with household pets and service animals prior to, during, and following a major disaster or emergency."

Homeland Security Presidential Directive 5 (HSPD-5) (February 28, 2003)

HSPD-5 is intended to "enhance the ability of the United States to manage domestic incidents." The Directive describes federal policies and objectives; identifies steps for improved coordination among federal, state, and local authorities; and tasks the Secretary of Homeland Security with developing a National Incident Management System and National Response Plan.

Homeland Security Presidential Directive 8 (HSPD-8) (December 17, 2003)

HSPD-8, as a companion to HSPD-5, "establishes policies to strengthen the preparedness of the United States to prevent and respond to" man-made and natural disasters and other emergencies. The Directive requires the Secretary of Homeland Security to develop a national domestic all-hazards preparedness goal, which establishes "measurable readiness priorities and targets" and "readiness metrics and elements." The Directive also requires relevant federal agencies to make financial assistance and support available to states, support the development of first responder equipment standards, and establish a training program to meet the national preparedness goals.

Emergency Management Assistance Compact (EMAC) of 1996
Pub. L. No. 104-321

EMAC facilitates resource sharing among member states during an emergency. The National Emergency Management Association (NEMA) administers EMAC, which has been enacted by every state. A governor's declaration of emergency and request for assistance triggers EMAC for the requesting state. An assisting state then responds to the request by providing the needed resources. Further, EMAC establishes that the requesting state is responsible for compensating the assisting state for any expenses incurred.

Legal Authorities Specific to Public Health Emergencies

Section 319 of the Public Health Service Act: Public Health Emergencies
42 U.S.C. § 247d

This section of the Public Health Service Act authorizes the Secretary of the Department of Health and Human Services (HHS) to determine that a public health emergency exists if "1) a disease or disorder presents a public health emergency; or 2) a public health emergency, including significant outbreaks of infectious diseases or bioterrorist attacks, otherwise exists." From the determination of a public health emergency flows the ability of the Secretary to "take such action as may be appropriate" and to use funds from the Public Health Emergency Fund (when appropriated). The public health emergency determination remains effective until the Secretary either declares that the emergency no longer exists, or at the expiration of ninety days, whichever occurs first. If the Secretary determines that the same or additional facts continue to warrant a public health emergency, he or she may renew the declaration for ninety-day periods. As amended by the Pandemic and All-Hazards Preparedness Reauthorization Act of 2013, Pub. L. No. 113-5, section 319 also allows the Secretary, upon request by a governor or tribal organization, to authorize the temporary reassignment of state and local public health department or agency personnel funded in whole or in part through programs authorized under the Public Health Service Act for the purpose of immediately addressing a federally declared public health emergency.

Section 311 of the Public Health Service Act: General Grant of Authority for Cooperation
42 U.S.C. § 243

This provision of the Public Health Service Act states that the Secretary of HHS shall assist states and local authorities in the prevention and suppression of communicable diseases and to help state and local authorities enforce quarantine regulations. This section also authorizes the Secretary to accept state and local authorities' assistance with enforcement of federal quarantine regulations. Further, this section authorizes the Secretary to develop a public health emergency management plan and, at the request of a state or local authority, extend temporary assistance regarding public health emergencies.

Section 319F-2 of the Public Health Service Act: Strategic National Stockpile and Security (the Stockpile)
42 U.S.C. § 247d-6b; 42 U.S.C. § 300hh-10(c)(3)(b)

The Stockpile (including drugs, vaccines, biological products, medical devices, and other supplies) is maintained by the Secretary of HHS, in collaboration with CDC's Director, and in coordination with the Secretary of Homeland Security, to provide for the emergency health security of the United States. The Secretary may deploy the Stockpile to respond to an actual or potential public health emergency, protect the public health or safety, or as required by the Secretary of Homeland Security, respond to an actual or potential emergency. The responsibility and authority to coordinate the Strategic National Stockpile has been assigned to the Assistant Secretary for Preparedness and Response under 42 U.S.C. § 300hh-10(c)(3)(b).

Public Health Security and Bioterrorism Preparedness and Response Act of 2002 Pub. L. No. 107-188

The Act amends the Public Health Service Act to "improve the ability of the United States to prevent, prepare for, and respond to bioterrorism and other public health emergencies." The Act requires the Secretary of HHS to "develop and implement" a coordinated strategy in the form of a national preparedness plan. The Act also establishes the position of Assistant Secretary for Public Health Emergency Preparedness (renamed the Assistant Secretary for Preparedness and Response, see Pandemic and All-Hazards Preparedness Act below), who is responsible for coordinating the operations of the National Disaster Medical System and other emergency response activities within HHS. Additionally, several provisions for protection of the food and drug supply are included. Further, the Act directs the Secretary to establish and maintain the Emergency System for Advance Registration of Health Professions Volunteers (ESAR-VHP).

Pandemic and All-Hazards Preparedness Act of 2006
Pub. L. No. 109-417

The Act identifies the Secretary of HHS as the lead federal official for public health emergency preparedness and response, and establishes the Assistant Secretary for Preparedness and Response (formerly named the Assistant Secretary for Public Health Emergency Preparedness, see Public Health Security and Bioterrorism Preparedness and Response Act of 2002 above). The Act also provides new authorities for developing countermeasures, establishes mechanisms and grants to continue strengthening state and local public health security infrastructure, and addresses surge capacity by placing the National Disaster Medical System and the Emergency System for Advance Registration of Health Professions Volunteers (ESAR-VHP) under the purview of HHS.

Pandemic and All–Hazards Preparedness Reauthorization Act (PAHPRA) of 2013
Pub. L. No. 113-5; 42 U.S.C. §§ 247d, 300hh-1(b)(3)(E), 247d-3a(b)(2)(a)(iii), 247d-6d(i)(7)(iii), 21 U.S.C. § 360bbb-3, et seq.

PAHPRA reauthorized funding for provisions of the Pandemic and All-Hazards Preparedness Act of 2006, as well as amended several provisions of the Public Health Service Act and the Food Drug and Cosmetic Act. PAHPRA requires Pandemic and All-Hazards Preparedness Act fund recipients to account for children and "at-risk individuals" in their All-Hazards Public Health Emergency Preparedness and Response Plan, as well as coordinate with local Metropolitan Medical Response Systems, local Medical Reserve Corps, and the local Cities Readiness Initiative. Additional PAHPRA changes made to authorities described elsewhere in this document are contained in the entries addressing

- Section 319 of the Public Health Service Act: Public Health Emergencies;
- The Public Readiness and Emergency Preparedness (PREP) Act of 2005; and
- Emergency Use Authorization.

Section 1135 of the Social Security Act: Authority to Waive Requirements During National Emergencies
42 U.S.C. § 1320b-5

Section 1135 of the Social Security Act authorizes the Secretary of HHS to waive or modify certain requirements of Medicare, Medicaid, and the State Children's Health Insurance Program during certain emergencies. Section 1135 waivers require both 1) a declaration of national emergency or disaster by the President under the National Emergencies Act or the Stafford Act and 2) a public health emergency determination by the Secretary under the Public Health Service Act. Waivers may be requested by affected healthcare providers in the emergency area during the emergency period. The Secretary may make a waiver retroactive to the beginning of the emergency period or any subsequent date thereafter. The waiver generally expires at the termination of the applicable declaration of emergency or disaster under the National Emergencies Act or Stafford Act or determination of public health emergency under the Public Health Service Act. In addition, the Secretary may specify that the waivers terminate sixty days from publication, which may be extended, provided that neither the original sixty-day period nor any extension extends beyond termination of the applicable declaration or determination. Waivers related to the Emergency Medical Treatment and Active Labor Act and the Health Information Portability and Accountability (HIPAA) Privacy Rule (see below) are subject to different requirements and may terminate after seventy-two hours.

Public Readiness and Emergency Preparedness (PREP) Act of 2005
Pub. L. No. 109-148; 42 U.S.C. §§ 247d-6d, 247d-6e

The PREP Act authorizes the Secretary of HHS to issue a declaration that provides immunity from tort liability for claims of loss (except willful misconduct) caused by, arising out of, relating to, or resulting from administration or use of countermeasures to diseases, threats and conditions determined by the Secretary to constitute a present or credible risk of a future public health emergency. The immunity applies to entities and individuals involved in the development, manufacture, testing, distribution, administration, and use of such countermeasures. As amended by PAHPRA (see above), the PREP Act immunity explicitly applies to products or technology intended to enhance medical countermeasures, in addition to the countermeasures themselves. PAHPRA also extends immunity to countermeasures authorized under sections 564A and 564B of the Federal Food, Drug, and Cosmetic Act (see below). The Secretary's declaration includes, among other things,

- The countermeasures covered by the declaration;
- The category of diseases, health conditions, or health threats for which administration and use of the countermeasures recommended;
- The effective time period of the declaration;

- The population of individuals receiving the countermeasure;
- Limitations, if any, on the geographic area for which immunity is in effect;
- Limitations, if any, on the means of distribution of the countermeasure; and
- Any additional persons identified by the Secretary as qualified to prescribe, dispense, or administer the countermeasures.

The Act also authorizes a fund in the United States Treasury to provide compensation for injuries directly caused by administration or use of the countermeasure covered by the Secretary's declaration.

Emergency Use Authorization

<u>Section 564 of the Federal Food, Drug, and Cosmetic Act</u>
<u>21 U.S.C. § 360bbb-3</u>
Under section 564 of the Federal Food, Drug, and Cosmetic Act, if
1. The Secretary of HHS has determined that there is a public health emergency or a significant potential for a public health emergency that affects or may affect national security or the health of US citizens abroad that involves a chemical, biological, radiological, or nuclear (CBRN) agent or agents;
2. The Secretary of Homeland Security has determined that there is an actual or significant potential for a domestic emergency involving a heightened risk of attack with a CBRN agent or agents;
3. The Secretary of Defense has determined that there is an actual or significant potential for heightened risk to the military involving a heightened risk of attack with a CBRN agent or agents; or
4. The Secretary of Homeland Security has identified a material threat pursuant to section 319F-2 of the Public Health Service Act sufficient to affect national security or the health and security of U.S. citizens abroad that involves a CBRN agent or agents

The Secretary of HHS may, based upon one of the preceding determinations, declare that circumstances exist to justify an Emergency Use Authorization (EUA) for an unapproved drug, device, or biological product, or for an unapproved use of an approved drug, device, or biological product. Once an emergency is declared, the Food and Drug Administration (FDA) Commissioner may issue an EUA for a particular product or products, assuming other statutory criteria and conditions are met. The EUA expires when the declaration of emergency terminates or when authorization is revoked. The FDA Commissioner may impose conditions on the use of the drug or device.

<u>Section 564A of the Federal Food, Drug, and Cosmetic Act</u>
<u>21 U.S.C. § 360bbb-3a</u>
Enacted by the Pandemic and All-Hazards Preparedness Reauthorization Act of 2013 (see above), section 564A established streamlined mechanisms to facilitate certain med-

ical countermeasure preparedness and response activities without having to issue an EUA (which can be a time- and resource-intensive process). These new authorities, applicable to eligible FDA-approved medical products intended for use during a chemical, biological, radiological, or nuclear (CBRN) emergency, include

1. Allowing CDC, under delegated authority, to create and issue, and government stakeholders to disseminate, special emergency use instructions about the FDA-approved conditions of use for such medical countermeasures before a CBRN event occurs;
2. Permitting the FDA to waive otherwise applicable manufacturing requirements, such as storage or handling, to accommodate emergency response needs; allowing mass dispensing of medical countermeasures during an actual CBRN emergency event without requiring an individual prescription for each recipient of the medical countermeasure, if permitted by State law or if in accordance with an order issued by the FDA Commissioner; and
3. Expanding the current waiver authority for risk evaluation and mitigation strategies to encompass any element for medical countermeasures to mitigate the health effects of a CBRN emergency.

Section 564B of the Federal Food, Drug, and Cosmetic Act
21 U.S.C. § 360bbb-3b

Enacted by the Pandemic and All-Hazards Preparedness Reauthorization Act of 2013 (see above), section 564B permits federal, state, and local governments to pre-position medical countermeasures in anticipation of approval or clearance, or issuance of an EUA, enabling them to better prepare for potential rapid deployment during an actual chemical, biological, radiological, or nuclear emergency.

Public Safety and Security

Posse Comitatus Act of 1878
18 U.S.C. § 1385

The Posse Comitatus Act generally prohibits the use of federal military personnel in a law enforcement capacity within the United States unless authorized by the U.S. Constitution or an act of Congress. Certain exceptions exist, such as when the Department of Defense aids the Department of Justice in responding to an emergency situation involving a weapon of mass destruction [10 U.S.C.A. § 382].

Insurrection Act of 1807
10 U.S.C. §§ 331-335

The Insurrection Act grants authority to the President to call the National Guard into federal service in the event of an insurrection in any state or if a state fails to uphold the constitutional rights of its citizens.

Emergency Federal Law Enforcement Assistance Act of 2006
42 U.S.C. § 10501, et seq.

Under the Emergency Federal Law Enforcement Assistance Act, the Attorney General may provide law enforcement assistance, including federal personnel, in response to a governor's written request, when he or she determines that such assistance is necessary to provide an adequate response to a law enforcement emergency. To the extent federal personnel would be used to enforce state or local law, they should be deputized or otherwise authorized under state or local law to exercise the key law enforcement powers (arrest, search, seizure) involved in enforcing those laws.

Control of Communicable Diseases

Section 311 of the Public Health Service Act: General Grant of Authority for Cooperation
42 U.S.C. § 243

This provision of the Public Health Service Act states that the Secretary of HHS shall assist states and local authorities in the prevention and suppression of communicable diseases and to help state and local authorities enforce quarantine regulations. This section also authorizes the Secretary to accept state and local authorities' assistance with enforcement of federal quarantine regulations. Further, this section authorizes the Secretary to develop a public health emergency management plan and, at the request of a state or local authority, extend temporary assistance regarding public health emergencies.

Section 361 of the Public Health Service Act: Regulations to Control Communicable Diseases
42 U.S.C. § 264

This section of the Public Health Service Act authorizes the Secretary of HHS to make and enforce regulations "to prevent the introduction, transmission, or spread of communicable diseases" into the states and possessions of the United States from foreign countries or possessions or from one state into another. This section also authorizes the apprehension, detention, examination, and conditional release of individuals with certain communicable diseases that are specified in an executive order of the President (see Executive Order 13296, as amended by Executive Order 13375). The process prescribed for isolating or quarantining such individuals is provided for in 42 C.F.R. Parts 70 and 71 (see below). ·

Section 362 of the Public Health Service Act: Suspension of Entries and Imports from Designated Places to Prevent Spread of Communicable Diseases
42 U.S.C. § 265

This section of the Public Health Service Act authorizes the Secretary of HHS, if he or she determines that a communicable disease exists in a foreign country and that introduction of persons from this foreign country poses a serious danger of introducing the disease into the United States, to suspend in the interests of public health the "introduction of persons" from those foreign countries or places for the time necessary to avert the danger, in accordance with approved regulations. This provision may also be applied to the introduction of property (see below).

Interstate Quarantine
42 C.F.R. Part 70

These federal regulations allow the CDC Director to take measures to prevent the spread of communicable diseases from one state or possession into another, including in the event that the Director determines that the measures taken by the health authorities of a state (including political subdivisions) or possession are insufficient to prevent such communicable disease spread. These regulations also authorize the detention, isolation, quarantine, or conditional release of persons for purposes of preventing the interstate spread of communicable diseases listed in an executive order of the President. See Executive Order 13296, as amended by Executive Order 13375.

Foreign Quarantine
42 C.F.R. Part 71

These federal regulations allow the CDC Director to take measures to prevent the introduction, transmission, and spread of communicable diseases into the United States from foreign countries. Among other things, the regulations require the commander of an aircraft or master of a ship destined for a U.S. port to report the occurrence of any deaths or ill persons onboard to the nearest quarantine station. These regulations also authorize the Director to inspect and detain ships and planes arriving into the United States as may be necessary to prevent the spread of communicable diseases. The Director may also isolate, quarantine, or place arriving persons under public health surveillance whenever the Director reasonably believes that the person is infected with or has been exposed to any of the communicable disease listed in an executive order of the President. See Executive Order 13296, as amended by Executive Order 13375.

Executive Order 13295, Revised List of Quarantinable Communicable Diseases (April 4, 2003)

This Executive Order identifies the eight communicable diseases (cholera; diphtheria; infectious tuberculosis; plague; smallpox; yellow fever; viral hemorrhagic fevers; and Severe Acute Respiratory Syndrome (SARS)), for which an individual can be apprehended, detained, examined, or conditionally released by federal public health authorities under 42 C.F.R.. §§ 70 and 71.

Executive Order 13375: Amendment to Executive Order 13295 Relating to Certain Influenza Viruses and Quarantinable Communicable Diseases (April 1, 2005)

This Executive Order amends Executive Order 13295 by adding "influenza caused by novel or reemergent influenza viruses that are causing, or have the potential to cause, a pandemic" to the list of communicable diseases for which an individual can be apprehended, detained, examined, or conditionally released by federal public health authorities under 42 C.F.R.. §§ 70 and 71.

Penalties for Violation of Quarantine Law
42 U.S.C. § 271

This statutory provision states that violation of federal quarantine regulations is a crime punishable by a fine of not more $1,000 or by imprisonment for not more than one year, or both. Implementing regulations are found at 42 C.F.R. Part 71.2. These penalties are strengthened under the sentencing classification provisions of 18 U.S.C. §§ 3559 and 3571, which provide for more strict penalties for criminal violations that would otherwise be classified as Class A misdemeanors. Under these strengthened penalties, individuals may be punished by a fine of up to $100,000 per violation not resulting in the death of an individual, or up to $250,000 per violation resulting in the death of an individual [18 U.S.C. 3559, 3571(b)]. Organizations may be fined up to $200,000 per violation not resulting in the death of an individual and $500,000 per violation resulting in the death of an individual [18 U.S.C. 3559, 3571(c)].

Emergency Medical Treatment and Active Labor Act (EMTALA)
42 U.S.C. § 1395dd

EMTALA requires that hospitals accepting Medicare payments provide patients coming to the emergency department appropriate medical screening for emergency medical conditions without regard to citizenship, legal status, or ability to pay. If the patient is found to have an emergency medical condition, the hospital must either provide further examination and treatment until the patient is stabilized, or, if the hospital is unable to stabilize the patient, the hospital must arrange for transfer of the individual to a capable facility. Patients cannot be denied stabilizing treatment or discharged prematurely based on prior unpaid debts to the hospital. While patients cannot be held criminally liable, hospitals may seek judgments against non-paying patients in civil court for the amounts owed.

State Health Laws Observed by United States Officers
42 U.S.C. § 97

This provision states that U.S. Coast Guard and customs officers, as well as "military officers commanding in any fort or station upon the seacoast," shall observe quarantines and health laws imposed by states regarding the arrival of vessels, and according to their respective powers, aid in the execution of such state health laws and quarantines as directed from time to time by the Secretary of HHS.

Quarantine Duties of Consular and Other Officers
42 U.S.C. § 268(b)

These statutes state the duty of Customs and Border Protection and the U.S. Coast Guard to aid in the execution of federal quarantine and the enforcement of federal quarantine rules and regulations.

Immigration Authority
8 U.S.C. §§ 1182 and 1222, 42 U.S.C. § 252

Under these provisions, the Department of Homeland Security and HHS are charged with conducting physical and mental examinations of arriving aliens. Under 8 U.S.C. § 1182, aliens are inadmissible in to the United States on health-related grounds if determined to have a communicable disease of public health significance, certain mental or physical defects, to be a drug abuser or addict, or to have failed to present documentation of vaccination against vaccine-preventable diseases as set forth in the statute. The process that HHS prescribes for conducting the medical examinations is provided for in 42 C.F.R. Part 34 (see below).

Medical Examination of Aliens
42 C.F.R. Part 34
CDC administers this regulation, which describes the medical examination that aliens must undergo before they may be admitted to the United States. The medical examination applies to aliens outside the U.S. applying for an immigrant visa; aliens arriving in the U.S.; aliens required by DHS to have a medical examination; and applicants in the U.S. applying for adjustment of their immigration status to that of permanent legal resident. Aliens determined to have a communicable disease of public health significance are generally inadmissible unless granted a waiver by DHS.

Managing Transportation

Transportation Security Administration Authority to Cancel or Ground Flights
49 U.S.C. §§ 114 and 44905(b)
The Transportation Security Administration has the authority to cancel a flight or prevent planes from landing if "a decision is made that a particular threat cannot be addressed in a way adequate to ensure, to the extent feasible, the safety of passengers and crew of a particular flight or series of flights."

Federal Aviation Administration Authority to Restrict Airport Access or Airspace
49 U.S.C. §§ 40101(d), 40103(b), 44701, and 46105(c)
The Federal Aviation Administration (FAA) has authority to stop, redirect, or exclude flights in United States airspace for public safety and has the authority to restrict airport access due to emergency conditions on the ground. If the FAA Administrator believes it necessary, he or she may "prescribe regulations and issue orders immediately to meet the emergency."

Managing Animals, Food, and Other Property

Control of Communicable Diseases
21 C.F.R. Part 1240
Similar to the regulations governing interstate quarantine, these regulations allow the FDA Commissioner to take measures to prevent the spread of communicable diseases from one state or possession into another in the event that the Commissioner determines that the

measures taken by the health authorities of a state (including political subdivisions) or possession are insufficient to prevent such communicable disease spread. These regulations also govern the interstate transport of mollusks, milk, turtles, certain birds, garbage, and drinking water.

Foreign Quarantine
42 C.F.R. Part 71
In addition to allowing the CDC Director to take measures to prevent the introduction, transmission, and spread of communicable diseases into the United States from foreign countries, by regulating the entry of people into the United States, these regulations also govern the importation of certain animals, including dogs, cats, turtles, and nonhuman primates.

Section 361 of the Public Health Service Act: Regulations to Control Communicable Diseases
42 U.S.C. § 264
For purposes of carrying out and enforcing regulations enacted under section 361 of the Public Health Service Act, this section states that the Secretary of HHS "may provide for such inspection, fumigation, disinfection, sanitation, pest extermination, destruction of animals or articles found to be so infected or contaminated as to be sources of dangerous infection to human beings . . ."

Section 362 of the Public Health Service Act: Suspension of Entries and Imports from Designated Places to Prevent Spread of Communicable Diseases
42 U.S.C. § 265
This section of the Public Health Service Act authorizes the Secretary of HHS, if he or she determines that a communicable disease exists in a foreign country and that introduction of property from this foreign country poses a serious danger of introducing the disease into the United States, to suspend in the interests of public health the "introduction of property" from those foreign countries or places for the time necessary to avert the danger, in accordance with approved regulations.

Pets Evacuation and Transportation Standards (PETS) Act of 2006
Pub. L. No. 109-308; 42 U.S.C. §§ 5170(b), 5196, 5196(b)
The PETS Act amends the Stafford Act to require the FEMA Director to ensure that state and local emergency preparedness plans "take into account the needs of individuals with household pets and service animals prior to, during, and following a major disaster or emergency."

Liability, Workers' Compensation, and Licensure

Federal Tort Claims Act
28 U.S.C. §§ 1346(b), 2671–2680

The Act waives the doctrine of sovereign immunity so that the United States can be held liable for the negligent acts or omissions of federal employees committed within the scope of their federal employment. Claims based on discretionary functions or intentional torts are explicitly precluded. Further, suits by military personnel for injuries sustained during service (also known as the Feres doctrine) have been deemed by the courts as outside of the Act. To proceed against the United States, the Attorney General must certify that the federal employee was acting within the scope of his office or employment, or, if the Attorney General refuses, the employee may petition the court to make this finding and certify. Once certified, the United States replaces the employee as the party defendant in the suit.

Federal Employee Compensation Act of 1993
Pub. L. No. 103-3; 5 U.S.C. § 81

The Federal Employee Compensation Act provides workers' compensation to civilian federal employees injured or killed while performing their duties. An injured employee or the family of an employee killed while performing his duties is entitled to related medical services and benefits unless the employee intended to bring about the injury or death, caused the injury or death through the employee's own willful misconduct, or the injury or death was proximately caused by the employee's intoxication.

Public Readiness and Emergency Preparedness (PREP) Act of 2005
Pub. L. No. 109-148; 42 U.S.C. §§ 247d-6d, 247d-6e

The PREP Act authorizes the Secretary of HHS to issue a declaration that provides immunity from tort liability for claims of loss (except willful misconduct) caused by, arising out of, relating to, or resulting from administration or use of countermeasures to diseases, threats and conditions determined by the Secretary to constitute a present, or credible risk of a future public health emergency. The immunity applies to entities and individuals involved in the development, manufacture, testing, distribution, administration, and use of such countermeasures. As amended by PAHPRA (see above), PREP Act immunity also explicitly applies to products or technology intended to enhance medical countermeasures, in addition to the countermeasures themselves (see Pandemic and All–Hazards Preparedness Reauthorization Act (PAHPRA) of 2013 above). PAHPRA also extends immunity to countermeasures authorized under sections 564A and 564B of the Federal Food, Drug, and Cosmetic Act (see above). The Secretary's declaration includes, among other things, the countermeasures covered by the declaration; the category of diseases, health conditions, or health threats for which administration and use of the countermeasures recommended; the effective time period of the declaration; the population of individuals receiving the countermeasure; limitations, if any, on the geographic area for which immunity is in effect; limitations, if any, on the means of distribution of the countermeasure; and any additional persons identified by the Secretary as qualified to prescribe, dispense, or administer the countermeasures. The Act also authorizes a fund in the United States Treasury to provide compensation for injuries directly caused by administration or use of the countermeasure covered by the Secretary's declaration.

Volunteer Protection Act of 1997
Pub. L. No 105-295; 42 U.S.C. §§ 14501–14505

The Volunteer Protection Act supports and promotes the activities of organizations that rely on volunteers by providing the volunteers some protections from liability for economic damages for activities relating to the work of the organizations. Under the Act, to be found not liable for the injury caused by a negligent act or omission of the volunteer, the volunteer must have been acting within the scope of his or her responsibilities in the nonprofit or government agency. The volunteer must have appropriate licensure or certification if required for the volunteer's duties; he or she must not have acted with gross negligence, reckless disregard, willful or criminal misconduct, or flagrant indifference; and the injury cannot have occurred while the volunteer was intoxicated. Further, the injury cannot have occurred while the volunteer was operating an automobile or other vehicle for which the state requires an operator's license and insurance. This Act does not limit the liability of the nonprofit or government agency. The Act does not limit an injured party's ability to sue for non-economic damages, provide immunity to the non-profit organization or government entity supervising the volunteer, nor limit a nonprofit or government entity's ability to bring a civil action against the volunteer. States may opt out of the Volunteer Protection Act.

Emergency Management Assistance Compact (EMAC) of 1996
Pub. L. No. 104-321

EMAC facilitates resource sharing among member states during an emergency. The National Emergency Management Association (NEMA) administers EMAC, which has been enacted by every state. A governor's declaration of emergency and request for assistance triggers EMAC for the requesting state. An assisting state then responds to the request by providing the needed resources, including personnel. EMAC stipulates that a provider who is licensed or certified in one state will be considered licensed or certified in the receiving state subject to limitations described in the requesting state's governor's order. EMAC provides for protection of officers or employees of the assisting state from tort liability for negligent acts or omissions unless the officer or employee acted with gross negligence, recklessness, or willful misconduct. EMAC also requires that each state provide for worker's compensation in instances of injury or death for their own employees.

Personal Health Information and Privacy

Privacy Act of 1974
5 U.S.C. § 552a

The Privacy Act describes the fair collection, maintenance, use and dissemination by a government agency of records containing personal identifiers (i.e. name, social security number, date of birth, etc.). Generally, the Act requires that information compiled in a federal record for a specific individual may not be used for another purpose without consent of the individual. The Act prevents disclosure of information contained in the record without an individual's written consent, unless the disclosure is one of the twelve exceptions expressly stated within the Act. Under most circumstances, individuals are allowed to request access to their own records and to challenge inaccurate information. The Act also outlines the civil remedies available if a government agency makes an unauthorized disclosure of an individual's personal information.

Health Information Portability and Accountability Act (HIPAA) of 1996: Privacy Rule
Pub. L. No. 104-191

The HIPAA Privacy Rule protects certain patient information (including health insurance and billing information, medical records, and conversations with providers) from being disclosed by covered entities (including most health insurance companies, health care providers, and health information clearinghouses) for reasons other than providing treatment and care, billing and payment, protecting the public's health (such as through surveillance of specific diseases), or reporting required information to police (such as gunshot wounds). Information cannot be disclosed outside of the HIPAA provisions without the patient's express written permission. Covered entities must have safeguards in place to protect patient health information to ensure that it is not mishandled. If a Section 319 Emergency has been declared, the Secretary of HHS may waive certain sanctions for non-compliance with HIPAA. Note that CDC is not a covered entity under HIPAA, nor are state or local public health departments unless they also treat patients. Regulations are found at 34 C.F.R. Part 160 and Subparts A and E of 164.

Family Educational Rights and Privacy Act (FERPA) of 1973
Pub. L. No. 93- 380, as amended; 20 U.S.C. § 1232g

FERPA applies to all educational agencies and institutions receiving funds under any program from the United States Department of Education, which encompasses virtually all public schools and universities, as well as some private schools. The school or agency may not disclose student records without a parent's or eligible student's written consent (an eligible student is either eighteen years or older or is attending a postsecondary institution at any age). FERPA also gives parents and eligible students the right to access and review records. Parents and eligible students may request explanation of items in the record, seek amendment to records for information that is "inaccurate, misleading, or in violation of the student's privacy" and may request a hearing to challenge the content of the record if the school or agency does not agree to the amendment. Disclosure to teachers and other relevant employees of the school or agency without consent of the parent or eligible child is allowed for legitimate educational purposes; disclosure without consent is also allowed in several express purposes, including "in connection with an emergency if knowledge of the information is necessary to protect the health or safety of the student or other individuals." For this exception, the school or agency must make a determination that there is an "articulable and significant threat" to the health and safety of the student or other individuals, taking into consideration a totality of the circumstances. Regulations are found at 34 C.F.R. Part 99.

Related Federal Guidance

National Response Framework (January 2008; updated May 2013)
The National Response Framework is a guide to how the United States conducts all-hazards response, and is intended to capture specific authorities and best practices for managing incidents that range from the serious but purely local, to large-scale terrorist attacks or catastrophic natural disasters. In addition to the core document, the framework contains Emergency Support Function (ESF) Annexes which group federal resources and capabilities into functional areas to serve as the primary mechanisms for providing assistance at the operational level. Common roles of federal agencies during emergencies are grouped together into fifteen ESFs with different responsibilities based on these roles. Within each ESF, there is at least one primary agency, support agencies, and an ESF coordinator that is selected to oversee the ESF.

- ESF #8 is designated for Public Health and Medical Services. The U.S. Department of Health and Human Services (HHS) is the Primary Agency and Coordinator for ESF #8. ESF #8 outlines the roles of the Primary Agency and each Supporting Agency when providing assistance to state, tribal, and local governments during public health emergencies or threats.
- ESF#13 is designated for Public Safety and Security. The U.S. Department of Justice is the Primary Agency and Coordinator for ESF#13. This ESF is activated in situations requiring extensive public safety and security and where state, tribal, and local government resources are overwhelmed or are inadequate or for federal-to-federal support.

The Framework also contains Incident Annexes that describe the concept of operations to address specific contingency or hazard situations or an element of an incident requiring specialized application of the Framework. The Biological Incident Annex outlines the actions, roles, and responsibilities associated with a human disease outbreak of known or unknown origin requiring federal assistance. HHS is the coordinating agency for this annex. The Food and Agriculture Incident Annex describes the roles and responsibilities associated with incidents involving agriculture and food systems that require a coordinated federal response. Both HHS and the Department of Agriculture are the coordinating agencies for this annex.

Source: Centers for Disease Control and Prevention, 2014, https://www.hsdl.org/?view&did=753211

CONGRESSIONAL PRIMER ON RESPONDING TO AND RECOVERING FROM MAJOR DISASTERS AND EMERGENCIES

Read the information here: http://fas.org/sgp/crs/homesec/R41981.pdf

PANDEMIC AND ALL-HAZARDS PREPAREDNESS REAUTHORIZATION ACT OF 2013

Read the information here: https://www.congress.gov/bill/113th-congress/senate-bill/242/text

GOOD SAMARITAN LAW IN FLORIDA

768.13 Good Samaritan Act; immunity from civil liability.—
(1) This act shall be known and cited as the "Good Samaritan Act."
(2)(a) Any person, including those licensed to practice medicine, who gratuitously and in good faith renders emergency care or treatment either in direct response to emergency situations related to and arising out of a public health emergency declared pursuant to s. 381.00315, a state of emergency which has been declared pursuant to s. 252.36 or at the scene of an emergency outside of a hospital, doctor's office, or other place having proper medical equipment, without objection of the injured victim or victims thereof, shall not be held liable for any civil damages as a result of such care or treatment or as a result of any act or failure to act in providing or arranging further medical treatment where the person acts as an ordinary reasonably prudent person would have acted under the same or similar circumstances.
(b)1. Any health care provider, including a hospital licensed under chapter 395, providing emergency services pursuant to obligations imposed by 42 U.S.C. s. 1395dd, s. 395.1041, s. 395.401, or s. 401.45 shall not be held liable for any civil damages as a result of such medical care or treatment unless such damages result from providing, or failing to provide, medical care or treatment under circumstances demonstrating a reckless disregard for the consequences so as to affect the life or health of another.
2. The immunity provided by this paragraph applies to damages as a result of any act or omission of providing medical care or treatment, including diagnosis:
a. Which occurs prior to the time the patient is stabilized and is capable of receiving medical treatment as a nonemergency patient, unless surgery is required as a result of the emergency within a reasonable time after the patient is stabilized, in which case the immunity provided by this paragraph applies to any act or omission of providing medical care or treatment which occurs prior to the stabilization of the patient following the surgery.
b. Which is related to the original medical emergency.
3. For purposes of this paragraph, "reckless disregard" as it applies to a given health care provider rendering emergency medical services shall be such conduct that a health care provider knew or should have known, at the time such services were rendered, created an unreasonable risk of injury so as to affect the life or health of another, and such risk was substantially greater than that which is necessary to make the conduct negligent.
4. Every emergency care facility granted immunity under this paragraph shall accept and treat all emergency care patients within the operational capacity of such facility without regard to ability to pay, including patients transferred from another emergency care facil-

ity or other health care provider pursuant to Pub. L. No. 99-272, s. 9121. The failure of an emergency care facility to comply with this subparagraph constitutes grounds for the department to initiate disciplinary action against the facility pursuant to chapter 395.

(c)1. Any health care practitioner as defined in s. 456.001(4) who is in a hospital attending to a patient of his or her practice or for business or personal reasons unrelated to direct patient care, and who voluntarily responds to provide care or treatment to a patient with whom at that time the practitioner does not have a then-existing health care patient-practitioner relationship, and when such care or treatment is necessitated by a sudden or unexpected situation or by an occurrence that demands immediate medical attention, shall not be held liable for any civil damages as a result of any act or omission relative to that care or treatment, unless that care or treatment is proven to amount to conduct that is willful and wanton and would likely result in injury so as to affect the life or health of another.

2. The immunity provided by this paragraph does not apply to damages as a result of any act or omission of providing medical care or treatment unrelated to the original situation that demanded immediate medical attention.

3. For purposes of this paragraph, the Legislature's intent is to encourage health care practitioners to provide necessary emergency care to all persons without fear of litigation as described in this paragraph.

(d) Any person whose acts or omissions are not otherwise covered by this section and who participates in emergency response activities under the direction of or in connection with a community emergency response team, local emergency management agencies, the Division of Emergency Management, or the Federal Emergency Management Agency is not liable for any civil damages as a result of care, treatment, or services provided gratuitously in such capacity and resulting from any act or failure to act in such capacity in providing or arranging further care, treatment, or services, if such person acts as a reasonably prudent person would have acted under the same or similar circumstances.

(3) Any person, including those licensed to practice veterinary medicine, who gratuitously and in good faith renders emergency care or treatment to an injured animal at the scene of an emergency on or adjacent to a roadway shall not be held liable for any civil damages as a result of such care or treatment or as a result of any act or failure to act in providing or arranging further medical treatment where the person acts as an ordinary reasonably prudent person would have acted under the same or similar circumstances.

History.—ss. 1, 2, ch. 65-313; s. 1, ch. 78-334; s. 62, ch. 86-160; s. 46, ch. 88-1; s. 4, ch. 88-173; s. 42, ch. 88-277; s. 1, ch. 89-71; s. 37, ch. 91-110; s. 33, ch. 93-211; s. 3, ch. 97-34; s. 1164, ch. 97-102; s. 2, ch. 2001-76; s. 3, ch. 2002-269; s. 65, ch. 2003-416; s. 1, ch. 2004-45; s. 441, ch. 2011-142.

Source: The Florida Senate, 2011, https://www.flsenate.gov/Laws/Statutes/2011/768.13

EMERGENCY MANAGEMENT AND LAW

William Charles Nicholson, Esq.

Abstract

The following chapter relates the history of law and emergency management, discusses vulnerability and steps to be taken for its reduction, defines various concepts from a legal perspective, and examines gaps in knowledge between the two fields. The chapter also notes how law may improve emergency management and identifies considerations that are paramount to the future. The major argument to be presented is that law and emergency management are inherently intertwined and that legal norms in the disaster field are changing and having a significant impact on the profession.

Introduction

In many ways, emergency management could not exist without the law. In the United States, legal enactments provide the authorities and funding for emergency management. Definitions of critical emergency management terms have been established in legal enactments. Although their interaction may be difficult at times, lawyers and emergency managers need one another. A major obstacle is the mutual ignorance that all too often characterizes their relationship. When attorneys, emergency managers, and leaders of units of government take the time to build a relationship that encompasses all phases of emergency management, the result can be shelter from liability as well as greater life safety and improved property protection.

History of Law and Emergency Management

The history of disasters in the United States is intertwined with the law (FEMA, 2005a). On the federal level, as early as 1803, Congress enacted legislation to provide relief from a severe fire in a New Hampshire town. The Congressional Act of 1803 is generally thought of as the first piece of disaster legislation. During the next century, specific legal enactments authorized funding for the response to disaster events one incident at a time. The 1930s brought about an organized federal approach to disaster law. The Reconstruction Finance Corporation was authorized to generate disaster loans for the repair and reconstruction of some public facilities after an earthquake. This authority was extended later to other varieties of disaster. The Bureau of Public Roads, under a 1934 law, was empowered to provide funding for highways and bridges damaged by natural disasters. Another important piece of legislation, the Flood Control Act, expanded the authority of the U.S. Army Corps of Engineers to put into effect flood control projects. This approach to disaster assistance improved on the prior "one at a time" practice of creating legal authority. Yet problems remained. The ever increasing size of the national government meant that sometimes federal agencies with different pieces of disaster authority found themselves working at cross purposes. As a result, Congress enacted legislation requiring better greater cooperation between federal agencies and authorizing the President to coordinate these activities.

The subsequent history of disasters reveals that they steadily grew in both number and magnitude. The federal government was faced with enormous disasters in the 1960s and early 1970s. The Federal Disaster Assistance Administration, which was located in the Department of Housing and Urban Development, coordinated these efforts. Hurricanes Carla (1962), Betsy (1965), Camille (1969), and Agnes (1972), as well as large earthquakes in Alaska (1964) and San Fernando in California (1971) put natural disasters in the forefront of national attention, and resulted in legislation. The 1968 National Flood Insurance Act gave homeowners new assistance, while the 1974 Disaster Relief Act regularized the procedure for issuance of Presidential disaster declarations.

Despite this legal progress, there was still not a unified framework for emergency and disaster practices. By the 1970s, disasters, hazards and emergencies were the business of over 100 federal agencies. On the state and local level, similar structures were in place. The result was a confusing welter of groups and efforts that often competed with or duplicated one another. At the request of the National Governor's Association, President Jimmy Carter moved to consolidate federal emergency functions.

In 1979, President Carter's issued an executive order unifying federal disaster activities under the newly created Federal Emergency Management Agency (FEMA). FEMA incorporated many bodies, including the Federal Insurance Administration, the National Fire Prevention and Control Administration, the National Weather Service Community Preparedness Program, the Federal Preparedness Agency of the General Services Administration and the Federal Disaster Assistance Administration from HUD. Civil defense moved to FEMA from the Defense Civil Preparedness Agency in the Department of Defense.

In the aftermath of the first attack on the World Trade Center (1993) and the Oklahoma City bombing (1995), FEMA's "all-hazards" approach to disaster management was overshadowed by a concentration on homeland security matters. The Homeland Security Act of 2002 (HS Act) united 22 federal agencies, programs and offices, including FEMA, to create the Department of Homeland Security (DHS). Creating DHS was another legal step in unifying disaster preparedness and response. DHS' mission focuses on terrorism, including prevention, vulnerability reduction, minimizing damage, and assisting in recovery from terrorism attacks (107th Congress, 2002, § 1(a-c)). Also included in the Department's responsibilities is carrying out all functions of entities transferred to the Department, including acting as a focal point regarding natural and manmade crises and emergency planning (107th Congress, 2002, § 1(d)).

Some experienced emergency management observers believe that the focus at DHS is too terrorism-oriented (Nicholson, 2003a), with troubling impact on the all-hazards preparedness mission that FEMA has traditionally espoused (Waugh, 2002). This is an issue that has two sides, but whatever perspective one endorses, to a great extent the argument revolves around the nature of legal enactments and their interaction with policy. From the view of statutory construction, however, the fact that the Department's terrorism responsibilities are listed as the first three parts of its mission while other hazards are lumped together in fourth place means that Congress intended DHS' terrorism responsibilities to be more important than those dealing with other hazards.

Defining and Reducing Vulnerability

The National Response Plan (NRP) (National Response Plan, 2005), and the National Incident Management System (NIMS) (National Incident Management System, 2005) do not define "vulnerability." In the FEMA publication *Building Design for Homeland Security*, "vulnerability" is defined as "any weakness that can be exploited by an aggressor or, in a non-terrorist threat environment, make an asset susceptible to hazard damage" (FEMA, 2005b). The publication discusses vulnerability assessment as well as what steps to take once vulnerabilities have been identified in order to mitigate against the identified threat.

The persuasiveness of authority for the term "vulnerability" is somewhat less than if it were defined directly in the NRP or NIMS. Its promulgation by FEMA and general use in the profession, however, indicate that an American Court under the commonly accepted business practice doctrine (discussed at greater length below) would find them influential.

Recently, a pair of Australians made an interesting suggestion for an increased role for legal enactments in vulnerability reduction (Handmer & Monson, 2004). Their approach features a definition of vulnerability as "a multi-faceted concept incorporating issues of livelihood, housing, security, and gender, among many others" (Handmer & Monson, 2004). The piece suggests that a link between vulnerability and law exists when laws set out rights to adequate housing and livelihood, for example. In addition to the familiar constraints of public and private law, social norms, custom, and international law are posited as having the potential to regulate vulnerability (Handmer & Monson, 2004). The article focuses on human rights as found in national public law, since such laws have been enforceable by the citizenry against their government. Enforcing other types of law is a much less certain endeavor.

Vulnerability is a "function of susceptibility to loss and the capacity to recover" (Handmer & Monson, 2004). Due to their more positive connotations, some prefer the terms resilience or capacity to vulnerability. The most vulnerable people are those whose basic human needs, like adequate food, shelter, health care, and education, are unmet. These needs are defined by the piece as "fundamental human rights."[1] The rights based approach works from the bottom – originating with the affected groups –as opposed to from the top – through government, Courts, and experts. The approach identifies the sources of vulnerability (failure to meet certain rights) and contains a way to reduce them (through legal enforcement of rights).

The article posits that international law may provide a method for expansion of enforceable human rights, through more inclusive interpretation. For example, it suggests that the right to life, liberty and security of every person under the *Universal Declaration of Human Rights* might expand to include protecting the "security of the person" from other harm, like natural disasters. Such an approach overemphasizes the force of international law, whose power extends only to those matters by which individual nations agree to be bound. Nations unilaterally may change their adherence to such agreements, other than in matters of torture and genocide. The article acknowledges an "implementation gap" on human rights, even in wealthy nations as well as the virtual impossibility of enforcing naked (that is, without incorporation into domestic law) international law. While some may espouse universal human rights, their practice is far from uniform around the world.

Three South African cases are interesting illustrations of the authors' premises. The first establishes a constitutional obligation to provide disaster relief, but states that a hearing is not required for all who object to the way relief is given (Handmer & Monson, 2004). The exceptional circumstances in a disaster allow the government to forego more onerous procedures than would normally apply to decision making. While the United States has never held disaster relief to be a constitutionally protected right (and the possibility of that ever happening in the US is highly unlikely, to say the least), the ability of the government to avoid procedural inconveniences is well established here.[2] The second decision revolves around access to housing and health care. Like many other nations with constitutions established or heavily revised in the second half of the twentieth century,[3] South Africa's constitution lists a range of rights to be provided within its available resources, including housing and health care. The residents in this case were squatting on private land, from which they were cruelly ejected, after which they were relocated into intolerable conditions. They appealed to the Constitutional Court. That tribunal held that, despite the challenges in enforcing them, "these are rights, and the Constitution obliges the State to give effect to them" (Public Law, No Publication Year).

The third case discusses the right to treatment for HIV patients. Some scholars view AIDS as a type of disaster (Varley, 1994). Clearly, the illness's effect on public health budgets has been disastrous. This case provided that South Africa had the constitutional obligation to provide HIV treatment to pregnant women to help prevent transmitting HIV to their unborn children. The South African Constitution recognizes a right to access to public health care services and requires the state to take reasonable steps, within its available resources, to achieve the progressive realization of this right (Public Law, No Publication Year). The Court found that the government was not going far enough in making appropriate medication available.

The South African cases illustrate how far a country may go in guaranteeing and enforcing human rights that go well beyond those afforded in the United States. Other nations with similar constitutions might pursue the same approach. In Europe, human rights established by the European Union cannot be enforced in the European Court of Human Rights, which enforces the European Convention on Human Rights. That convention does not recognize, for example, a right to adequate housing or health care. The best approach in Europe, as well as in Australia, is posited to be through legislation rather than Constitutional change (Public Law, No Publication Year). This is because, as in the United States, it is very difficult to amend the Constitution.

Parenthetically, it must be observed that the desire to resist the faddish causes of the moment and preserve existing property and other legal relationships is an important reason that Constitutions are difficult to amend.

Also, as a practical matter, establishing the redistribution of wealth in the manner envisioned by the expansion of fundamental human rights to include disaster relief, housing, and medical care is most likely to result in national bankruptcy for those countries that decide to put it into action. The limit placed on such services by the "progressive realization" language cited by the South African Court decisions may mean that the process of bankruptcy will be prolonged rather than immediate, but that does not make it less probable.

The Legal Perspective

As might be expected, hazards, disasters, and emergency management have definitions established by law. Definitions are found in various locations, most importantly including glossaries in the National Response Plan (NRP) (National Response Plan, 2005) and the National Incident Management System (NIMS) (National Incident Management System, 2005). States also define some of these terms. Federal and state law also determines responsibilities for preparedness.

When finalized, the NRP and NIMS will be the end product of a process that began with the passage of the HS Act of 2002. On February 28, 2003 President Bush issued Homeland Security Presidential Directive 5 (HSPD 5) (The White House, 2003). HSPD 5 directs all Federal agencies to take specific steps for planning and incident management. HSPD 5's major goal is to establish a single, comprehensive approach to domestic incident management. The effect of this unified approach will be efficient and effective operation of all levels of government as regards disasters. The Directive specifies the lead agencies for terrorism events and other major disasters. HSPD 5 directs all Federal agencies to work together with DHS to institute the NRP and NIMS. NIMS is the operational portion of the NRP (Homeland Security Presidential Directive 5, 2003). In this manner, legal authority for creating the NRP and NIMS flows from the HS Act of 2002 through HSPD 5 to DHS (Nicholson, 2003b). Failure to comply with the mandates of the NRP and NIMS subjects emergency response and emergency management groups to sanctions, in the form of losing federal grant funds (Homeland Security Presidential Directive 5, 2003).

Given that the NRP and NIMS establish enforceable standards, their definitions have the effect of law for those entities that do not wish to lose their federal funding. For the few entities that do not elect to preserve their federal funding, the NRP and NIMS definitions will also have legal effect as industry standards. The "commonly accepted business practice" doctrine operates to establish elevated standards of care when a large number of similarly situated concerns take supplemental actions. Here, adoption of NRP and NIMS by an overwhelming majority of emergency management groups would be strong evidence to a Court that it should hold all emergency management organizations to these norms.

The NRP and NIMS define "hazard" as something that is potentially dangerous or harmful, often the root cause of an unwanted outcome (National Response Plan, 2005; National Incident Management System, 2005). To define "disaster," the NRP and NIMS refer to the Stafford Act's definition of a "major disaster" as:

> Any natural catastrophe (including any hurricane, tornado, storm, high water, wind-driven water, tidal wave, tsunami, earthquake, volcanic eruption, landslide, mudslide, snowstorm, or drought) or, regardless of cause, any fire, flood, or explosion, in any part of the United States, which in the determination of the President causes damage of sufficient severity and magnitude to warrant major disaster assistance under this act to supplement the efforts and available resources of States, local governments, and disaster relief organizations in alleviating the damage, loss, hardship, or suffering caused thereby (National Response Plan, 2005; National Incident Management System, 2005).

States typically have their own definitions of disaster.[4]

The NRP and NIMS do not define "emergency management." Two on line courses offer definitional assistance that is consistent. The FEMA on line course Introduction to Emergency Management does not offer a simple designation. Rather, it discusses the nature of comprehensive emergency management, building from the simple image of a homeowner responding to a broken water pipe and a flooded basement. The course sums up the modern emergency management's focus as follows:

> Today the emphasis is on the protection of the civilian population and property from the destructive forces of natural and man-made disasters through a comprehensive program of mitigation, preparedness, response, and recovery (FEMA, 2005c).

FEMA's on line Principles of Emergency Management course defines the term rather straightforwardly as "Organized *analysis, planning, decision-making, and assignment of available resources* to mitigate, prepare for, respond to, and recover from the effects of all hazards" (FEMA, 2005d). States also have their definitions for emergency management, which correspond to the federal approach described above.[5]

The persuasiveness of authority for the term "emergency management" is somewhat less than if it were defined directly in the NRP or NIMS. Its promulgation by FEMA and general use in the profession, however, indicate that a Court under the above discussed commonly accepted business practice doctrine would find it influential.

The HS Act of 2002 is somewhat contradictory in setting out responsibilities for preparedness. The role of FEMA is defined to include its Stafford Act functions as well as reducing the loss of life and property and protecting the nation from "all hazards" by leading and supporting the nation in a comprehensive, risk-based emergency management program.[6] The law tasks the Office of Domestic Preparedness (ODP) with terrorism preparedness, in contrast to FEMA, which is specifically entrusted with preparing for and mitigating the effects of non-terrorist-related disasters in the United States.[7] The statute's reader wonders whether the "all hazards" language is mere window dressing, given the division of roles in the description of ODP's tasking.

The end result must be confusion to emergency management, similar to that engendered by Congress' decision to break off planning for release of extremely hazardous substances (EHS) from "all hazards" emergency management in 1986. The federal Emergency Planning and Right to Know Act (EPCRA) requires state and local units of government to split off an important part of emergency management to another entity. EPCRA is contained in the Superfund Amendment and Reauthorization Act of 1986 (SARA Title III) (USC, 2005, §§ 11001-11050). EPCRA mandates that a State Emergency Response Agency (SERC) must ensure planning for EHS releases (USC, 2005, § 1001(a)). The SERC creates emergency planning districts and superintends Local Emergency Planning Committees (LEPCs), (USC, 2005, § 1001(b) (c)) which do the planning for EHS releases (USC, 2005, § 1001(a)).

Emergency management has been able to incorporate LEPC plans as annexes to emergency operations plans. LEPCs and emergency management generally work well together. It remains to be seen whether the same approach will be applied as successfully to terrorism planning at all levels of government.

The Interaction Between Law and Emergency Management

The relationship between law and emergency management may be characterized as one mutual need. Mitigation in particular is an area where the two disciplines have the potential to interact very well. Regrettably, in spite of the fact that the law creates emergency management, in general the understanding of emergency managers and lawyers may be described as mutual ignorance. Some are not even aware that their activities are governed by both federal and state law (Pine, 1991).

Many business and government leaders are uninformed regarding the laws that control their behavior. Sometimes, emergency managers may pay no attention to the law. They may vociferously declare themselves to be "too busy saving lives and protecting property to bother with all that legal mumbo jumbo." Such an attitude is peculiar, given emergency management's "all hazards" character. Analysis of the instructive resources accessible to most emergency managers, however, renders their stance more comprehensible. Despite the fact that emergency management is a legal product on the federal, state and local levels, FEMA's educational materials have historically been deficient regarding coverage of legal issues (Nicholson, 2003c). As a result, matters of liability constitute the greatest unanticipated and unexamined vulnerability that emergency management confronts.

One characteristic shared by top attorneys is their knowledge and understanding of their customer's industry in general, as well as the specifics that set the client's business apart from the rest. Sadly, emergency management lawyers possess minimal assets outside of statutes and interpretations thereof as source material to utilize when counseling their clients on even simple legal matters (Nicholson, 2003d). The wise attorney will recognize his or her ignorance and pursue knowledge of the client's organization. It will be necessary to hunt up resources that go beyond the Continuing Legal Education that lawyers usually see as their main font of information. One way for the emergency management lawyer to go farther is to enroll in the Emergency Management Professional Development Series offered by the Federal Emergency Management Institute (FEMA, 2005e).

How Legal Advice Can Improve Emergency Management

An integrated emergency management system is composed of a conceptual framework that increases emergency management capability through networking. To achieve increased capability, there must be prior networking, coordination, linkages, and partnerships. There must also be creative thinking about resource shortfalls. All hazards threatening a community must be identified so that needs may be compared with resources (FEMA, 2005e). This process requires emergency managers to be pro-active risk managers as opposed to reactive risk ignorers.

Given the all-encompassing nature of law's relationship with emergency management as discussed above, potential liability is a hazard that confronts all emergency management organizations and the units of government that they serve. Potential claims in the aftermath of disasters include wrongful death, negligent planning or actions during the disaster, civil rights violations resulting from improper use of authority, exceeding the scope of proper practice for emergency management, failure to properly distribute aid, monetary damages resulting from loss of business during an evacuation, and many more.

The advance networking required to address the legal hazard entails joining together with legal counsel to avert prospective liability. Properly trained legal counsel may offer beneficial input prior to the emergent event that gives rise to possible liability. Networking with legal counsel in such a manner defines "litigation mitigation" (Nicholson, 2003e). Litigation mitigation has three complimentary objectives:

1. reduced exposure to legal claims;
2. improved life safety; and
3. enhanced property protection.

Typically, legal counsel looks at the first element as his or her main concern. To an emergency manager, all three components are of critical significance. Actually, life safety and property preservation are natural byproducts of legal protection.

If litigation mitigation makes so much sense, one may inquire as to why it is not more prevalent. Several impediments prevent litigation mitigation. A few are intentionally inflicted, while others are the product of the natural evolution of groups with different traditions.

One important obstacle to pro-active connections with attorneys results from groups' usual approach to the use of legal counsel. By tradition, governmental employees look on the attorney like a "legal firefighter." The lawyer gets the call following the legal conflagration's eruption. All too frequently, the client only contacts the attorney after the arrival of legal documents indicating commencement of a lawsuit. The other side of fire fighting is fire prevention, just as the other side of emergency response is mitigation. For emergency management, the attorney could prove to be the equivalent of a fire inspector. Like the inspector, the attorney often may recognize the tinder for a legal inferno and highlight economical approaches that might reduce the hazard.

To the person in the street, lawyers may have an almost priestly appearance - they employ their incomprehensible terminology and execute their esoteric rites. Unfortunately, some attorneys revel in the feeling of exclusivity. In the same way, certain emergency managers use acronyms with meanings shrouded in obscurity to those not initiated in the fraternity. Clearly, unusual language and rituals distinguish both groups from the laity as well as each another. This method is the antithesis to the networking, coordination, linkages, and partnerships essential to creating an integrated emergency management system. It is essential for legal counsel and emergency manager to rely on and comprehend each other as equal partners for litigation mitigation to be successful.

Attorneys also find themselves unable to locate resources that explain the process for engaging in litigation mitigation. Their professional training at law schools does not include this topic, in general. The majority of such institutions rely on a "case study" approach first created hundreds of years ago. Another barrier is the emphasis placed by law schools on if a case is ready to take to Court. Undertaking a pro-active pursuit such as mitigation litigation is contrary to the training and long-standing traditions of the law.

Another factor in lessening the likelihood of networking partnerships between emergency managers and lawyers is the developing nature of the legal market. On one hand, corporate clients insist on a firm that can "do it all," resulting in ongoing pressure to make firms ever larger. Simultaneously, business clients often look at firms as sources of skilled operators who can manipulate the legal system rather than as places to go for trustworthy counselors. Often, companies pay no attention to lawyers' guidance unless it matches with what they wish to hear. The networking and trust needed for a quality litigation mitigation association do not exist in such circumstances. Rather, the lawyer is viewed as a remote, unfamiliar "legal information engineer" who is a tool instead of a partner (Caplan, 2003).

Another major obstacle between attorneys and emergency managers is cost. Although an emergency manager will typically have access to the advice of a city or county attorney, he or she may need more specialized assistance, which may cost a significant amount. A specialist attorney's professional advice may run as much as several hundred dollars an hour, or more. Clearly, lawyers run more per hour than some other types of mitigation. Still, considering the down side of a lack of litigation mitigation, one is hard pressed to see a valid argument against this enhanced safety. An option that may provide for cost controls is negotiating an arrangement with a firm to provide discounted hourly rates in return for an assured number of hours yearly.

From the government side, several significant obstacles exist. Smaller units of government may have attorney advisors who are local practitioners. These lawyers often collect decreased hourly wages for their government work compared with what they collect for normal hourly fees. The result of this arrangement may be that government work gets done only when ordinary business is lacking. This schedule often results in a conflict with the unit's desire for the attorney's help. Another difficulty is that rural units hardly ever make available funding for Continuing Legal Education (CLE) for their lawyer employees or contractors. The untrained country attorney may prove to be unable to give the high-level guidance the unit needs. The lack of CLE training necessary to bring the lawyer up to speed merely emphasizes the difficulty. The lawyer in such circumstances might be in danger of committing malpractice by advising beyond his or her ability. In some cases, the attorney advising the local unit receives the contract for legal services thanks to political activism instead of any actual knowledge of the practice area. A unit's attorney is often appointed on a political basis, even when the City Manager is a merit position. The effect of this situation may not be ineffective counsel, but it may result in regular changes. The potential exists here for recurring legal fees for getting on top of things as well as conflicting legal guidance.

Future Developments

In late 2004, the 9-11 Commission officially endorsed adoption of the National Fire Protection Association 1600 "Standard on Disaster/Emergency Management and Business Continuity Programs, 2004 Edition" (NFPA 1600) (NFPA, 2004) as the national preparedness benchmark. On December 17, 2004, (The White House, 2004) President Bush signed the Intelligence Reform and Terrorism Prevention Act of 2004 (IRTP Act) (Intelligence Reform and Terrorism Prevention Act, 2004) which recognizes NFPA 1600 as a "voluntary" national preparedness norm. NFPA 1600 and other documents such as the Capability Assessment for Readiness (CAR), constitute the core of the Emergency Management Accreditation Program (EMAP) (EMAP, 2005). The accreditation procedure includes application, self-assessment, on-site assessment by an outside review team, committee and commission review of conformity with the EMAP Standard, and re-certification every five years. Adoption of NFPA 1600 is not yet mandatory. It might be said that EMAP is well on its way to becoming the United States' *de facto* emergency management standard. As other emergency management programs are accredited under the standard, it becomes more likely that a Court might hold all emergency management groups to the NFPA 1600 criterion. One nationally known expert believes that "synergy is already building between NFPA 1600, EMAP and the NIMS Integration Center. It's just a matter of time before they are incorporated into NIC's requirements."[7] In fact, mandatory adoption of NFPA 1600 into NIMS will be an important part of standards to be set by the NIMS Integration Center.[8] Emergency management professionals will need to understand and comply with the full dimension of their legal obligations under NIMS, including NFPA 1600 and EMAP.

Other legal needs that will doubtless receive more attention in the future include liability issues in the aftermath of terrorism events. In the wake of the 9-11 attacks, insurance policies are being re-written to exclude terrorism coverage or to make premiums for adding it prohibitively expensive. The result is that businesses and units of government find themselves to be self-insured for this huge potential liability. Every state should examine its immunity statutes to see if the exclusions for third party acts are broad enough to protect from liability from terrorism events. Going hand in hand with that examination, of course, will be the need for units of government to ensure that their steps to provide for the safety of visitors and employees in their offices are appropriate for the dangers involved. As with the private sector, this will involve examining what similar units of government are doing, and being at least as safe. For example, state governments that do not provide for screening of people and parcels entering their premises might be exposed to liability in the event of a suicide terrorist bomber entering their premises unchallenged and causing death or injuries.

Interstate and intrastate mutual aid are currently the focus of examination by emergency response and emergency management across the nation, with NEMA making significant efforts to ensure that common language is available for both. Mutual aid agreements will be required under NIMS in the near future.[8]

Notwithstanding the obstructions discussed previously, litigation mitigation offers benefits that make its adoption highly advisable. As a mitigation step, it is a natural part of comprehensive emergency management. This approach is challenging. Both the attorney and the emergency management client must be willing to commit to a partnership that is based on mutual trust and respect. Both groups need to obtain knowledge of pertinent legal standards so that they may support one another. The attorney must understand the client's business in order to provide the best legal advice. Litigation mitigation must be actively practiced to fully address vulnerability to the hazard of liability.

Whether a rights-based approach to vulnerability is a trend that will grow in the future or a fad confined to nations with significant socialist leanings is a matter well worth following. Most likely, an impetus to create such rights worldwide will result in significant resistance from those nations whose assets are likely to be redistributed by such an approach. As those nations (like the United States) are powerful, their opposition may make difficult reaching a common agreement on universal enactment of fundamental human rights.

Conclusion

Law and emergency management are inextricably bound together. In the United States, emergency management law has a history of over 200 years. That history reveals emergency management law as ever more all embracing. Some nations have taken emergency management much farther, incorporating disaster relief, housing, and health care as "fundamental human rights" protected by Constitutional guarantee. This approach changes emergency management law into a social engineering standard that acts to redistribute wealth.

Emergency management legal standards in the United States are in the process of evolution as well. The NRP, NIMS, NFPA 1600, and EMAP are all working together to bring national uniformity to the practice of emergency management.[9] In the U.S., legal norms for emergency management focus on greater professionalization and better execution of traditional functions. Concentrating on the nuts and bolts of emergency management, rather than creating new rights that incidentally affect the discipline, appears to be the direction of future legal development in the United States.

Endnotes

[1] Id. at 46. One feels constrained to point out that such needs are typically "rights" only in socialist countries.

[2] See, e.g., Indiana Code 10-14-3-12 (d) (1) (2005).
(d)In addition to the governor's other powers, the governor may do the following while the state of emergency exists: (1) Suspend the provisions of any regulatory statute prescribing the procedures for conduct of state business, or the orders, rules, or regulations of any state agency if strict compliance with any of these provisions would in any way prevent, hinder, or delay necessary action in coping with the emergency.

[3] E.g. Zimbabwe, Zambia, Algeria, Angola, Armenia, and India. "Public Law in Vulnerability Reduction" 54.

[4] See, e.g., Indiana Code 10-14-3-1(a) (2005).
"Disaster"
Sec. 1. (a) As used in this chapter, "disaster" means an occurrence or imminent threat of widespread or severe damage, injury, or loss of life or property resulting from any natural or manmade cause.
  (b) The term includes the following:
    (1) Fire.
    (2) Flood.
    (3) Earthquake.
    (4) Wind.
    (5) Storm.
    (6) Wave action.
    (7) Oil spill.
    (8) Other water contamination requiring emergency action to avert danger or damage.
    (9) Air contamination.
    (10) Drought.
    (11) Explosion.
    (12) Riot.
    (13) Hostile military or paramilitary action.
As added by P.L.2-2003, SEC.5.

[5] See, e.g., Indiana Code 10-14-3-2 (2005).
"Emergency management"
Sec. 2. As used in this chapter, "emergency management" means the preparation for and the coordination of all emergency functions, other than functions for which military forces or other federal agencies are primarily responsible, to prevent, minimize, and repair injury and damage resulting from disasters. The functions include the following:
  (1) Firefighting services.
  (2) Police services.
  (3) Medical and health services.
  (4) Rescue.
  (5) Engineering.
  (6) Warning services.
  (7) Communications.
  (8) Radiological, chemical, and other special weapons defense.
  (9) Evacuation of persons from stricken areas.
  (10) Emergency welfare services.
  (11) Emergency transportation.
  (12) Plant protection.
  (13) Temporary restoration of public utility services.
  (14) Other functions related to civilian protection.
  (15) All other activities necessary or incidental to the preparation for and coordination of the functions described in subdivisions (1) through (14).

[6] HS Act § 507 ROLE OF FEDERAL EMERGENCY MANAGEMENT AGENCY.
(a) IN GENERAL.—The functions of the Federal Emergency Management Agency include the following:
(1) All functions and authorities prescribed by the Robert T. Stafford Disaster Relief and Emergency Assistance Act (42 U.S.C. 5121 et seq.).
(2) Carrying out its mission to reduce the loss of life and property and protect the Nation from all hazards by leading and supporting the Nation in a comprehensive, risk-based emergency management program—

[7] HS Act § 430 (c) RESPONSIBILITIES.—The Office for Domestic Preparedness shall have the primary responsibility within the executive branch of Government for the preparedness of the United States for acts of terrorism, including—
(6) as the lead executive branch agency for preparedness of the United States for acts of terrorism, cooperating closely with the Federal Emergency Management Agency, which shall have the primary responsibility within the executive branch to prepare for and mitigate the effects of non-terrorist-related disasters in the United States;

[8] Telephone interview May 9, 2005 with Kay C. Goss, CEM, Electronic Data Systems Corporation, US Government Solutions, Senior Advisor for Homeland Security, Business Continuity Planning, and Emergency Management Services.

[9] Interview with Acting Director Gil Jamieson, NIMS Integration Center, Washington, DC (June 3, 2005). "I see the prospects of their being part of NIMS for emergency management. I have met with both the NFPA 1600 committee and the EMAP people, and I endorse the process, but it needs to evolve and be more inclusive of NIMS."

References

Caplan. (2003, April 18). Law firms become big business as well. *Wilmington News Journal*, A17.

EMAP. (2005). Recent and upcoming activities. http://www.emaponline.org/What/Implementation/Description_Full.cfmhttp://www.emaponline.org/

FEMA. (2005a). http://www.fema.gov/about/history.shtm

FEMA. (2005b). Vulnerability assessment. http://www.fema.gov/pdf/fima/155/e155_unit_iv.pdf

FEMA. (2005c). Emergency management: Setting the scene. http://www.training.fema.gov/emiweb/downloads/is1_Unit1.pdf

FEMA. (2005d). Principles of emergency management. FEMA's independent study. http://www.training.fema.gov/emiweb/downloads/IS230.doc

FEMA. (2005e). Professional development series. http://www.training.fema.gov/emiweb/PDS/

Handmer, J., & Monson, R. (2004, November). Does a rights based approach make a difference? The role of public law in vulnerability reduction. *International Journal of Mass Emergencies and Disasters, 22*(3), 43.

Homeland Security Presidential Directive 5. (2003, February 28). Paragraph 16.

Intelligence Reform and Terrorism Prevention Act. (2004). S.2845 ENR. http://thomas.loc.gov/cgi-bin/query/D?c108:4:./temp/~c108150E9Q:: [Henceforth IRTP Act].

National Incident Management System 127. (2005). http://www.fema.gov/nims/

The National Response Plan 63. (2005). http://www.dhs.gov/dhspublic/interapp/editorial/editorial_0566.xml

NFPA. (2004). NFPA 1600 standards on disaster/ emergency management and business continuity programs. http://www.nasttpo.org/NFPA1600.htm

Nicholson, W. C. (2003a). *Emergency response and emergency management law* (pp. 236–238). Charles C. Thomas.

Nicholson, W. C. (2003b). Integrating local, state and federal responders and emergency management: New packaging and new controls. *Journal of Emergency Management, 1*(15), 15.

Nicholson, W. C. (2003c). Legal issues in emergency response to terrorism incidents involving hazardous materials: The Hazardous Waste Operations and Emergency Response ("HAZWOPER") standard, standard operating procedures, mutual aid and the incident command system. *Widener Symposium Law Journal, 9*(2), 295, 298–300.

Nicholson, W. C. (2003d). *Emergency response and emergency management law: Cases and materials.* Charles C. Thomas.

Nicholson, W. C. (2003e). Litigation mitigation: Proactive risk management in the wake of the West Warwick Club fire. *Journal of Emergency Management, 1*(2).

Pine, J. (1991). Liability issues (Chapter 11). In *Emergency management, principles and practice for local government.* International City Management Association.

United States Code. (2005). §§ 11001-11050; § 11001 (a, b, c); § 11003 (a).

Varley, A. (1994). *Disasters, development and the environment.* John Wiley.

Waugh, W. L., Jr. (2002). The "all-hazards" approach must be continued 2. *Journal of Emergency Management, 1*(2), 11.

The White House. (2003, February 28). *Homeland Security Presidential Directive 5, Subject: Management of Domestic Incidents.* Author.

The White House. (2004, December 17). *President signs Intelligence Reform and Terrorism Prevention Act.* Author.

107th Cong. 2002. Homeland Security Act of 2002, H.R. 5005 (enacted) [hereinafter HS Act] § 1(a-d).

Source: https://training.fema.gov/hiedu/aemrc/booksdownload/ddemtextbook/

LEGAL ISSUES IN EMERGENCY MANAGEMENT[1]

William C. Nicholson, Esquire

This chapter provides an overview of the many legal issues involving emergency management. It explains concept of negligence, and explores its specific application to emergency manage-

---

1. Note: This chapter is not legal advice, and William C. Nicholson is not your attorney. For legal advice, consult your own lawyer.

ment. The chapter examines relevant sources of federal, state, and local law and immunities. Also discussed are NFPA 1600 and its evolution toward becoming the legal standard through EMAP. Legal duties of emergency managers and daily challenges in such areas of law as torts, contracts, ethics, and human resources are also covered. Legal aspects of mutual aid, standard operating procedures, and incident command, including the NRP and NIMS, are considered in some detail. The chapter explores legal issues in working with volunteers, planning responsibilities, and declaring an emergency, as well as response and recovery issues.

Introduction

Local authorities face many decisions in connection with emergency management activities. Unfortunately, the essential nature of emergencies and disasters is that something is going wrong or is about to go wrong. Whether the event springs from an occurrence or imminent threat of widespread or severe damage, injury, or loss of life or property resulting from any natural or manmade cause,[2] the choices that must be made by local officials frequently are not easy to make. Indeed, often the options from which a course of action must be selected are all unpleasant. Sometimes, different plaintiffs will see the same action as wrong for the opposite reasons.

For example, a flood threatens a city and limited resources mean that one of two residential areas may be preserved through sandbagging and diking. One region has many low-income residents and property values that are minimal. The other area is a wealthy enclave with extremely high property values. Assuming all residents can be safely evacuated, the choice that must be made is still not a happy one. Whether the selection is to preserve the higher property values or the greater number of residences, many citizens will be dissatisfied that their neighborhood was not saved. In this case, as with many emergency management decisions, either group may have the basis for a lawsuit. The legal challenge for leaders of local government, as for emergency management as a whole, lies in taking proactive steps to avoid bad choices like the one discussed above. Of course, not every bad choice can be prevented. Still, with close involvement of legal counsel in all phases of emergency management, the situation may be vastly improved. This approach is known as "litigation mitigation" (Nicholson, 2003a).

Litigation mitigation has three goals:
- reduced exposure to legal claims;
- improved life safety; and
- enhanced property protection.

Lawyers are trained to look at the first of these three factors as their main concern. A leader of local government must view all three as of fundamental importance. Actually, reduction of legal exposure naturally results in higher life safety and property protection.

---

2. Indiana Code 10-14-3-1(a) (2004) definition of a disaster.

The fact is that the array of laws that regulate the conduct of local government may be bewildering. Emergency managers sometimes disregard legal issues and vociferously declare that they are "too busy saving lives and protecting property to bother with all that legal nonsense." Such a line of attack is peculiar, given the "all hazards" nature of emergency management. Unfortunately, educational materials are generally deficient when it comes to treatment of legal issues (Nicholson, 2003b). Liability issues have, in fact, been called the "great unplanned for hazard faced by emergency management" (Nicholson, 2003a).

Sources of Emergency Management Law

Emergency management law in the US is rooted in all three levels of government—federal, state and local. While all three types of legal responsibility may result in liability, the most likely source is state law, specifically the tort concept known as negligence. Immunities allow protection for emergency managers under certain circumstances. The NFPA and post-9/11 federal law have created new standards that apply to all emergency managers. The availability of federal funds for emergency management results in setting criteria for state and local emergency management performance.

Many other laws affect emergency management's daily activities. Some of these laws spring from duties peculiar to the discipline, such as obligations to plan, train, and exercise. Emergency managers who are government employees have obligations that arise from their service, like complying with government ethics rules and special requirements for procurement. Other important legal considerations arise from general managerial responsibilities, and affect managers in both the private and public sectors. These include issues such as personnel law and contract law.

Negligence

Negligence is a common law doctrine that has evolved over the years. Its basic principle is this: every person has a general obligation to act in a reasonable manner at all times, considering the circumstances. When one acts (or fails to act) unreasonably and that act (or failure to act) is the legal cause of an injury to a person or property, liability ensues.

Table 14-1. Elements of Negligence

Element	Explanation
Duty	Obligation to act in a reasonable manner
Breach of Duty	Unreasonable action or failure to act
Legal Causation	Frequently referred to as "proximate cause," this simply means that the harm happened as a reasonably close result of the act or failure to act
Personal injury or property damage	Occurs
Result	Liability

In the emergency management context, negligence usually arises from the failure to perform (or unreasonably bad performance of) specific governmental duties. The unit of government may incur liability from failure to properly train or supervise emergency management workers. Other frequent sources of liability include failure to perform the duties that are generally accepted as being part of emergency management's responsibilities. (See the discussion below of NFPA 1600 and EMAP.)

Types of activity that may give rise to negligence liability vary. They include failure to adhere to a plan (Lerner, 1991), executive level decision making (poor choices, poor planning, bad emergency response), or an Incident Commander's lack of wisdom.

Another frequent cause of liability is the failure to comply with a legal duty, such as OSHA law. Also, a violation of law may be used as proof in a civil suit requesting damages for personal injury or wrongful death. When the elements of the violation are the same as the elements required for civil liability and the burden of proof is the same for both, the only issue in a civil trial may be the measure of damages.[3]

Immunities

Units of government enjoy immunity, or protection from legal liability, for many of their activities. This immunity is not, however, unlimited. During an emergency, the needs of a small group of people (their personal lives, businesses and property) frequently must be considered and balanced against society's greater interest. Disaster response statutes and common law provide customary defenses and immunities for protection of emergency responders who are working in the capacity of a governmental employee (Lerner, 1991).

Immunity under state law. To protect from litigation, state legislatures incorporate within their laws tort liability immunities for official acts.[4] Such acts must be within the employee's scope of employment for immunity to apply.[5] State disaster or emergency statutes[6] often contain more specific immunity provisions to protect government executives engaged in critical decision-making procedures in emergencies (Swanson, 2000). Some states have gone further by establishing broad immunities shielding a variety of players (i.e., the state, political subdivisions, or local governmental entities) who act during an emergency response, rather than solely individuals involved in the decision-making process.[7] Such provisions are typically contained in a state's emergency management laws.

---

3. *See, e.g.,* Meridian Ins. Co. v. Zepeda, 734 N.E. 2d 1126, 1130-31 (Ind. App. 2000). "... a criminal conviction may be admitted in evidence in a civil action and may be conclusive proof in a civil trial of the factual issues determined by the criminal judgment." *Id.*
4. *See, e.g.,* IND. CODE § 34-13-3-3 (2004), which includes a long list of actions for which government and its employees are immune.
5. *See, e.g.,* IND. CODE § 34-13-3-3 (2004), which requires that actions must be within the scope of employment if they are to be protected.
6. Howard D. Swanson, *The Delicate Art of Practicing Municipal Law Under Conditions of Hell and High Water*, 76 N.D. L. REV. 487, 490 n.10 (2000) lists citations for emergency management statutes in various jurisdictions.
7. *See, e.g.,* IND. CODE § 10-14-3-15(a) (2004). "Any function under this chapter and any other activity relating to emergency management is a governmental function. The state, any political subdivision, any other agencies of the state or political subdivision of the state, or, except in cases of willful misconduct, gross negligence, or bad faith, any emergency management worker complying with or reasonably attempting to comply with this chapter or any order or rule adopted under this chapter, or under any ordinance relating to blackout or other precautionary measures enacted by any political subdivision of the state, is not liable for the death of or injury to persons or for damage to property as a result of any such activity."

Some states make available particular immunity provisions directed at emergency workers, whether volunteers or employees. Also, immunities exist for people owning or controlling real estate or motorized vehicles who voluntarily authorize the usage of their property during an emergency. "Good Samaritan" statutes may also provide immunity to certain classes of emergency medical responders, although such statutes often do not apply if the responder is operating in an official capacity.

Immunities under federal law. General tort immunity may also bar a civil lawsuit springing from an emergency or disaster response. For the federal government, two tort immunity doctrines may apply: "governmental function" and "discretionary action."

The "governmental function" analysis guards long-established or inherent governmental activities including measures assigned by constitution or statute and actions like collecting taxes, law enforcement, and legislation. Such actions are usually characterized as being performed solely by a governmental entity, done for the benefit of the public, with no private sector equivalent.[8] The government does not make a profit from such acts. Emergency planning and response acquires its immunity from tort liability as a traditional or inherent governmental function.

The Federal Tort Claims Act (FTCA) contains the "discretionary action" exclusion. The "discretionary" immunity centers on a particular governmental act or decision instead of the type of activity undertaken. Its purpose is to protect governmental employees at the policy level from worrying about lawsuits during disaster planning and response. If, however, the action objected to does not involve a permitted use of policy judgment, the government will not be protected.

The United States Supreme Court in *Berkovitz v. US*[9] created a two-part test for use of the "discretionary immunity" exemption found in FTCA. The first step requires analyzing the nature of the conduct. If the questioned conduct is not an optional matter but instead is an action mandated by a federal statute or policy, then the discretionary immunity exemption will not apply to the conduct. The employee has no choice but to follow the directives. The Court reasoned that, in the absence of choice—no judgment made, there is no discretion in the conduct to protect. The second step only applies if there is no statutory, regulatory, or procedural policy instruction mandating a course of action. The conduct must involve a quantity of judgment, which then may be determined to be the sort of judgment that the discretionary immunity exemption was designed to guard. The exemption shields only governmental actions and decisions based on public policy (i.e., social, economic, or political policy). If the activity was not founded on public policy, then the suit may continue.

---

8. 57 Am. Jur. 2d *Municipal, County, School and State Tort Liability* § 57 (2001).
9. Berkovitz v. United States, 486 US 531 (1988).

Most states recognize some form of this test within their own statutes. Where state courts have mentioned repetitively that the discretionary immunity exemption provided by their code is essentially the same as the discretionary immunity exemption within the Federal Tort Claims Act, the "discretionary immunity" test applies (Fraiser, 1999).

In the recent *Commerce and Industry Insurance Company v. Grinnell Corporation*[10] decision, the 5th Circuit Court of Appeals reversed summary judgment by a lower court, finding that the "discretionary immunity" test was inappropriately employed. The Circuit Court held that specific regulations and distinct fire department policies decreed procedures for firefighters to follow at a warehouse fire, and that the firefighters violated them.[11] The Court stated that the city could not be allowed the immunity exemption provided by La. Rev. Stat. Ann. § 9:2798.1 (West, 1997) and remanded the case for further proceedings.

The *Commerce and Industry Insurance Company* decision may indicate the potential future evolution of cases brought against emergency management organizations for improper actions during emergencies or disasters. In an emergency response such as that in the *Commerce and Industry Insurance Company* case, the courts may hold the organization and its employees responsible for actions that fall outside established regulatory standards (such as the requirement to have a current plan and standard operating procedures). Emergency management may be hard pressed to rely on discretionary immunity to protect the unit of government and employees from liability.

Courts interpret statutory waivers of government immunity extremely narrowly. They look closely into the facts underlying the alleged waiver.[12] Also, tort immunities may not always apply. They are virtually never to be had if death, injury, or damages result from conduct other than negligence, including willful conduct, gross negligence, wanton disregard, or bad faith on the part of government employee or entities.[13]

NFPA 1600:[14] *The New Standard for Emergency Management*

On April 29, 2004, the American National Standards Institute (ANSI) recommended to the 9/11 Commission that NFPA 1600 be established as the national preparedness standard. On July 22, 2004, the 9/11 Commission formally endorsed NFPA 1600 and urged that compliance with NFPA 1600 be taken into account by the insurance and credit rating industries

---

10. Commerce and Indus. Ins. Co. v. Grinnell Corp., 280 F.3d 566 (5th Cir. 2002).
11. Alleged negligent actions and omissions included: (1) attempting to restore electrical power before an electrical inspection had been conducted, in violation of code and policy; (2) turning off the sprinkler system without posting personnel with two-way radios at the sprinkler valves, in contravention of a specific regulation; (3) opening the large bay doors before the fire was declared out, despite wind velocities of 21 mph; (4) failing to "overhaul" any of the upper level racks even though they had been subjected to intense heat; and (5) departing the scene "under these conditions" within six minutes after declaring the fire out, without leaving adequate personnel and equipment for a fire watch.*Id.* at 569.
12. Caillouette v. Hercules, Inc., 827 P.2d 1306, 1311-13 (N.M. App. 1992). The New Mexico Department of Public Safety was found not to have waived immunity on the facts of the case in a wrongful death action arising from a hazmat cleanup incident.
13. *See, e.g.*, Ind. Code § 10-14-3-15(a) (2004). "[E]xcept in cases of willful misconduct, gross negligence, or bad faith, any emergency management worker complying with or reasonably attempting to comply with this chapter or any order or rule adopted under this chapter, or under any ordinance relating to blackout or other precautionary measures enacted by any political subdivision of the state, is not liable for the death of or injury to persons or for damage to property as a result of any such activity."
14. NFPA 1600 (2004 Edition) may be accessed on at: www.nasttpo.org/NFPA1600.htm.

in assessing a company's insurance rating and creditworthiness. The 9/11 Commission also believes "compliance with the standard should define the standard of care owed by a company to its employees and the public for legal purposes."[15]

NFPA 1600 establishes a shared set of norms for disaster management, emergency management, and business continuity programs. It also recognizes ways to exercise plans and makes available a listing of resource organizations within the fields of disaster recovery, emergency management and business continuity planning. One vital aspect of NFPA 1600 is its requirement that all emergency management and business continuity programs must comply with all relevant laws, policies and industry practice.[16]

Incorporating NFPA 1600 Through EMAP

The National Emergency Management Association (NEMA) has also endorsed NFPA 1600 as an appropriate standard for emergency management. As early as 1998, NEMA passed a resolution signaling its support of NFPA 1600,[17] which provides the foundation for EMAP.[18] The accreditation process includes application, self-assessment, on-site assessment by an outside review team, committee and commission review of compliance with the EMAP Standard, and re-certification every five years.

EMAP has moved rapidly from a concept first expressed in 1997 through pilot tests and assessments through certification of units of government, the first of which was awarded in 2003.

Table 14-2. EMAP Timeline

Date	Activity
April 2002	EMAP opened for registration and for state applications
Summer-Fall 2002	Local pilot tests
2003	EMAP conducted 20 state/territorial baseline assessments
June 2003	Two states are conditionally accredited: Arizona and North Dakota
September 2003	First two jurisdictions receive EMAP accreditation: Florida and District of Columbia
January 2004	Continue state/territorial baseline assessments and begin conducting local on-site assessments for programs seeking accreditation

EMAP is supported by a large number of important players in emergency management, including the National Emergency Management Association, International Association of Emergency Managers, Federal Emergency Management Agency, US Department of Transportation, Association of State Flood Plain Managers, Institute for Business and Home Safety, International Association of Fire Chiefs, National Association of Counties, National Association of Development Organizations, National Conference of State Legislatures,

---

15. The 9/11 Commission Report 398 (2004).
16. NFPA 1600 § 5.2 (2004 Edition).
17. NFPA 1600 Standard Resolution, found at www.nemaweb.org/?335.
18. EMAP Recent and Upcoming Activities, found at www.emaponline.org/What/Implementation/Description_Full.cfm.

National Governors Association, National League of Cities, and the US Environmental Protection Agency.

Although EMAP accreditation is voluntary, the fact that it is endorsed by such a wide variety of authorities means it is well on its way to becoming the *de facto* standard for emergency management in the United States. The more programs become accredited under the standard, the more likely a Court will be to hold all emergency management to the norm. Accepted industry practices frequently move from *de facto* to *de jure* acceptance through common law adoption in the Courts.[19] Clearly, potential liability could result from not performing to the standards set by EMAP. The wise emergency management program manager will take prompt steps to ensure that his or her program is accredited under EMAP.

The Local/State/Federal Interface

Local emergency management organizations' planning, training and exercising responsibilities are contained in the Performance Partnership Agreement (PPA) and the Cooperative Agreement (CA) with FEMA. These documents explain the stipulations that must be accomplished before the federal government, through the state emergency management agency, will release emergency management funds to local units of government. The PPA is a strategic plan, and is revised on a five year timetable. The CA is an accord revised every year that creates goals for emergency management statewide in the federal fiscal year, which runs from October 1 through September 30. The duties of local emergency management are referred to as "Outputs," whose fulfillment the state supervises and reports to FEMA. Each SEMA co-operates with local emergency managers to condense these outputs into detailed assignments, which are called "Compliance Requirements." These standards act as a form of private law, binding states and localities that receive funds to obey federal mandates.

Some counties do not choose to comply with the terms of the PPA and CA, and hence do not receive federal funding through Emergency Management Performance Grants (EMPGs). The vast majority of counties nationwide comply with the documents. This creates an industry benchmark that compliments NFPA 1600. A court may hold this to be a standard of care, creating potential legal liability for those units of government with non-compliant LEMAs.

Legal Duties of Emergency Management Directors

Local and state emergency management directors have many legal duties. The basis for these duties includes both specific emergency management law and other laws of general

---

19. Indeed, custom and usage within an industry need not be complete or general where improved safety standards, which EMAP provides for emergency management, are involved. See *TJ Hooper*, 60 F 2d 737 (2d Cir. 1932), certiorari denied, *Eastern Transportation Co. v. Northern Barge Corp.*, 287 US 662 (1932), where in 1932, despite the absence of statutes, regulations or even custom as to radio receiving sets, Judge Learned Hand found a vessel unseaworthy for lack of one. Two barges had been lost in a storm and the tugs and their tows might have sought shelter in time had they received weather reports by radio. This case may show which way the wind blows for the future of emergency management certification under EMAP.

application, such as Occupational Safety and Health Administration (OSHA) law, contract law, personnel law, and government ethics law.

State Emergency Management Law

Every state has some form of emergency management law. Such laws typically include specifications that:
- Set up a state emergency or disaster management agency;
- Specify state and local organization roles in responding to disasters;
- Assign executive authority to declare a state of emergency;
- Explain special executive powers that result from such a declaration; and
- Allow cooperation in the form of mutual aid with neighboring jurisdictions.

These statutes also address many other aspects of disaster preparedness and response. Typically, such laws provide a rather detailed set of responsibilities for emergency managers. For example, in Indiana, the local emergency manager must fulfill a variety of duties during all phases of emergency management. The specifically enumerated duties are limited to preparing and keeping current the emergency plan, preparing and distributing a list of emergency duties for all officials, and documenting the chain of command for continuity of government purposes.[20]

Other duties are found elsewhere in the law. The definition section lays out the broad scope of the discipline's responsibilities. "'Emergency management' means the preparation for and the coordination of all emergency functions, other than functions for which military forces or other federal agencies are primarily responsible, to prevent, minimize, and repair injury and damage resulting from disasters. The functions include the following:

1. Firefighting services.
2. Police services.
3. Medical and health services.
4. Rescue.
5. Engineering.
6. Warning services.
7. Communications.
8. Radiological, chemical, and other special weapons defense.
9. Evacuation of persons from stricken areas.
10. Emergency welfare services.
11. Emergency transportation.
12. Plant protection.
13. Temporary restoration of public utility services.
14. Other functions related to civilian protection.

---
20. Indiana Code 10-14-3-17 (h)

15. All other activities necessary or incidental to the preparation for and coordination of the functions described in subdivisions (1) through (14)."[21]

As can be easily seen, while the enumerated duties appear to be limited, their scope is all-inclusive. Also, keeping a "current plan" is a specific responsibility, whose failure to fulfill may expose the emergency manager and his/her jurisdiction to liability.

Local Emergency Management Ordinance

The local emergency manager is obliged to understand and obey all relevant local ordinances, particularly those directed at his or her functions. The emergency management ordinance serves a number of functions. This local law can:
- "Fill in the blanks" in state law for local emergency management;
- Delineate the local line of succession;
- Specify grants of emergency authority to the leaders of the unit of government;
- Provide a structure for governmental emergency management activities;
- Act as a teaching tool to help all government employees understand their roles during a disaster;
- Provide legal support to the emergency operations plan; and
- Assure that proper steps are taken at all phases of emergency management to save lives and protect property.

Attached to this chapter as an appendix is a model ordinance drafted by the municipal attorney for Grand Forks, North Dakota, in the wake of catastrophic flooding that took place in spring 1997 (Swanson, 2000). While this is a fine place to start with an ordinance, one must recall the NFPA 1600 and NIMS standards discussed at various points in this chapter, and ensure consistency with their requirements.

Other Legal Duties

The local emergency manager must bear in mind the mandates of NFPA 1600 and NIMS, as well as numerous other laws that must be complied with to prevent legal blame. These other laws are detailed below.

Understanding Contract Law to Prevent Claims

Every emergency manager enters into contracts for purchase of goods and personal services. The basics of contract law are straightforward, consisting of three elements:
- The offer, typically in the form of "I will sell you these goods or perform these services for this amount of money."

---

21. Indiana Code 10-14-3-2(a).

- Acceptance, "I accept your offer." and
- Consideration, or the fee paid for the services.

Difficulties may arise when the parties do not have a mutual understanding of exactly what is offered or the nature and character of the consideration. To facilitate mutual understanding, frequently referred to as a "meeting of the minds", contracts are typically written rather than oral. Having the agreement in writing allows both parties to see clearly the subject matter of their bargain.

One key thing to remember is that the party that creates the initial draft of the contract will typically end up with a document that reflects his or her desires more than those of the other party. This is why emergency managers should strive whenever possible, particularly with expensive purchases, to assure that their attorney drafts the contract. For some, this step is a given, as units of government may have standardized contracts for purchase of goods or services.

Frequently, the contractor will have a standard contract of its own that will be proposed to be the first draft. The contractor may say that they always use this contract, and threaten to walk away if it is not used. Unless one company uniquely produces the subject matter, it is not a bad idea to let the contractor walk away in this instance. Remember that the purchaser has the upper hand for the most part in negotiations, because he or she has the money, and the contractor must have work to prosper. Another tack is to take the contractor's document and use pieces of it in crafting one's own contract.

Sometimes, the contract officer will be tempted to use the contractor's document as is, because it will mean less work for that busy individual. One must be extremely careful in reading such texts and always be ready to delete unacceptable language. Their wording commonly will contain indemnification requirements, waivers of inadequate performance, arbitration clauses, and other language that dilutes the obligations of the contractor. Their language also may include requirements that are contrary to existing state or local law.

The emergency manager and his or her attorney or contract officer should carefully scrutinize the contents of standardized contracts when big-ticket items are involved. Modification of standard language is often appropriate in such situations. Examples of modification to ensure the prompt and proper performance by the contractor are discussed in detail below.

Prompt performance is often a big concern. Three steps are available that can be a big incentive for rapid completion of the work or delivery of the goods. The first is a schedule for performance, with times for completion of different tasks or delivery of a certain amount of goods, and partial payment scheduled to match. One thing to watch out for is that each piece of the job must be carefully inspected for conformance with contract standards before acceptance. The second item, penalties for late delivery or performance, is actually a disincentive for delayed compliance. The third item is extra pay for early performance. The combination of these three elements in a contract can be very helpful when the emergency program needs something yesterday.

One key part of drafting a contract for purchase of goods is performance standards. These are particularly important when the items purchased are being custom built, as is the case with antenna systems, for example. The emergency manager and the subject matter expert need to get together to discuss in fine detail exactly what is desired, and how it is expected to operate when the entire system is installed. They then need to meet with the attorney or contracting officer to make sure that the standards are put together in complete form, leaving nothing out. If this preparatory step is properly taken, one is much more likely to end up with the end product desired.

When purchasing a complex and expensive system, there may be political pressure to award different contracts to various people within the jurisdiction, with the goal of "spreading the wealth." While this may sound like a good idea, in actuality it could be the cause of unending headaches. When a system, such a communications network, is installed, all of its parts must mesh and work together properly for it to perform as advertised. If multiple contractors have performed the work and there is a problem, they may all point fingers at one another as the cause of the problem, and refuse to cooperate in fixing things. This can be both inconvenient and politically embarrassing. One good way to avoid this problem is to insist on getting quoted on a "turn key" system with proper guarantees in the contract that it will perform as advertised prior to acceptance by the purchaser. In this situation, it is important when setting up a schedule of partial payments that a significant portion, usually 25–33%, be held back until verification tests, possibly by a third party, have been performed to ensure that the entire system works as advertised. There are five contract modifications that can benefit the emergency manager:
- Schedule delivery dates with partial payments upon acceptance of the goods or services.
- Impose penalties for late performance.
- Provide rewards for early performance.
- Define detailed operation standards for equipment.
- Try to get a "turn key" system.

Remember that when the actual product differs from the contents of a written contract, the party whose expectations are frustrated will have a number of legal options. First, there may be a cause of action for damages or specific performance. Second, the contract may be repudiated, or cancelled. Third, if part of the contract has been complied with, and some performance is contrary to the contract requirements, there may be payment for partial performance only.

Personnel Law Issues for Emergency Management

All employers face the potential of dealing with workers who act in ways that are contrary to the requirements of the best interests of the organization, whether it be a unit of government, private business, or other entity. Indeed, personnel issues may consume a large percentage of the emergency manager's time. While employment law is a subject with many potential intricacies, understanding the basics will be of great benefit to the emergency manager. Knowing the fundamental outlines of this area of law will assist in planning ahead to avoid personnel disputes, an important aspect of litigation mitigation. This knowledge will also provide insight into the best way to react when problems do occur.

Ideally, both the employer and employee should understand that it is to their mutual benefit to cooperate in helping the enterprise to succeed. Unhappy workers mean lower performance and decreased satisfaction for the head of the organization. The boss benefits when the group does well, so it is in his or her best interest to assist in that effort. Actually, however, disputes between people at different levels of authority are a daily part of economic and social life. As such, employment law may be very political.

Employment law includes a lot of governmental regulation, both federal and state. The employer frequently also has extensive standards for employees. This is particularly the case where, as with emergency response and emergency management, the job entails significant potential hazards. Four kinds of legal rules govern the daily life of employees. These include:
- Statutes, which often authorize administrative agencies to take action.
- The body of law that comprises the rules, regulations, and rulings of administrative agencies.
- Common law tort and contract rules.
- State and federal constitutional specifications that delineate employee rights, mostly regarding government employees.

Statutes that govern the employment relationship are of two types: those that govern collective action (union activity); and those that cover all employees. Collective action is governed by the National Labor Relations Act,[22] specific laws regarding federal employment, and other laws not relevant to the limited purposes of this chapter. On the federal side, employees of DHS have extremely limited rights compared to their counterparts in other agencies, which was the subject of vigorous debate during the adoption of the HS Act. State regulation of union activities is frequently preempted by the broad federal statutes.

Torts

Work-related torts cover an assortment of interests, and are discussed briefly below.

Invasion of privacy. An employee has only a limited expectation of privacy at work. Generally, however, conduct that can be described as "snooping" by the employer goes too far. This does not mean that the employer cannot obtain information on the employee that directly affects workplace performance (like performing reasonable and impartial testing for drugs

---
22. 29 USC §§ 151-169 (2004).

or alcohol) or may endanger the employer's reputation or the safety of other employees. Also, one must recall that emergency management is a public safety role, where employees may have access to classified information. As such, a greater degree of intrusion into the employee's affairs may be appropriate. It is very important to consult with legal counsel before taking intrusive action.

Defamation. Employers may not do harm to their employees' fame, character, or reputation by means of false or malicious declarations. The declaration may be in the form of gestures or action rather than words. In one case, an employer fired the employee, stood over him while he packed him belongings, and escorted him to the door. This was found to be defamatory activity, because it implied that the employee was dishonest and untrustworthy.[23]

False imprisonment. False imprisonment means detaining a person without cause and not permitting him or her liberty to leave, when the person knows that he or she may not leave. This was found to exist in a case where a security guard and the owner of the security service kept a grocery clerk in a room and would not let her use the telephone other than to receive one call during a three hour interrogation. The guard put himself between her and the door and told her he would decide if she was going to jail.[24]

Intentional infliction of emotional distress. To prove intentional infliction of mental distress: first, the employer must act in an extreme and outrageous way; second, the employer must have intended to cause emotional distress or had a substantial certainty that it would ensue; third, substantial emotional distress must result from the employer's behavior. Courts have differing ideas about what is outrageous. In one case, the employer ordered the employee to lower his trousers and expose himself to fellow employees. The trial court found for the employee, the appeals court reversed, and the state supreme court reversed again, holding for the employee.[25]

Fraudulent misrepresentation. Fraudulent misrepresentation happens when an employer falsely makes a statement of opinion, fact, law, or intention, intending the employee to act based on it. One employer told an employee that if the employee would accept a job in California, the employer would buy his house. After accepting the transfer, the employee tried to get the employer to buy the home, and was fired. The employer's lie changed the way the employee evaluated the job offer, and recovery was permitted.[26]

Intentional interference with contractual relations. The employer here must act, with knowledge of an existing or possible contract between the employee and a third party, with the intent of interfering with it, and actually cause the harm intended. This tort must be carefully kept in mind by emergency manager supervisors in this time when many contractors are

---

23. *Bolton v. Minnesota Dept. of Human Services*, 527 NW 2d 149 (Minn. App. 1985).
24. *Buckel v. Rodriguez*, 891 P2d 16 (Or. App. 1995).
25. *Madani v. Kendall Ford, Inc.*, 818 P 2d 930 (Or. 1991).
26. *Palmer v. Beverly Enterprises*, 823 F 2d 1105 (7th Cir. 1987).

attempting to "cherry pick" the best emergency management employees to work for them. Interfering with this process, despite understandable anger with the employee, may expose the supervisor and employer to liability.

Malicious prosecution. For this action to succeed, one must prove that the antagonist began a legal action, the antagonist lost the case, the antagonist did not have probable cause to begin the case, the antagonist began the case with "malice," and the case caused harm for which damages may be had. Either employer or employee may use this theory, but courts do not like this type of action. When successful, however, large damages may be won.

Abuse of process. Like malicious prosecution, this kind of case springs from misuse of the legal system, and may be used by either employer or employee. One must prove that the adversary used the legal system due to a secret bad motive and that the process was used for a purpose other than that for which it was designed. This can occur, for instance, when one plants evidence to discredit a person and calls the police to arrest the person.

Blacklisting. This tort involves preventing or trying to prevent an employee from getting future employment. The employee must establish that the employer did this out of malice. Employers have a limited privilege to talk about matters that concern them both. Giving a bad reference is the classic example of this. If false information is given out, there will be a basis to get damages. If the statements are on overall "suitability," they may be held to be mere opinion or information.[27]

Constitutional Provisions

The United States Constitution defines the relationships between the federal and state governments, as well as between these government and its citizens. It does not regulate conduct between citizens. It is therefore not relevant in many employment relationships. The Constitution does, however, regulate employment relationships in the public sector, as these are between the government and its citizens. Constitutional provisions control government emergency management programs.

As a general matter, no level of government may exercise its power to take away constitutionally guaranteed rights of employees. The rights of privacy, free speech, and association are those most often at issue.

Right to privacy. Searching a government employee's desk has been found unconstitutional.[28] As mentioned above, however, the fact that emergency management is a public safety entity may create greater opportunities for oversight of employees. Again, the jurisdiction's attorney should be consulted prior to any such action.

---

27. *Austin v. Torrington Co.*, 180 F 2d 416 (4th Cir. 1987), *cert. denied*, 484 US 977 (1987).
28. *O'Connor v. Ortega*, 480 US 709 (1987).

Free speech and association. The Supreme Court has ruled that hiring, promotions, transfers, and recalls of a low ranking government employee may not be based on support for a particular political party.[29] The employee's first amendment rights of free speech and association are improperly limited by such a requirement, unless party membership can be shown to be a proper prerequisite for effective performance in the job. This would be a difficult matter to prove. The Fourteenth Amendment's equal protection clause stops racial discrimination by government employers.

Regulations of Special Interest to Emergency Management.
There are many governmental regulatory programs that affect employment, and their full scope is well beyond this chapter. Some must be mentioned if only in passing because of their effect on emergency management activities.

Health and safety: OSHA. Occupational Safety and Health Administration (OSHA)[30] regulations apply to all workplace activities, including those of government entities. The OSHA statute permits states to have responsibility for workplace safety if their programs meet specific guidelines.[31] The state standards must be at least as strict as those of the federal government. The emergency manager should become familiar with the regime in place covering his or her workplace.

OSHA imposes two duties on employers:
- Provision of a hazard-free workplace, and
- Compliance with OSHA standards.[32]

The OSH Act gives employees several important rights:
- To question unsafe conditions and request a federal inspection,
- To assist OSHA inspectors,
- To bring an action to make the Secretary of Labor seek injunctive relief where there is imminent danger to employees,
- To gain access to records about the employee's health an exposure to hazardous substances.[33]

Employers of 11 or more employees must keep records of occupational diseases and injuries.[34] Failure to do so is a very serious matter that may result in huge fines.

Health and Safety: Workers Compensation. Government and private sector employees are typically compensated for their on-duty injuries through workers compensation schemes,

---

29. *Rutan v. Republican Party of Illinois*, 497 US 62 (1990).
30. In 1970, Congress enacted the federal Occupational Safety and Health Act of 1970 ("OSH Act"). 84 Stat. 1590 (codified at 29 USC 553, 651-678 (2002)). The OSH Act specifically authorized the Secretary of Labor to promulgate national health and safety standards. 29 USC 655(a).
31. 29 USC § 667.
32. 29 USC § 634(a).
33. 29 USC § 657.
34. 29 USC § 657 (c).

which vary from state to state. These programs include "exclusive remedy" clauses, which prevent all but a very small number of lawsuits against employers for workplace injuries. The big exception occurs when the employer clearly intends to harm workers. Federal civilian employees are covered by the Federal Employees Compensation Act (FECA).[35]

Progressive Discipline

Many employment contracts utilize a system called "progressive discipline" to deal with employees who perform below par or contrary to the employer's rules. Such programs typically call for a graduated set of penalties before en employee may be terminated. An example follows:
- First offense: verbal reprimand.
- Second offense: written reprimand.
- Third offense: uncompensated suspension for up to a maximum period, typically two weeks.
- Fourth offense: termination.

Frequently in such programs, the written reprimand and suspension periods will be accompanied by a plan for correction. This is a sort of "mini contract" in which the manager specifies areas of shortfall, and the employee agrees to correct shortcomings on a schedule. Failure to comply with the plan may result in further discipline.

One challenge with this system is its requirement that managers actually manage. All too often, an underperforming employee may be given one verbal reprimand after another, with no written documentation. Eventually, the sum of failures to perform may be sufficient for termination, but the fact that these events have not been noted in the employee's file may mean that the employee stays on for additional time while a sufficient record for termination is compiled. Such a situation may be the basis for discipline of the manager by his or her superiors. It certainly is frustrating for the attorney who must explain the need for such documentation and fight against the employee's appeal.

Of course, where an employee's actions are illegal or bring the employer into disrepute, like running a gambling ring from one's desk, immediate termination may be appropriate. Similarly, putting oneself or fellow employees at risk through unsafe behavior, like a heavy equipment operator who drinks on the job, may also be grounds for immediate termination. Any possible deviation from the system must, however, be discussed with legal counsel before taking place.

Avoiding Ethical Lapses in Emergency Management

Both government and business employees are bound by ethical standards. The difference between the two is that ethical standards for business are largely self-imposed, while those

---
35. 5 USC §§ 8101-8151.

binding government employees may be matters of law or policy. Government ethics guidelines apply to the actions of employees whether they are at work or not. The reason for this intrusion into employees' private lives is that they are seen as representing the government at all times.

Public service is a public trust, therefore, government employees must behave in ways that will promote trust by the general public. The following statements are minimum standards of conduct for government employees to follow. (Taken from the Indiana Ethics Commission standards.)

- Employees are to be impartial in the discharge of their duties.
- Decisions and policies must not be made outside the proper channels of government.
- Public office is not to be used for private gain.
- Employees may not make unapproved use of government property, personnel, or facilities.
- Employees may not use government time for other than official duties.
- Employees may not benefit financially from information of a confidential nature gained through government employment.
- Employees may not solicit or accept outside payments for the performance of official duties.
- An employee may not accept a gift, favor, service, entertainment, food or drink which could influence the employee's action.
- Payment for an appearance, speech, or article may not be accepted if the appearance, speech, or article could be considered part of the employee's official duties.
- An employee may not accept payment of expense for travel, conventions, conferences, or similar activities that could influence the employee's action.
- Employees may not have outside employment incompatible with their government employment or against their agency's rules.
- Supervisors may not solicit political contributions from employees they supervise.
- An employee may not solicit political contributions from persons or entities that have a business relationship with the employee's agency.

The Hatch Act

The Hatch Act applies to state and local employees of the executive branch. They must be principally employed in connection with programs financed in whole or in part by loans or grants made by the United States or a federal agency. Emergency management agencies that operate using the federal funds made available through the Emergency Management Performance Grants as well as employees whose salary is partially paid by programs like the Chemical Stockpile Emergency Preparedness Program (CSEPP) are subject to the Hatch Act. State law and agency regulations also apply to such employees. State and local laws do not affect the Hatch Act's prohibitions.

Covered state and local employees may:
- Run for public office in nonpartisan elections
- Campaign for and hold office in political clubs and organizations
- Actively campaign for candidates for public office in partisan and nonpartisan elections
- Contribute money to political organizations and attend political fundraising functions

Covered state and local employees may not:
- Be candidates for public office in a partisan election
- Use official authority or influence to interfere with or affect the results of an election or nomination
- Directly or indirectly coerce contributions from subordinates in support of a political party or candidate

Violation of the Hatch Act may result in significant penalties. If the Merit Systems Protection Board finds a violation that calls for discharge from employment, the agency must either remove the employee or surrender a part of the federal assistance equal to two years salary of the employee. If the Board decides the violation does not warrant the employee's firing, there will be no penalty (for further information, see www.osc.gov/hatchact.htm).

Mutual Aid Agreements

Mutual aid agreements (MAAs) are a key part of emergency management. They are mandated by a number of standards, including NFPA 1600 and NIMS. Their importance to the EOP is obvious: they allow multiplication of resources. The proper contents for intra-state and inter-state mutual aid agreements are found on the Emergency Management Assistance Compact (EMAC) Web site (www.emacweb.org). These are:
- Definitions of key terms used in the agreement;
- Roles and responsibilities of individual parties;
- Procedures for requesting and providing assistance;
- Procedures, authorities, and rules for payment, reimbursement, and
- Allocation of costs;
- Notification procedures;
- Protocols for interoperable communications;
- Relationships with other agreements among jurisdictions;
- Workers compensation;
- Treatment of liability and immunity;
- Recognition of qualifications and certifications; and
- Sharing agreements, as required.

Authorized officials from each of the participating jurisdictions will collectively approve all mutual-aid agreements.

EMAC is the benchmark for interstate agreements. Various states have adopted slightly differing versions of EMAC.[36] One issue that EMAC does not address is the credentialing of visiting emergency responders such as Emergency Medical Technicians and doctors. This was reportedly a matter of such controversy when EMAC was written that the decision was made to allow each state to deal with the issue separately.[37] It is unfortunate that there is not a uniform national approach to this issue in EMAC.

For those who become federally certified under the authority of NIMS, nationwide credentialing will be a part of the package.[38] This approach will do a great deal to lessen potential confusion in the aftermath of an emergency or disaster.

The EMAC web page also contains a model intrastate agreement.[39] Some states already have made provision for an intrastate agreement. For example, Indiana has an intrastate mutual aid program that applies to every political subdivision of the state that does not opt out by adopting an ordinance or resolution stating that it does so.[40]

Jurisdictions that request mutual aid assistance must be aware of potential legal claims that may arise from doing so. While the model agreements discussed above will cover issues like who is responsible for injuries to members of the assisting unit, case law indicates that the requesting entity may be responsible for their workers compensation claims if they are injured during the response.[41]

Standard Operating Procedures

Emergency response groups employ SOPs to direct their members during daily operations (Brunacini, 1985, p. 16). One vital reason for the mutual aid agreement is to guarantee that responding entities, whether public or private, abide by SOPs or standard operating guidelines (SOGs) during mutual aid responses (Federal Emergency Management Agency—United States Fire Administration, 1999).[42] When writing SOPs, MAAs should be considered, similarly, when drafting MAAs, SOPs must be assessed. Many other texts, plans and agreements must be evaluated as well when developing SOPs, including the requirements

---

36. See, e.g., Indiana Code 10-14-6 Interstate Emergency Management and Disaster Compact (2004).
37. See, e.g., Indiana Code §§ 10-14-3-3 and10-14-3-15(b) for one approach. Section 10-14-3-3 defines "emergency management worker" as any full-time or part-time paid, volunteer, or auxiliary employee of: (1) the state; (2) other: (A) states; (B) territories; or (C) possessions; (3) the District of Columbia; (4) the federal government; (5) any neighboring country; (6) any political subdivision of an entity described in subdivisions (1) through (5); or (7) any agency or organization;performing emergency management services at any place in Indiana subject to the order or control of, or under a request of, the state government or any political subdivision of the state.
Sec. 15. (b) Any requirement for a license to practice any professional, mechanical, or other skill does not apply to any authorized emergency management worker who, in the course of performing duties as an emergency management worker, practices a professional, mechanical, or other skill during a disaster emergency.
38. NIMS at 46. "Personnel certification entails authoritatively attesting that individuals meet professional standards for the training, experience, and performance required for key incident management functions. Credentialing involves providing documentation that can authenticate and verify the certification and identity of designated incident managers and emergency responders."
39. See emacweb.org/docs/Wide%20Release%20Intrastate%20Mutual%20Aid.pdf
40. Indiana Code 10-14-3-10.6.
41. See, e.g., *Thomas v. Lisbon*, 550 A.2d 894 (S.Ct. Conn. 1988).
42. Federal Emergency Management Agency—United States Fire Administration (1999). [hereinafter Developing SOPs] "Mutual or automatic aid agreements . . . help [to] ensure that agreements are enforced and joint operations are coordinated."

of the Hazardous Waste Operations and Emergency Response ("HAZWOPER") Standard. Like mutual aid agreements, SOPs must be written to be successful. They have to be enforced to succeed (Brunacini, 1985, pp. 16-17).

The NFPA characterizes an SOP as " 'an organizational directive that establishes a standard course of action'" (Federal Emergency Management Agency—United States Fire Administration, 1999, p. 2). A comprehensive collection of SOPs specifies in a comprehensive way how an emergency response organization will operate during an event, working as a "game plan" prior to the event (Brunacini, 1985, p. 16). SOPs must be drafted with intelligent risk management as their main goal to make sure that safety is the norm expected by all involved. Safety-specific SOPs are unqualified mandates that must be abided by, no matter what else is going on.

For individual responders, SOPs provide comprehensible declarations of employer standards and act as a detailed description of expectations. Managers use SOPs for several reasons: examining their operations from a strategic viewpoint, recording needed changes, detailing regulatory compliance, creating intentions, as well as bettering training and measuring performance. According to Brunacini (1985, p. 18), "Standard operating procedures become the basis for much of the use of the regular management process. The standard steps of the system development/training/application/ review/revision are used in the development, application, and ongoing management of SOPs." They communicate legal and administrative mandates to members of emergency response groups. At a sizeable event with multiple responding agencies involved, SOPs become even more important.

Fire departments were the first emergency response organizations to utilize SOPs during emergency response. As departments grew beyond their casual roots, they began to address safety issues through internal controls. These requirements, originally termed "rules of engagement," protected firefighters during daily fire actions. The more contemporary terminology for these guidelines is standard operating procedures. As fires have become more complicated, SOPs have developed from measures that are "chiseled in stone" to SOGs. SOGs permit increased flexibility in responding to difficult fire scenes, encouraging the full exploitation of firefighters' knowledge, skills and abilities. Other emergency response groups learned from the fire service's knowledge, likewise developing ever more highly developed SOPs and SOGs. For hazmat responses, employers must encompass SOPs in their written safety and health program.[43]

Legally, SOPs are a form of "private law," that is, they are created by an organization and delineate the obligations of its members. For those people, the SOP is a rule of law, and violation can have serious consequences. These results can be internal penalties. Violations can also be the basis for a lawsuit for negligence, since the SOP is, at least, a site-specific industry standard. Indeed, many SOPs reflect generally accepted safe practices, and their

---
43. 29 CFR § 1910.120(b)(1)(ii)(F).

violation could well result in liability. Failure to adopt SOPs is not a way to avoid these potential liabilities. The only legal safe harbor is to adopt good SOPs and enforce them.

The Role of ICS

Concern that the nation required a common method for management of incidents led the Congress, in the Homeland Security Act of 2002,[44] to require adoption of IMS.[45] In response to the Congressional directive, DHS released NIMS on March 1, 2004 (see www.dhs.gov/interweb/assetlibrary/NIMS-90-web.pdf). Use of ICS is required by both NFPA 1600[46] and NIMS.[47] As mentioned above, the emergency manager is therefore obligated to ensure that it is utilized in emergency responses. HAZWOPER, which has been in existence for over 20 years, requires all hazmat responses to make use of ICS[48] and requires the Incident Commander (IC) to categorize, to the extent possible, all hazardous substances or conditions at hand and address site analysis, use of engineering controls, maximum exposure limits, hazardous substance handling procedures, and use of any new technologies.[49] The IC's duties at this point consist of identifying the substance and controlling the hazard.

The IC must put into practice suitable emergency operations, and ensure that the personal protective equipment (PPE) worn is appropriate for the hazards present.[50] There are particular requirements for breathing equipment.[51] "[T]he number of emergency response personnel at the emergency site, in those areas of potential or actual exposure to incident or site hazards . . . , [must be limited] to those who are actively performing emergency operations."[52]

The "buddy system" in twos or more must be used.[53] This necessitates that one is available to observe and, if required, save the other. Back-up workers must be prepared to provide support or rescue. Advance emergency medical personnel must also be present with medical equipment and transportation.[54]

Perhaps the most imperative obligation is naming a safety officer who is well-informed about operations at the incident scene.[55] He or she has the specific responsibility of identi-

---

44. Homeland Security Act of 2002, H.R. 5005, 107th Cong. (2002) (enacted).
45. Id. at § 501 (5) The HS Act requires "[b]uilding a comprehensive incident management system with Federal, state, and local government personnel, agencies, and authorities, to respond to... [terrorist] attacks and disasters."
46. NFPA 1600 § 5.8.
47. NIMS at 1-2.
48. 29 CFR § 1910.120(q)(3)(i) requires that during an emergency response the most senior emergency response official becomes the individual in charge of a site-specific Incident Command System (ICS). All emergency responders and their communications shall be coordinated and controlled through the individual in charge of the ICS assisted by the senior official present for each employer. Id.
49. 29 CFR § 1910.120(q)(3)(ii).
50. 29 CFR § 1910.120(q)(3)(iii) requires personal protective equipment to "meet, at a minimum, the criteria contained in 29 CFR § 1910.156(e) when worn while performing fire fighting operations beyond the incipient stage for . . . [the] incident."
51. 29 CFR § 1910.120 (q)(3)(iv).
52. 29 CFR § 1910.120(q)(3)(v).
53. 29 CFR § 1910.120(q)(3)(v).
54. 29 CFR § 1910.120(q)(3)(vi).
55. 29 CFR § 1910.120(q)(3)(vii). "The individual in charge of the ICS shall designate a safety official, who is knowledgeable in the operations being implemented at the emergency response site. . . ."

fying and evaluating hazards and providing direction respecting safety of operations. The safety officer has the power to alter, suspend, or terminate those activities.[56] The safety officer must immediately inform the IC of any action required to rectify hazards at an emergency scene. Case law demonstrates that the safety officer must be an individual other than the IC him or herself.[57]

Incorporating Volunteer Resources

Volunteers are a vital resource for emergency management. Properly managed, they can prove to be a key element is the successful response to an emergent situation. Their contributions are particularly important when funding for many types of preparedness and response activities are shrinking, as terrorism becomes the obsession of our national leadership. A number of legal issues may arise in connection with the utilization of volunteer resources.

Who Is a Volunteer?

The first question that must be addressed is the definitional issue—who is a volunteer? The answer is more complex than it might seem. One does not become a volunteer by simply showing up at the scene of an event. Rather, a person must be a member of an accredited organization or an integrated member of the emergency response team.

Incorporating Volunteers

The most important step that can be taken to prevent liability with regard to volunteers is properly integrating them into the emergency response organization. This may be done in a couple of ways. The best approach is to establish ongoing relationships with the major volunteer groups prior to a crisis. Like other emergency response groups, volunteer organizations need to be included in planning, training, and exercising. Their roles should be spelled out in the EOP. Typically, the parent organization ensures individual volunteers are properly trained and provides them with documentation so that they are identified appropriately during an incident. This removes a significant administrative burden from the IC at the incident scene.

Emergent Volunteers

One of the IC's biggest headaches may be the crowd of well-meaning emergent volunteers that often congregates at the scene. These people are frequently not affiliated with the groups with which the unit of government has existing mutual aid agreements. They may or may not be trained responders. One of the IC's major duties is access control. When

---

56. 29 CFR § 1910.120(q)(3)(viii).
57. *See Victor Microwave, Inc.,* 1996 OSAHRC LEXIS 57, at *44-47. Failure to designate a separate safety officer was found to be a serious violation.

trained responders arrive as the prearranged outcome of a mutual aid agreement, the result can be useful resources. Unfortunately, emergency responders converge on the incident scene at the location individually or in groups, despite not being asked for or even being actively discouraged. This happened both in New York and at the Pentagon after the 9-11 strikes. The IC must show decision and tact to maintain control of the site. One of the first responsibilities for an IC is organization of a perimeter, which should be controlled by law enforcement (Brunacini, 1985, p. 22). People trying to come into the perimeter without proper permission must be prevented from doing so and moved to a distant staging area (Brunacini, 1985, pp. 23-24). There, training and capabilities can be assessed, and their proper role, if any, can be assigned. In the event that they are found to be trained responders with needed skills, a record of the assessment must be made. They can then be officially rostered as approved responders. Taking these steps will protect the emergency response organization from liability, as it shows that they are taking reasonable steps to find out the competencies of the volunteers. Of course, there is an accompanying duty to assign the volunteers to duties for which they are qualified (Nicholson, 2003b).

The Volunteer Protection Act of 1997

Many members of Congress believe that the possibility of litigation may lessen the likelihood of people to volunteer for public service. In response, they enacted the Volunteer Protection Act of 1997 (VPA) to make available statutory immunity to increase the labor pool for voluntary entities.[58] The VPA preempts state laws providing higher levels of liability for volunteers than gross negligence. States may opt out of the VPA. In addition to shelter from negligence lawsuits, punitive damages may not be awarded against a volunteer acting within the scope of his/her responsibilities to a nonprofit organization, even when that volunteer is negligent or grossly negligent. The immunity does not attach to the volunteer's organization.

Notably, the VPA does not exempt volunteers from liability for any harm caused while driving a motor vehicle. This exclusion is important, since research indicates that half the claims involving emergency response organizations arise from vehicle accidents. While the VPA alters the basis for a lawsuit, it probably does not affect administrative actions taken on a negligence basis. Laws that name negligent conduct endangering persons as the basis for administrative penalties therefore continue to be valid.

The Planning Process

The first step in emergency management at all levels of government is planning. Correct planning signifies that resources, proper procedures, and trained personnel are organized

---

58. Pub. L. No. 105-19, 111 Stat. 218 (codified at 42 USCA. §§ 14501-14505 (West Supp. III 2002)). As is the case with any type of tort reform, the VPA has come in for significant criticism. *See, e.g.*, Andrew F. Popper, *A One-Term Tort Reform Tale: Victimizing The Vulnerable*, 35 Harv. J. on Legis. 123, 130-137 (Winter 1998). "An underlying principle of tort law is that the threat of personal liability creates individual accountability and thereby enhances the quality of goods and services. Accordingly, the common law imposes a minimum level of due care on people who choose to volunteer. The Volunteer Protection Act changes that standard, and in so doing, reduces the incentive to provide quality services." *Id.* at 134-35 (citations omitted).

when a disaster occurs. Emergency response plans may vary widely in size and comprehensiveness, depending on the nature of the jurisdiction they serve and the planning philosophy of the drafters.

Proactive Preparation for Federal Assistance

One matter that can make a tremendous difference in the amount and quality of assistance that a jurisdiction receives from the federal government is the legal enactments it has in place regarding infrastructure replacement. Building and fire codes should be up to date, and require that all new or rebuilt structures comply with current codes. Standards for replacement of infrastructure, such as bridges and highways, must specify that new construction or repairs shall conform to currently accepted best practices. The reason for these legal steps is that federal aid will pay for reconstruction or repair only to the extent that the unit of government imposes the same requirements on itself or private parties.

Good financial controls will also make a tremendous difference when the time comes to request federal reimbursement. The federal government will only pay for items for which properly documented receipts exist. Although these matters may seem beyond the scope of traditional emergency management planning, having them in place is an excellent example of how proper planning on the legal side can result in significant financial benefits.

Potential Liabilities Arising from the Duty to Plan

As described above, the common custom is to create and maintain an EOP. If possessing such a plan improves response, the next query must be whether lack of a plan would be the basis for a lawsuit. Violation of a "specific and mandatory" statutory or other mandate to establish a plan would not be discretionary under *Berkovitz v. United States*, discussed above. All states have statutory requirements to prepare an EOP. Further, environmental law requires preparation of a response plan for releases of extremely hazardous substances.[59]

Failing to prepare a mandated plan will result in liability. In a case involving failure by the Nuclear Regulatory Commission to prepare a plan mandated by its own rules, the court found that the "choice" made by the agency's employee was a failure or refusal to follow safety standards, resulting in a lack of immunity. Where the challenged governmental activity involves safety considerations under an established policy rather than the balancing of competing public policy considerations, the rationale for the exception falls away and the US government will be held responsible for the negligence of its employees.[60]

---

59. The Comprehensive Environmental Response, Compensation, and Liability Act (CERCLA) section 104 (i), as amended by SARA, requires the Aganecy for Toxic Ssubstances and Disease Registry and the EPA to prepare a list, in order of priority, of substances that are most commonly found at facilities on the National Priorities List (NPL) established by the National Contingency Plan (NCP). The NCP provides guidelines and procedures needed to respond to releases and threatened released of hazardous substances, pollutants, or contaminates. Superfund Amendment and Reauthorization Act of 1986 (SARA or Superfund), 42 USC §§ 11001et seq. This act provided for broad Federal authority to respond directly to releases or threatened releases of hazardous substances that may endanger public health or the environment.
60. *Roberts v. United States*, 724 F.Supp. 778, 791 (D.DC 1989).

Another situation that may result in liability is where a plan exists, but may have been negligently drafted. Interestingly, at the federal level, planning is considered inherently discretionary, while operational activities are not. This means that cases brought under the Federal Tort Claims Act for bad plans (as opposed to the previous discussion where a mandatory plan was not created) will typically not succeed.[61]

The adoption of NFPA 1600, however, will most probably result in liability for negligently drafted plans. This is because the planning portion of NFPA 1600 details particular tasks. Several plans are mandated:

> **5.7.1*** The program shall include, but shall not be limited to, a strategic plan, an emergency operations/response plan, a mitigation plan, a recovery plan, and a continuity plan.[62]

The content of these plans is laid out with some particularity. The emergency response plan is described as follows:

> **1.7.2.2** The emergency operations/response plan shall assign responsibilities to organizations and individuals for carrying out specific actions at projected times and places in an emergency or disaster.[63]
>
> All of the plans required by NFPA 1600 have several shared components:
>
> **5.7.3 Common Plan Elements.**
>
> **5.7.3.1** The functional roles and responsibilities of internal and external agencies, organizations, departments, and individuals shall be identified.
>
> **5.7.3.2** Lines of authority for those agencies, organizations, departments, and individuals shall be established or identified.[64]

NFPA 1600 also requires other steps be taken that are a normal part of planning, such as hazard identification, risk assessment, and impact analysis.[65] As mentioned previously, NFPA 1600 also imposes a duty to adhere to current laws, policies, and industry practices.[66] This means the requirements of NFPA 1600 are a moving target. Avoidance of liability for bad planning will therefore require constant attention to evolving standards.

In addition to NFPA 1600, NIMS sets mandatory standards for emergency management programs that wish to receive federal funds, including Emergency Management Perfor-

---

61. See, e.g., *In Re: Ohio River Disaster Litigation*, 862 F.2d 1237 (6th Cir. 1988).
62. NFPA 1600 § 5.7.1 (2004 Edition).
63. NFPA 1600 § 5.7.2.2 (2004 Edition).
64. NFPA 1600 § 5.7.3 (2004 Edition).
65. NFPA 1600 § 5.3 (2004 Edition).
66. NFPA 1600 § 5.2 (2004 Edition).

mance Grants (EMPGs),[67] after October 2004.[68] NIMS requires EOPs, corrective action and mitigation plans, and recovery plans.[69] NIMS' requirements for EOPs are rather extensive.[70] These are to:

- Define the scope of preparedness and incident management activities necessary for the jurisdiction.
- Describe organizational structures, roles and responsibilities, policies, and protocols for providing emergency support.
- Facilitate response and short-term recovery activities
- Drive decisions about long-term prevention and mitigation efforts or risk-based preparedness measures directed at specific hazards.
- Be flexible enough for use in all emergencies.
- Describe the purpose of the plan, situation and assumptions, concept of operations, organization and assignment of responsibilities, administration and logistics, plan development and maintenance, and authorities and references.
- Contain functional annexes, hazard-specific appendices, and a glossary.
- Predesignate jurisdictional and/or functional area representatives to the IC or UC to facilitate responsive and collaborative incident management.
- Include preincident and postincident public awareness, education, and communications plans and protocols.

NIMS establishes a national industry standard. Even though NIMS frames its mandates as suggestions, using the term "should" rather than "must", the requirement of NFPA 1600 that plans incorporate industry standards, however, renders these voluntary elements mandatory. NIMS complements NFPA 1600, and sets the benchmark for planning. Failure to plan to its requirements may well result in liability.

Since 9/11, states have expanded their statutory schemes to include specific enactments addressing terrorism. In particular, states that list planning requirements frequently have added planning for terrorist events to their laws.[71] This is an example of the evolving nature of planning requirements. As experienced emergency managers say, the plan is never final, but rather a "living document."

Failure to Follow the Plan

Assuming that a good plan has been established, failure to follow it in the wake of an emergency may subject the emergency manager to liability. In federal court, the response hinges on whether the plan is interpreted as setting a compulsory course of action. An EOP could

---

67. EMPG description on the web at: http://www.fema.gov/preparedness/empg.shtm
68. Homeland Security Presidential Directive 5, § 20 Subject: Management of Domestic Incidents, The White House, February 28, 2003. http://www.whitehouse.gov/news/releases/2003/02/20030228-9.html
69. NIMS at 36-37.
70. NIMS at 36-37.
71. See, e.g., Fla. Stat. § 252.34 (2004) emergency management responsibilities, Fla. Stat. § 395.1056 (2004) requiring hospitals to plan for terrorism events.

be construed as a "specific and mandatory" obligation, although it is an internal document with no direct legal consequences for the public. That result may be gotten from *Berkovitz*, which refers to "statute, regulation or policy."[72] Violating an internal policy, therefore, may give a basis to sue if the policy "leaves no room for implementing officials to exercise independent policy judgment".[73]

Determining whether a document limits an official's choice or only informs his or her discretionary judgment requires close scrutiny. EOPs generally contain a range of substance varying from general to specific. A general tasking for protecting the public (e.g., to the county commissioners) clearly envisages the use of discretion. Conversely, where the plan contains detailed lists of actions, there may be no opportunity to do other than required by the list, except if the plan permits deviation. Some plans have mandatory, automatic protective measures—like evacuating the public. As noted in Chapter 10, nuclear power plants classify emergencies as an Unusual Event, Alert, Site Area Emergency, or General Emergency. Neighboring areas may include language in their plans that particular measures, such as activating sirens or evacuating a given radius in the region of the plant, must automatically occur when the plant gets to the Site Area Emergency or General Emergency, whether or not any radioactive material has been released. Failing negligently to take the required actions could expose the emergency manager to tort liability.

Planning for Special Risks

Hazardous Materials Releases

The acts of all responders to emergencies, particularly those involving hazmat—such as a weapons of mass destruction (WMD) event, are closely regulated by both OSHA[74] and the EPA.[75] Emergency managers should take steps to ensure responders understand the applicability of these rules to their activities, and ensure safety mandates are followed.

Both public and private groups have responsibility for first response to a hazmat incident. Usually, in-plant response teams will be first at industrial incidents. OSHA's rule for Process Safety Management of Highly Hazardous Chemicals mandates these teams. This rule's purpose is preventing or minimizing the consequences of catastrophic releases of toxic, reactive, flammable, or explosive chemicals.[76] Offsite spills or airborne releases occurring on public property such as highways or exceeding the boundaries of an industrial facility, the first response organization is normally the fire service. The highly dangerous nature of

---

72. *Berkovitz* at 536.
73. *Berkovitz* at 547.
74. Occupational Safety and Health Standards 29 CFR §1910.120 (q) (1998) covers employees who are engaged in emergency response to hazardous substance releases no matter where it occurs except that it does not cover employees engaged in operations specified in paragraphs (a)(1)(i) through (a)(1)(iv) of this section. Nor does it cover those emergency response organizations that have developed and implemented programs equivalent to this paragraph for handling releases of hazardous substances pursuant to section 303 of the Superfund Amendments and Reauthorization Act of
75. Environmental Protection Agency (EPA) 40 CFR § 372.18 (1995) deals with the enforcement and compliance guidelines for toxic chemical release reporting and community right-to-know
76. 29 CFR § 1910.119 deals with preventing or minimizing the consequence of catastrophic release of hazardous materials in the industrial setting.

hazmat requires sophisticated technical expertise of responders (Federal Emergency Management Agency/United States Fire Administration, 2000).

Planning Structure for Extremely Hazardous Substances. The requirements of the Emergency Planning and Right to Know Act (EPCRA) mandate a separate structure for planning for extremely hazardous substances (EHS) releases. EPCRA is part of Title III of the Superfund Amendment and Reauthorization Act of 1986 (SARA Title III).[77] States frequently enact EPCRA's requirements into their own laws to provide a supporting state structure for the program.[78] EPCRA creates a structure consisting of LEPCs, which report to, and are lesser parts of, SERCs. The LEPC also has specific roles that are directed by law, some of which coincide with the LEMA's duties.

SERC and LEPC duties. The SERC has four responsibilities. First, it promotes emergency planning and provides information about potential chemical hazards statewide. Second, it helps the state to obey the obligations imposed by SARA Title III. Third, it sets up and oversees the operation of state emergency planning districts. Fourth, it collects and issues information needed for successful emergency response planning.

SARA Title III requires LEPCs to do the following:
- Prepare an EHS release plan.
- Revise the plan annually.
- Evaluate resources needed to develop, implement and exercise the plan.
- Make recommendations for additional needed resources.
- Submit the plan to the SERC.[79]

LEPC and LEMA interface. In contrast to the LEPC, LEMAs are clearly part of local government. As mentioned, the LEPC's planning requirement under EPCRA is expressly limited to SARA Title III chemical releases. The LEPC's plan cannot, however, stand alone, for LEPCs are not the only bodies charged by law with planning for emergencies. NFPA 1600 and state laws require LEMAs to prepare and keep current a local EOP for its area.

Under the all hazards approach, emergency managers must consider possible emergencies concerning hazmat. The EOP must include a current appendix for response to hazmat incidents. Possible hazmat emergencies incorporate the EHSs covered by SARA Title III, as well as an assortment of other substances. Required planning compliance requirements for LEMAs will typically include submitting the local EOP, in its entirety, including the SARA Title III plan as a hazard-specific appendix.

The overlapping planning responsibilities of LEPCs and LEMAs may occasionally result in some doubling of effort, and even disputes as to the proper approaches to the nine planning

---

77. 42 United States Code §§ 11001-11050 (2004).
78. See, e.g., Indiana Code 13-25-2 (2004).
79. 42 USC § 11003.

elements required of LEPCs. In order to join together the planning responsibilities of local emergency management and those of LEPCs, it makes sense for the SARA Title III plan to be a hazard-specific appendix to the EOP. Nonetheless, the SARA Title III plan continues to be the LEPC's responsibility. As an appendix, the SARA Title III plan should make use of the rest of the EOP. Subjects required to be part of the LEPC plan—such as community notification, evacuation, training, and exercising—should refer to the corresponding portions of the EOP, rather than being duplicated in the LEPC's plan.

The shared goals of saving lives and protecting property unite LEMAs and LEPCs, just as they link the SEMA and SERC. All involved must, however, work with both mutual deference and awareness of the legal limits on LEMAs and LEPCs. Working carefully together, LEMAs and LEPCs can ensure that the best feasible steps have been taken to plan for incidents involving EHSs.

Terrorism

Terrorism is an unfortunate danger of modern life. Some emergency managers believe, in fact, that terrorism has become the single hazard tail that wags the all hazards dog of their professional life. Requirements for terrorism planning, however, are not new. Indeed, they pre-date the 9/11 attacks by a number of years. In 1995, President Clinton issued Presidential Decision Directives 39,[80] which detailed ways of dealing with terrorism, including planning. FEMA promulgated the Federal Response Plan (FRP) Terrorism Incident Annex[81] in 1999 to ensure the FRP would provide a structure to fully respond to terrorism incidents.

Congress, in the Homeland Security Act of 2002, Public Law 107-296 (HS Act),[82] requires DHS to build a comprehensive national incident management system with federal, state, and local government personnel, agencies, and authorities, to respond to terrorist attacks and disasters; and consolidate existing federal government emergency response plans into a single, coordinated national response plan.[83] On February 28, 2003 President Bush issued HSPD 5, which states:[84]

> to prevent, prepare for, respond to, and recover from terrorist attacks, major disasters, and other emergencies, the United States Government shall establish a single, comprehensive approach to domestic incident management. The objective of the United States Government is to ensure that all levels of government across the Nation have the capability to work efficiently and effectively together, using a national approach to domestic incident management.[85]

---

80. Presidential Decision Directive 39, US Policy on Counterterrorism (June 21, 1995)
81. Federal Response Plan Terrorism Incident Annex, *available at* http://www.fema/gov/pdf/rrr/frp/frptem.pdf (1999). "The purpose of this annex is to ensure that the Federal Response Plan (FRP) is adequate to respond to the consequences of terrorism within the United States, including terrorism involving WMD." *Id.* at 1.
82. Homeland Security Act of 2002, H.R. 5005, 107th Cong. (2002) (enacted) [hereinafter HS Act].
83. HS Act §§ 501(5) and (6)..
84. Homeland Security Presidential Directive 5, Subject: Management of Domestic Incidents, The White House, February 28, 2003. http://www.whitehouse.gov/news/releases/2003/02/20030228-9.html
85. HSPD 5 § 3.

To accomplish the preparedness goals of that policy, DHS directs in the NIMS that planning be performed for all types of incidents, including acts of terrorism.[86] The consequences of failing to plan as directed by the HS Act are discussed above.

School Violence

In the wake of events like the Columbine High School massacre in Colorado, the federal government enacted the Safe and Drug-Free Schools and Communities Act of 1994 (Safe Schools Act).[87] The Safe School Act requires schools to develop appropriate school safety plans that will help control student-on-student violence. The Safe Schools Act is a federal grant program that focuses on preventing violence and drug abuse in schools. These goals are achieved through federal aid to states so that they can make grants to local educational agencies and community organizations. Federal money also goes to support private, non-profit organizations and colleges and universities that develop anti-violence and anti-drug initiatives.

Unfortunately, as frequently happens when funds become available to fulfill a mandate, some unscrupulous contractors came on the scene touting questionable school safety plans. Comparing these "plans" often revealed them to be "one size fits all" documents. A form plan that does not take into account the particular characteristics of a school is an inadequate plan. The potential liabilities that flow from embracing an inadequate plan are discussed above.

Training and Exercising the EOP

Typically, training and exercising are matters for which LEPCs may legitimately expend funds. States often require LEPCs to include training[88] and exercising[89] their plans.

Training Responsibilities

The PPA often sets objectives for training such as developing and delivering training to individuals and groups with important emergency management duties, focusing on deficiencies in their ability to respond to identified risks. Such training is often required to be accomplished at all levels of government as well as the private sector, and to include on the job training for local emergency management organization staff from unaffected areas during genuine emergencies.

For every year, the CA contains specific requisites that help the state and its local units of government achieve the objectives specified in the PPA. The training specifications of the

---

86. NIMS at 1, 35-37 (planning elements).
87. Safe and Drug-Free Schools and Communities Act of 1994 (Safe Schools Act) 20 USC §§ 7101 *et.seq* (2004).
88. See, e.g., Indiana Code 13-25-2-5(c)(8) (2004).
89. See, e.g., Indiana Code 13-25-2-5(c)(9) (2004).

CA often set training objectives such as:
- Train a state's quick reaction team,
- Provide support to state agencies in creation of SOPs,
- Conduct training for state and local agencies in specific hazards such as earthquakes or hurricanes,
- Deliver training through the SEMA,
- Develop new training,
- Provide a robust public awareness program, and
- Accomplish SARA Title III training.

Required training compliance requirements for local emergency management organizations may include one SEMA training course annually for each staff member for whom the federal government provides salary reimbursement.

Exercising Responsibilities

EPCRA requires that an LEPC's plan must be exercised at least once annually. A SERC may create a policy permitting the exercise to be a tabletop, functional, or full-scale exercise. The SERC may require a 30 day advance notification and brief description of the exercise to be conducted. Sometimes, a SERC will permit an incident response to be used as a substitute for an exercise.

For local emergency management, the PPA may set exercise objectives such as:
- Establish a comprehensive exercise program to test and assess all aspects of the state's emergency management system, including federal programs, such as the Radiological Emergency Planning (REP), Chemical Stockpile Emergency Preparedness (CSEP), earthquake, hazmat, and terrorism;
- Conduct statewide tabletop exercises that incorporate federal, state and local response personnel; and
- Conduct critiques to assess shortcomings and identify corrective actions.

A CA may require exercises during a given federal fiscal year such as:
- Participate in federally created exercises that evaluate federal response planning concepts,
- Observe all exercises and create a procedure to correct shortcomings, and
- Require that all participants in the federal reimbursement program meet the exercise standards set by FEMA, including correction of deficiencies.

Required exercise compliance requirements for local emergency management may include one actual incident, one full scale exercise, one functional exercise, or two table top exercises. All incidents or exercises must meet established criteria. Working together, LEMAs

and LEPCs should be able to combine their requirements in joint exercises that will satisfy both the SERC and SEMA. These exercises should immediately be followed by critiques that identify where the emergency response system worked correctly and where it needs improvement. The failure to apply lessons learned from exercises in the form of revisions to the EOP, procedures, facilities, equipment, and training may result in liability if the uncorrected deficiencies result in property damage or personal injury in a subsequent actual incident.

Declaring an Emergency

Many types of events are characterized as emergencies, from a one car accident with minor injuries and property injury to a hurricane or terrorist attack. Clearly, the resources necessary to respond to an event vary considerably depending on its type, and magnitude. Happily, the vast majority of incidents are closer to the one car accident end of the spectrum than to a catastrophe. In most instances, therefore, assistance from beyond a jurisdiction's borders is not required.

Emergency managers should know what resources are available locally. In compliance with NFPA 1600 and NIMS, there should also be established MAAs to obtain help from neighboring jurisdictions. When a major incident occurs, however, the emergency manager knows how long readily obtainable resources will last. There is not a requirement that every available resource be exhausted before help from higher levels of government may be obtained. As a general matter, local capabilities must be in either actual or imminent danger of being overwhelmed before a successful request for aid may be made.

One need not wait for an incident to occur before asking for help. The timing of a request for assistance from the next higher level of government is determined by whether a unit of government (or any part thereof) is experiencing or is in imminent danger of experiencing a natural or manmade emergency or disaster. The procedure for asking for help from the next higher level of government is similar, whether the requestor is at the local or state level. The requirements for both include a written declaration, which must contain six elements.
- A statement that a disaster is current or imminent.
- A description of the threat.
- A statement that resources are or soon will be exhausted.
- The extent of damage.
- The types of assistance requested.
- A request for assistance.

The request must be made through the proper channels. Local government may request help from the state. The state must be the entity that asks the federal government for assistance.

Federal Support to States

FEMA processes a governor's request for Presidential Disaster Declaration (PDD) or Emergency Declaration under the Stafford Act. Governors submit these requests to FEMA indicating the extent of damage and the types of federal assistance required. FEMA then forwards the governor's request to the White House, simultaneously notifying the Secretary of DHS, along with a recommended course of action. Concurrent with a PDD of a major disaster or emergency and official appointment of an FCO, FEMA designates the types of assistance to be made available and the counties eligible to receive assistance. In catastrophic incidents, the declaration process can be expedited. In some cases, the Stafford Act authorizes declarations without a governor's request. [90]

Effect of Declaring an Emergency

Declaring an emergency activates the emergency response and disaster recovery components of the EOPs of the affected political subdivision or area. Additionally, it typically will activate specific powers for the head of government to take a variety of actions for the duration of the declaration. These may include any of the following:
- Deploying and using any forces to which the plan or plans apply;
- Using or distributing any supplies, equipment, materials, and facilities assembled, stockpiled, or arranged to be made available under any law relating to disaster emergencies;
- Authorizing the governor to act as the commander-in-chief of the organized and unorganized militia and of all other forces available for emergency duty;
- Suspending the provisions of any regulatory statute prescribing the procedures for conduct of government business, or the orders, rules, or regulations of any agency if strict compliance with any of these provisions would in any way prevent, hinder, or delay necessary action in coping with the emergency;
- Using all available resources of the unit of government reasonably necessary to cope with the emergency;
- Transferring the direction, personnel, or functions of departments and agencies or units for performing or facilitating emergency services;
- Subjecting to any applicable requirements for compensation, commandeer or use any private property if the governor finds this action necessary to cope with the emergency;
- Assisting in the evacuation of all or part of the population from any stricken or threatened area in the jurisdiction if the head of the unit of government considers this action necessary for the preservation of life or other disaster mitigation, response, or recovery;
- Prescribing routes, modes of transportation, and destinations in connection with evacuation;
- Controlling ingress to and egress from a disaster area, the movement of persons within the area, and the occupancy of premises in the area;

---

90. This information is from the National Response Plan, Draft #2 at 61 (April 28, 2004).

- Suspending or limiting the sale, dispensing, or transportation of alcoholic beverages, firearms, explosives, and combustibles;
- Making provision for the availability and use of temporary emergency housing;
- At the state level, allowing persons who hold a license to practice medicine, dentistry, pharmacy, nursing, engineering, and similar other professions as may be specified by the governor to practice their respective profession in the state during the period of the state of emergency if the state in which a person's license was issued has a mutual aid compact for emergency management with the state;
- Giving specific authority to allocate drugs, foodstuffs, and other essential materials and services.[91]

When to Declare

Generally, an emergency should be declared when doing so will benefit the jurisdiction. In most states, the head of the unit of government makes the declaration, with advice from the emergency manager. An unnecessary declaration may be the source of liability. This would be most likely if the declaration were clearly unneeded and the special powers that accrue to the head of the unit of government, such as ignoring normal contracting requirements or taking private property, were used in an objectionable way. This is an unlikely scenario; to succeed, a suit would need to prove that the declarer acted in a grossly negligent or malicious manner. A delayed declaration could result in hindering prompt assistance from higher jurisdictions that possess manpower and equipment that could prevent a bad situation from further deteriorating. If the delay resulted in property damage, personal injury, or death, liability might result.

As discussed above, different states approach the matter of emergency management immunities in their own ways. In some states, a delay in declaring will be accompanied by a postponement of immunities for the emergency response organization. In other states, in contrast, all activities connected with emergency management, whatever phase may be involved, are protected by immunity statutes.

Legal Issues in Evacuation

One of the most challenging aspects of emergency response is the fact that often a decision must be made between options that are universally unattractive. Sometimes, different plaintiffs will see the same action as wrong for the opposite reasons. Evacuation is a good example of this phenomenon. Legal authorities for declaring an evacuation are found in state and local emergency management acts and ordinances. Such laws often grant the head of government the authority to force people to evacuate their homes and businesses. Often, evacuation may be the best protective step that can be taken. Unfortunately, evacuation can be very expensive and disruptive for households and businesses. Further, it creates safety hazards. Evacuation illustrates the fundamental challenge to the person making choices during responses—reacting

---

91. This list is adapted from Indiana Code 10-14-3-12 (2004).

appropriately to situational demands while avoiding needless disturbance to daily life. Public policy decisions such as deciding whether and how broadly to evacuate are the sorts of action that should typically be covered by discretionary function immunity.

Sometimes, people refuse to evacuate. Options at that point are not attractive. Does one spend vital time trying to convince the recalcitrant resident to evacuate when there are others to be saved? Does one spend limited resources on arresting and confining the person (risking a potential suit for false arrest)? One effective approach has been to require those refusing to evacuate to fill in a "next of kin" form so that the government may inform their survivors after they die (the implication is that failing to leave will render death inevitable). The form also should contain waiver of liability language so that the government will not be responsible for the person's death. One reason that people may not wish to leave is that their companion animals may not accompany them to Red Cross shelters. Many jurisdictions are addressing this issue by making advance agreements for assistance with veterinarians to care for such animals.

Sometimes, it is necessary to reenter the evacuation area for vital tasks during the emergency. At this point, this nature and criticality of the task must be evaluated to ascertain whether it is worthwhile to risk lives and legal liability to permit such action. To be on the safe side from a legal perspective, only when the danger has passed should reentry be allowed.

Legal Issues During Disaster Recovery

The legal requirements for ending a state of emergency may be found in emergency management laws and ordinances. Typically, the event is terminated by action of law after incident conditions have stabilized. Renewal of the state of emergency may be possible by a simple declaration by the head of government, or it might take ratification by the legislative body.

There are three varieties of federal major disaster recovery assistance:
- Mitigation,
- Individual Assistance, which applies to individuals and households, and
- Public Assistance, which applies to infrastructure owned by local government.

If a Small Business Administration emergency has been declared, low interest loans may be available to businesses. The interested reader to should refer to additional very lengthy federal publications covering this issue. Answers to some basic questions and referral to more extensive materials may be found on the FEMA web site at: www.fema.gov/rrr/qanda.shtm

Transitioning from Recovery to Mitigation

Emergency managers have a legal obligation to ensure lessons learned from an incident are incorporated into the community's hazard mitigation practices. NIMS requires corrective action plans and mitigation plans, as well as recovery operations plans, new developments that go beyond the traditional EOPs. Corrective action plans are intended to put into practice measures based on lessons learned from actual incidents or training and exercises. Mitigation plans explain actions that can be taken prior to, during, or after an event to reduce or eliminate risks to persons or property or to lessen the actual or possible effects or consequences of an incident. Recovery plans explain measures beyond quick damage assessment and any that may be needed to supply urgent life support for victims. Long-term recovery planning entails identifying strategic priorities for restoration, improvement, and growth. This includes rebuilding to withstand future calamities. The discussion above of legal steps that may be taken in the planning stage is relevant at this point as well.

Conclusion

Emergency managers must comply with a wide variety of legal responsibilities that spring from federal and state statutes, local ordinances, case law, and policies. Some of these apply specifically to emergency management, having been drafted specifically for the discipline. Further obligations apply to all government managers, and still other standards pertain to all management personnel.

Avoidance of liability requires creating a proactive partnership with legal advisors that runs through all phases of emergency management. In mitigation, updating fire and building codes to address local hazards can mean a less severe effect from a disaster. Before a disaster strikes, an attorney can help draft plans, evaluate training standards, and monitor exercises for potential legal issues, as well as assure that EOP revisions are sufficient from a legal standpoint. During emergency response, the attorney may advise the leader of the unit of government and emergency manager on potential legal effects of various options. During disaster recovery, the lawyer can help to make sure that expenses are properly documented and that the transition into mitigation is properly performed. Only when emergency managers and the attorneys who advise them understand each other's responsibilities and contributions can they work together to diminish the potential for litigation.

Appendix 14-A
Model Local Disaster or Emergency Ordinance[92]

Section 1-0101. Intent
It is the intent of this article to provide the necessary organization, powers, and authority to enable the timely and effective use of all available City resources to prepare for, respond to and recover from emergencies and/or disasters, whether natural or man made, likely to affect the health, security, safety, or property of the inhabitants of the City. It is intended to grant as broad of power as permitted.

---

92. Note: This ordinance is found in: Howard D. Swanson, *The Delicate Art of Practicing Municipal Law Under Conditions of Hell and High Water*, 76 N.D. L. REV. 487 (2000)

Section 1-0102. Definitions
(1) Civil emergency: Conditions of unrest including, but not limited to riot, civil disturbance, unlawful assembly, hostile military or paramilitary action, war, terrorism, or sabotage.
(2) Disaster: The occurrence of widespread or severe damage, injury, or loss of life or property resulting from any natural or manmade cause including but not limited to flood, fire, cyclone, tornado, earthquake, severe high or low temperatures, blizzard, landslide, mudslide, hurricane, building or structural collapse, high water table, water pollution, air pollution, epidemic, riot, drought, utility emergency, sudden and severe energy shortages, volcano, earthquake, snow, ice, windstorm, waves, hazardous substance spills, chemical or petroleum spills, biological material release or spill, radiological release or spill, structural failure, public health emergency or accidents.
(3) Emergency: Any occurrence or threat of natural or man made disaster of a major proportion in which the safety and welfare of the inhabitants of the City or their property are jeopardized or placed at extreme peril that timely action may avert or minimize.
(4) Utility emergency: Any condition which endangers or threatens to endanger the safety, potability, availability, transmission, distribution, treatment, or storage of water, natural gas, fuel or electricity through their respective systems.

Section 1-0103. Authorization to issue declaration of emergency or disaster
The Mayor is authorized to declare a local emergency or disaster if the Mayor finds that the City or any part thereof is suffering from or is in imminent danger of suffering a natural or manmade emergency or disaster.

Section 1-0104. Filing of declaration
Any declaration of an emergency or disaster by the mayor shall be promptly filed with the City Auditor and the public shall be notified through general publicity of said declaration.

Section 1-0105. Term of declaration
The declaration of a local emergency or disaster shall be in effect as determined by the Mayor for a period of up to thirty (30) days. This period may be extended only upon the approval of the City Council.

Section 1-0106. Succession of authority
If the Mayor is unavailable, the President of the City Council shall have the same authority as is granted to the Mayor hereunder, followed by the Vice President of the City Council, the Chair of the Public Safety Committee, the Chair of the Public Service Committee, the Chair of the Finance Committee, the Chair of the Urban Development Committee, and then followed by the next most senior member of the City Council.

Section 1-0107. Powers
Upon the issuance of an emergency or disaster declaration, the Mayor may exercise the following powers, including, but not limited to:

(1) an order establishing a curfew during such hours of the days or nights and affecting such categories of persons as may be designated.

(2) an order to direct and compel the evacuation of all or a part of the population from any stricken or threatened areas within the City if the Mayor deems this action is necessary for the preservation of life, property or other disaster or emergency mitigation, response or recovery activities and to prescribe routes, modes of transportation and destination in connection with an evacuation.

(3) an order controlling, restricting, allocating or regulating the use, sale, production or distribution of food, water, fuel, clothing, and other commodities, materials, goods, services and resources.

(4) an order requiring the closing of businesses deemed nonessential by the Mayor.

(5) an order suspending or limiting the sale, distribution, dispensing, or transportation of alcoholic beverages, firearms, explosives and/or combustible products and requiring the closing of those businesses or parts of businesses insofar as the sale, distribution, dispensing or transportation of these items are concerned.

(6) an order prohibiting the sale or distribution within the City of any products which, the mayor determines, could be employed in a manner that would constitute a danger to public health or safety.

(7) an order closing any streets, alleys, sidewalks, public parks, public ways or other public places.

(8) an order closing the access to any buildings, streets, alleys, sidewalks or other public or private places.

(9) establish and control routes of transportation ingress or egress.

(10) control ingress and egress from a disaster or emergency area.

(11) subject to requirements for compensation, commandeer or utilize private property if necessary to cope with emergency or disaster conditions.

(12) appropriate and expend funds, exclude contracts, authorize the obtaining and acquisition of property, equipment, services, supplies and materials without the strict compliance with procurement regulations or procedures.

(13) transfer the direction, personnel or functions of City departments and agencies for the purposes of performing or facilitating emergency or disaster services.

(14) utilize all available resources of the City as may be reasonably necessary to cope with the emergency or disaster whether in preparation for, response to or recovery from an emergency or disaster.

(15) suspend or modify the provisions of any ordinance if strict compliance thereof would in any way prevent, hinder or delay necessary action in coping with any emergency or disaster.

(16) accept services, gifts, grants and loans, equipment, supplies and materials whether from private, nonprofit or governmental sources.

(17) temporarily suspend, limit, cancel, postpone, convene, schedule, or continue all meetings of the City Council, and any City committee, commission, board, authority or other City body as deemed appropriate by the Mayor.

(18) suspend or limit the use of the City's water resources.
(19) suspend or limit the burning of any items of property within the City limits and up to two (2) miles outside the corporate City limits.
(20) require emergency services of any City officer or employee. If regular City forces are determined to be inadequate, then to acquire the services of such other personnel as are available, including citizen volunteers. All duly authorized persons rendering emergency services shall be entitled to the privileges and immunities as provided by state or local law.
(21) hire or contract for construction, engineering, architectural, building, electrical, plumbing, and/or other professional or construction services essential to continue the activities of the City without the advertising of bids or compliance with procurement requirements.
(22) make application for local, state or federal assistance.
(23) terminate or suspend any process, operation, machine, device or event that is or may negatively impact the health, safety and welfare of persons or property within the City of Grand Forks.
(24) delegate authority to such City officials as the Mayor determines reasonably necessary or expedient.
(25) requiring the continuation, termination, disconnection or suspension of natural gas, electric power, water, sewer or other public utilities.
(26) close or cancel the use of any municipally owned or operated building or other public facility.
(27) prescribe routes, modes of transportation and destination in connection with any evacuation.
(28) exercise such powers and functions in light of the exigencies of emergency or disaster including the waiving of compliance with any time consuming procedures and formalities, including notices, as maybe prescribed by law pertaining thereto.
(29) issue any and all such other orders or undertake such other functions and activities as the Mayor reasonably believes is required to protect the health, safety, welfare of persons or property within the City of Grand Forks or to otherwise preserve the public peace or abate, clean up, or mitigate the effects of any emergency or disaster.

Section 1-0108. Enforcement of orders

A. The members of the police department and such other law enforcement and peace officers as may be authorized by the Mayor are further authorized and directed to enforce the orders, rules and regulations made or issued pursuant to this chapter.
B. During the period of a declared emergency or disaster, a person shall not:
(1) enter or remain upon the premises of any establishment not open for business to the general public, unless such person is the owner or authorized agent of the establishment.
(2) violate any of the orders duly issued by the Mayor or authorized personnel.
(3) willfully obstruct, hinder, or delay any duly authorized City officer, employee or volunteer in the enforcement or exercise of the provisions of this chapter, or of the undertaking of any activity pursuant to this chapter.

Section 1-0109. Authority to enter a property

During the period of a declared emergency or disaster, a City employee or authorized agent may enter onto or upon private property if the employee or authorized agent has reasonable grounds to believe that there is a true emergency and an immediate need for assistance for the protection of life or property, and that entering onto the private land will allow the person to take such steps to alleviate or minimize the emergency or disaster or to prevent or minimize danger to lives or property from the declared emergency or disaster.

Section 1-0110. Location of governing body meetings and departments

(1) Whenever an emergency or disaster makes it imprudent or impossible to conduct the affairs of the City at its regular locations, the governing body may meet at any place, inside or outside the city limits. Any temporary disaster meeting location for the governing body shall continue until a new location is established or until the emergency or disaster is terminated and the governing body is able to return to its normal location.

(2) Whenever a disaster makes it imprudent or impossible to conduct the affairs of any department of the City at its regular location, such department may conduct its business at any place, inside or outside the city limits and may remain at the temporary location until the emergency or disaster is declared ended or until the department is able to return to its normal location.

(3) Any official act or meeting required to be performed at any regular location of the governing body or of its departments is valid when performed at any temporary location under this section.

(4) The provisions of this section shall apply to all executive, legislative and judicial branches, powers and functions conferred upon the city and its offices, employees, and authorized agents.

Section 1-0111. Mutual aid agreements

(1) The Mayor may, on behalf of the City, enter into such reciprocal aid, mutual aid, joint powers agreements, intergovernmental assistance agreements or other compacts or plans with other governmental entities for the protection of life and property. Such agreements may include the furnishing or exchange of supplies, equipment, facilities, personnel and/or services.

(2) The governing body or any of its committees, commissions or authorities may exercise such powers and functions in light of the exigencies of the emergency or disaster and may waive compliance with time consuming procedures and formalities prescribed by law pertaining thereto.

(3) The foregoing shall apply to all executive, legislative and judicial powers and functions conferred upon the City and its officers, employees and authorized agents.

Section 1-0112. Severability

The provisions of this chapter are declared to be severable, and if any section, sentence, clause or phrase of this chapter shall for any reason be held to be invalid or unconstitutional or if the application of this chapter to any person or circumstance is held to be invalid or unconstitutional, such holding shall not affect the validity of the remaining sections, sentences, clauses and/or phrases of this ordinance.

Source: https://training.fema.gov/hiedu/aemrc/booksdownload/fem/

ADDITIONAL RESOURCES

IS-21.14 Civil Rights and FEMA Disaster Assistance
IS-33.14 FEMA Initial Ethics Orientation 2014
IS-800.b National Response Framework, An Introduction
IS-808 Emergency Support Function (ESF) #8 – Public Health and Medical Services
IS-813 Emergency Support Functions (ESF) #13 - Public Safety and Security Annex

CHILDREN, LAW AND DISASTER FROM THE AMERICAN BAR ASSOCIATION

Read the information here: https://books.google.com/books?id=ccrsdMt7aPQC&pg=PA56&lpg=PA56&dq=children,+law+and+disasters&source=bl&ots=L6vQv3NxVg&sig=4J7VdaWwzT2oiXP3JxRWlLwD_SQ&hl=en&sa=X&ved=0ahUKEwiti7Xgn_rKAhVEJh4KHX2YBCYQ6AEILjAD#v=onepage&q=children%2C%20law%20and%20disasters&f=false

Chapter Takeaways

Personal Notes

Disaster Conflict Management

James L. Greenstone, Ed.D., J.D., DABECI

Sharon C. Leviton, Ph.D., DABECI

Negotiation Success Factors: How They Work

The success of negotiations is contingent on many factors operating together. This is true regardless of type of bargaining or intervention undertaken. So, what are these factors? Here we will examine several that may have wide use. The focus here is specific, but the possible applications are broad regardless of the reader's orientation.

INTRODUCTION

On April 20, at 03:35 a.m., negotiators were deployed to support an officer who was already talking with a subject barricaded in his truck threatening to kill himself. Most of the issues seemed to revolve around family matters and husband/wife relational problems.

At 04:28 a.m., the primary negotiator began to speak directly with the subject.

John T Takai/Shutterstock.com

WHAT ACTUALLY HAPPENED

A sampling of some of the responses that the negotiator / crisis intervener made to the subject follows:
- Will you come out? If I give you my word? Will you come out of the truck?
- I want you to be there for them.
- Show Betty that you are sincere and want to make things better.
- We'll work through it together and we'll get Betty involved. It will be better for you and your children.
- Give me an opportunity to help you.
- I know a lot about you because I spoke with Betty. (Negotiator related what he knew.)
- I'm here because we (corrected) I don't want to see you get hurt.
- Will you promise me you will come out? (After he asked to hear her voice on the police radio.)
- I'm not here to tell you what you want to hear. I'm here to help you.
- I can't help you until I know that I am safe and that you are safe.
- I want to help you.
- Give her another opportunity.
- I'm trying to give you some options. We can work together to try to work this out.
- Once I know you are safe, we can begin working out everything else.
- I told you she cares about you. Give her the opportunity to show you.
- As long as you keep trying, there is always the possibility that things can work out.
- I want to see you work out things with Betty and things get better.
- Will you give me the opportunity to help you?
- I'm only here to help you. I'm concerned about you and want to be sure you are okay.
- I'll do everything I can to get you and Betty to work things out. Give me the opportunity.
- It's getting late, kids are tired, you're tired, I'm tired.
- If you're serious about making your marriage work, that is what you need to do (come out).
- Are you willing to work with me on that? If I give you my word?
- I can't do that right now. They won't let me.
- The problem is that you can't make things work from inside that truck.
- You've had problems in the past and you've always managed to work them out.
- Will you come out for me?
- Let's start to work this out.
- I can't hear you, Steven.
- I want to help you, but I can only do it when I know you are safe.
- This is what I want you to do, throw out the gun and come out.
- I know you want to do the right thing and that's the right thing to do (throw gun out and come out).
- I give you my word I will let you hear her voice if you come out.
- You're doing the right thing by wanting to talk to someone and work things out.

Steven came out at 06:09 a.m.

WHY DID THIS WORK?

Most observers know that it did not work:
a. Because all went perfectly;
b. Because the methods that were used were somehow scientific;
c. Because of "magic"; or
d. Because of super-human skills.

All may have worked out the way that it did due to luck. This author's guess is, however, that luck, combined with the following, allowed success to be achieved and at least one life to be spared. It is suggested that the reader consider the application of relevant factors to their own setting. Some may be more obvious than others:
- Perseverance
- Procedures
- Voice quality
- Identifying with a human need
- Reading the signs
- Team involvement
- Time, after starting to intervene
- Increasing pressure
- Calculating responses
- Winning attitude
- Going for a "win-win"
- Intelligence utilization
- Letting the victim know that his feelings were heard and understood
- Noting his investment in other parts of his life, e.g., Family, kitten, mission
- Knowledge of his psychological status
- Letting him know that he was not alone
- Persistence in not leaving until the victim was safe
- Care for the victim after he came out
- Making promises that could be kept
- Sowing seeds of doubt
- Accepting his concessions
- Taking his problems seriously
- Taking our problems and personal needs seriously
- Caring for each member of our team
- Inner confidence that we could make it happen
- Good leadership
- Team-team cooperation
- Determination
- Wearing down the victim

And, maybe a little more luck.

CONCLUSION

Remember: Good luck is usually the result of careful planning. And, that the above, perhaps with some modification, is useful in any type of negotiations, bargaining, or crisis intervention where the stakes are high.

RELATED RESOURCES

Greenstone, J. L., & Leviton, S. C. (2002). *The elements of crisis intervention: Crises and how to respond to them* (2nd ed.). Brooks/Cole.

Greenstone, J. L. (2005). *The elements of police hostage and crisis negotiations: Critical incidents and how to respond to them.* The Haworth Press.

Leviton, S. C., & Greenstone, J. L. (1997). *Elements of mediation.* Brooks/Cole.

Crisis Management for Mediators: The Unrecognized Elements

Mediators and negotiators may assume incorrectly that because disputants intellectually select mediation as their means of conflict resolution that it must follow that they have left their innermost feelings at the threshold of the mediation room. To the contrary, the individual's perception of his/her world will enter the mediation session and must be understood by the mediator. Without this appreciation of the client's perception of reality, the mediator cannot effectively deal with the behavior of the disputants. Here we will address the need for awareness of the potential for, and the prevention of, crises within the mediation process, and for appropriate intervention if prevention did not occur, and crisis behavior is exhibited. Such intervention may allow the mediation to go forward effectively.

It is not unusual that persons deciding to be mediators enter this field without adequate appreciation for the risks and stressors involved therein. This can be seen as the "coffee-klatch" mentality that is pervasive when it is assumed that those coming for mediation come to discuss their dispute in a calm and reasonable manner. While it is true that mediation stresses the need to handle disputes in this manner in order to achieve equitable results, it is often unrecognized that, because much emotion has often preceded the mediation, tension is often very high. Those coming to the mediator for help may be on the verge of experiencing crisis in their lives, will experience crisis after the mediation is complete. Because this seems to be so, Crisis Intervention training, the unrecognized elements, should be part of all training given to mediators.

DEFINITION OF A CRISIS

Crisis occurs when unusual stress in a person's life renders him unable to cope with the world utilizing those personal mechanisms normally available to him. Crisis Intervention is the effective intrusion into that person's life in order to defuse a potentially disastrous situation before physical and or emotional destruction results or is exacerbated.

The potential stress and tension may be at maximum levels before, during, or immediately following a mediation session. At these times, the client may experience extreme feeling of fear, anger, grief, hostility, helplessness, hopelessness, and or alienation from his or her self-concept, family, and society. He may experience a pervasive sense of anxiety which produces disorganization, and chaotic thinking. The person may feel overwhelmed and immobilized. At this point, the client will look to the mediator to provide structure in a world that seems to be falling apart. The mediator is often required by circumstances to take emotional control until the client can restore his or her own coping mechanisms and regain self-control. To the same degree that it is vital to stop bleeding from an artery or a vein to save the life of an accident victim, so it is equally vital to realize that people bleed emotionally also. If this emotional wound is not given immediate and effective attention, emotional scarring and even death may occur. It is at this point that the mediator's role is broadened to include Crisis Intervention.

The mediator's success as a crisis intervener will determine if the mediation process can continue. Until the crisis is past, the mediation cannot continue. The emphasis of Crisis Intervention is on immediate response rather than on short or long-term counseling. The goal of the mediator in this context is to (a) reduce emotional trauma and (b) to return the client to precrisis levels of functioning. Often an uncomfortable role for the mediator due to lack of training and preparation, it is nonetheless a vital role in determining the eventual success of the primary process. Therefore, awareness of the need, and for training in the process of intervention, must be considered as important to the training of the mediator as the writing of contracts or the settling of points at issue.

MEDIATION, CRISIS INTERVENTION, AND PSYCHOTHERAPY

According to Richard Evarts in 1983, Mediation is the intervention of a neutral third party, who, intervening at the request of the parties, assists the parties at dispute in finding their own way out of the dispute on the basis of equity through consensus.

Crisis Intervention is the immediate, timely, and skillful intrusion into a person's life, at that time in that person's life when the stress that the person may be experiencing is too great to be handled and managed through this person's usual coping mechanisms, in order to defuse the potentially destructive effects of the unusual stress and to return the person in crisis to levels of precrisis functioning; Emotional First Aid.

Psychotherapy may be defined in many ways according to the particular theoretical frame of reference of the therapist. Generally, it can be said that the focus of psychotherapy, even short-term therapy, is the resolution of personal problems and personal growth over time. This often involves several sessions over days or weeks and goes beyond current functioning in its scope.

Crisis Intervention focuses on the immediate situation with its goal being that of management and of returning the client to his or her level of precrisis functioning. Psychotherapy goes beyond this point and assists the individual to go beyond where she now is and to achieve even greater growth. Mediation cannot occur or continue in the face of crisis. The very nature of crisis would preclude any attempt on the part of the clients to see options or to problem-solve. Because mediation requires the ability as well as the willingness to seek and to explore alternatives, and because the nature of crisis prevents this, crises must be recognized as they occur in a mediation session, or prevented from occurring in the first place, if the ends of the mediation process are to be met.

HOW A CRISIS DEVELOPS

The Crisis Cube, referred to in previous chapters, represents the processes basic to the development of all crises. While all of us function more or less effectively during our daily lives, at the point when stress increases to the level that usual coping mechanisms are rendered ineffective, crisis occurs. This is the crisis point. The stress necessary for the crisis point to be reached may be caused by a single event, several events happening in a person's life at the same time, or by stressful events occurring serially. Whether one event or more than one event will cause enough stress to create a crisis varies with the individual involved. Each day of our lives, we face trying experiences with reasonable success depending on our abilities, backgrounds, and mental strengths. Differing amounts of stress are necessary to create a crisis depending on how well we have developed our abilities to cope. Moreover, no one is immune to the crisis experience. For some, a single event my create enough stress to produce a lack of structure and hence a crisis. For some, it may take several events to create this overwhelming experience. Either way, when the single, combined, or cumulative stress makes it impossible for the individual to handle life as usual, crisis becomes an inevitable reality.

At the point of crisis, the effectiveness of behavior begins to decline. The resulting behavior is seen as maladaptive in order to distinguish such behavior from mental illness which may resemble such behavior. The major difference here is that if the source of the crisis were to be removed, the crisis would cease. The same behavior representing mental illness would not immediately go away if the source of stress or conflict were removed. Maladaptive behavior is directly related to the immediate crisis and may or may not be representative of additional problems. Persons who are mentally ill may also suffer from crisis; those in crisis may or may not be mentally ill.

THE ROLE OF THE MEDIATOR

The mediator/intervener must attempt to interrupt the line of maladaptive behavior. The more timely and skillful the intervention, the quicker the victim can be helped to recognize and to utilize personal and societal resources, to return to his previous level of functioning, and consequently to be able to continue the mediation process with all necessary faculties. If the line of maladaptive behavior is not interrupted, functioning may continue to deteriorate. If there is any good news in all of this, it is that crises are self-limiting. They will not continue unabated. If the mediator did nothing to intervene, eventually the crisis experienced by the victim/client would cease. The problem with nonintervention is measured in degree of deterioration of functioning. There seems to be an inverse relationship between the timeliness of skillful intervention and the need for psychotherapy or other treatment for the victim subsequent to the management of the crisis. The longer the crisis continues, the greater the likelihood that additional or even on-going treatment will be necessary later. The obverse, obviously, is that if intervention is attempted in a skillful manner, additional harm may not be done. The old therapy training maxim that, "If you don't help them, at least don't hurt them," is not only inapplicable, but is also a fallacy. As a result of the mediator/intervener's contact with the client/victim, the client will be affected or changed in some way. One thing seems very clear: whatever happens, things will not be the same as a result of the intervention whether that intervention is skillful or lacking in effectiveness. If we are able to recognize the potential for crisis, learn how to prevent its advent, and finally be prepared to act should a crisis occur, the mediator can increase the possibility of success within the mediation process itself.

Such prevention, preparation, and available skills can also provide for the increased safety of all parties to the mediation or attendant to the process.

RECOGNITION OF MALADAPTIVE BEHAVIOR

A mediator's effectiveness is strengthened through the identification of those individuals who are about to experience crisis. The person who is prone to crisis can be characterized by several indicators. These include:

1. An alienation from lasting and meaningful personal relationships.
2. An inability to utilize life support systems such as family, friends, and social groups.
3. A difficulty in learning from life experiences so that the individual continues to make the same mistakes that he has made over and over again and which may have potentiated crises in the past.
4. A history of previously experienced crises which have not been effectively resolved.
5. Feelings of low self-esteem and/or a history of emotional disorders.
6. Provocative, impulsive behavior resulting from unresolved inner conflicts.
7. Poor marital relationships.
8. Excessive use of drugs, including alcohol abuse.
9. Marginal income.
10. Lack of regular or fulfilling work.
11. Unusual or frequent physical injuries.
12. Frequent changes of address.

Events Which May Precipitate a Crisis

When evaluating the crisis potential of a disputant, note that there are a number of events which may precipitate crises in an individual's life. Some of these are:

1. Accidents in the home.
2. Automobile accidents with or without injuries.

3. Being arrested, appearing in court or anticipating a mediation session.
4. Changes in a job situation or in income.
5. Changes in school status involving promotion or being held back in school. This can affect either the child involved or the parents.
6. Death of a significant person in one's life.
7. Divorce or separation or any of the attendant circumstances.
8. A delinquency episode.
9. Physical illness, terminal conditions or acute episodes of mental disorders.
10. Actual loss or impending loss of something significant in one's life.

The above lists are not exhaustive. They serve only to provide clues to the mediator in evaluating crisis potential. Any one incident may be sufficient to cause crisis in a person's life. For some, several problems occurring at the same time may be enough. For others, serial events, without management of any of these events, may push the stress level in an individual to crisis proportions. Individuals who seem most crisis-prone are those who are sensitive to relatively minor stressors.

CRISIS RECOGNITION

It should be clear that the effectiveness of the mediator requires an ability to recognize when a crisis is occurring as well as when the potentiality exists. Disputants may indicate crisis in different ways. Some cry out and become obvious about their suffering. Others may withdraw and become depressed. A person in crisis may evidence any of the following mental states reflecting possible crisis and resulting maladaptive behavior. This may be characterized by their verbal as well as behavioral responses:

1. BEWILDERMENT: "I've never felt this way before."
2. DANGER: "I'm so nervous and frightened."
3. IMPASSE: "I feel stuck. Nothing I do seems to help."
4. CONFUSION: "I can't think clearly."
5. DESPERATION: "I've just got to do something."
6. APATHY: "Nothing I do seems to help, so why bother anymore?"
7. HELPLESSNESS: "I can't take care of myself."
8. URGENCY: "I need help now!!"
9. DISCOMFORT: "I feel miserable. I'm restless and unsettled!!"
10. ANGER: "How could this happen to me?!!"

CRISIS INTERVENTION IN MEDIATION

The key to crisis intervention is awareness. Crisis prevention must be part of the mediator's toolbox as well, and requires increased awareness. The responsibilities of the mediator begin before the disputants enter the mediation session. The mediator who has not planned ahead and has buried himself behind the intake file while the clients are stumbling into the room, runs the risk of serious consequence. He or she may have unintentionally created additional stress for all involved by failing to adequately and effectively plan.

OFFICE ARRANGEMENT

The structure of our physical world contributes to increased stress. Once aware of the potential stressors in an office arrangement an alert mediator can eliminate or at least minimize these stressors. What follows is a list of potential environmental stressors within an office:

- Glass offices which do not allow privacy for its occupants.
- Open spaces where doors cannot be closed during times when privacy is needed.
- Lack of windows.
- Insufficient insulation to limit sounds or conversations from another room.
- Artificial or natural lighting that produces glare.
- Inadequate heating or cooling.
- Ringing telephones or other distractions during the session.
- Overstuffed furniture which hampers free movement.
- Too much clutter in the room producing a stifling effect.
- Sharp, hot, dissonant wall colors that can be provocative or anxiety producing.
- Intrusive background music.
- Cigarette, cigar, or pipe smoke, No Smoking Allowed.
- Fumes from disinfectants, furniture polish, or even cologne, perfumes or after shave lotions.
- Inadequate ventilation.
- Inadequate workspace.
- Poorly planned seating arrangement that creates either too much or too little space between clients and mediator.
- Wall treatments, window treatments, or furniture treatments that intrude.
- Inadequate accommodations for the elderly or handicapped.
- Inadequate security within or surrounding the office building.

This list is by no means exhaustive. The reader/mediator is urged to examine his/her own office space and to identify those areas that can exacerbate the stress already being experienced by clients when they enter the room. Such a search will additionally serve to minimize the mediator's own stress.

The time to perform this task is now.

FIELD TRIP THROUGH THE WAITING ROOM

The second step in preventing a crisis is to take a "field trip" through the reception area once the clients have arrived but before they are brought into the mediation room. This field trip can provide invaluable information for assessment purposes. What you see, hear, smell, and/or feel as you observe the clients will offer clues to what is about to happen and about what control you might be required to exert. Is the couple sitting together? Have they chosen to wait in separate rooms?

If children are present, with whom are they seated? Is there interaction? What is the quality of the interaction? Does either of the parties appear unusually anxious? Does either party exhibit maladaptive behavior? Is there discernible hostility? Do you smell alcohol? Do you sense drug abuse from what you observe? Is there a disparity in the way they are dressed that might impact on the equity of power? Do you sense anything unusual that you want to remember for later use? Do you see or sense something that would necessitate a weapons affidavit?

Use the information that you have gathered to set up the mediation room. Consider such things as the shape of the table, the placement of chairs, and the seating arrangement of the parties involved. Also, use the information to balance power and to determine what you want to address in your introduction of the session. You might have to address feelings before you can move to substantive issues. Use the information to determine whether or not you will proceed with the mediation. If you sense that something is wrong, take the necessary time to investigate before deciding to mediate. The field trip can be accomplished quickly if your antenna is well tuned. Probably the mediator's best tool for detecting potential violence or the presence of weapons is his/her own internal communication and sensing capabilities. All of us at one time or another have experienced inklings. These are partial awareness, which is not clear or complete in terms of our central awareness. The successful mediator is one who has developed the use of these sensing devices in the skillful art of negotiating. The mediator who develops the same sensors in the area of personal and client safety will be around long enough to be a successful mediator. Sensing that a husband and wife do not get along may not indicate that any special action on the part of the mediator is needed other than the mediation itself. Conversely, sensing that the actions, stances, and verbalizations may indicate the possibility that one or both of the parties intend to do injury to the other is a real cause for concern on the part of the mediator, and an indicator that quick, definitive and effective action must be taken. Each mediator must know that the potential for violence exists and that the mediation process cannot begin, continue, or culminate until the matters of safety and personal well-being are dealt with.

SEATING THE PARTIES

Parties should be brought in and seated so that the person who is most likely to become violent does not have to pass the other party on his way in. To accomplish this, seat the one least likely to become violent in the chair farthest from the doorway. Then bring in the other party and seat this person closer to the door. A secondary advantage in this is that should the second party be unable or unwilling to remain in the session, he can leave without posing any problems for the mediator or for the other party.

Usually, the mediator should follow the parties into the mediation room. Not only does this avoid having the mediator's back to the client at any time, but also the mediator can view the client from rear, thereby discovering additional information that might be useful from a safety standpoint. We refer to this check as a "visual frisk."

Once the clients have been seated in the mediation room, the mediator will take his place in such way that he can communicate with equal ease to each client and without appearing to show favoritism. The mediator should sit in a comfortable position slightly forward in his chair, with both feet flat on the floor. When using a table, the mediator's hands will normally be on the tabletop in front of him. When not using a table, the mediator's hands will rest comfortably on his knees or on the arms of the chair. It is important that the mediator convey openness and interest through body language. It is also crucial that the mediator be seated in a position offering the greatest flexibility to respond to whatever transpires during the session. Expecting the unexpected means being ready and being able to respond as needed. In the above arrangement, the mediator's hands are in front of him and his legs under him so that movement to interrupt or to correct the situation can be made instantly. If the parties leave their chairs in anger, either at one another or at the mediator, the mediator can also leave his chair quickly without being in a compromising position. A position that is too relaxed, or one in which the mediator's legs are tangled or crossed may not permit the needed response speed. Hands open or in front of the body and on the table will allow the mediator to protect herself if necessary, and also to respond to the hands of the clients should tempers and actions flare.

Crisis is not always exhibited verbally or in hostile, violent actions. It often takes the form of withdrawal or emotional shutting down. A person in crisis during a mediation session may remain physically in the room but emotionally withdraw from the proceedings. This withdrawal might be demonstrated by gradual turning of the shoulders or body away from the table, a blank stare that lasts for a period of time, nonparticipation in the process, a sudden, blanket agreement to anything and everything being suggested, or a flattened effect. The mediator cannot continue without the involvement of both parties. It is the job of the mediator to sense the withdrawal and to attempt to deal with it. Caucusing at this point is often an effective way to help the victim deal with the stressors that precipitated the crisis. Sometimes just reaching out by physically touching the victim's shoulder or arm and speaking in a soothing, reassuring tone can bring the person back to the session without the need for a caucus. Sometimes a simple statement such as "We need you" or "We can't go on without you," will encourage the victim to verbalize his feelings and bring him back to the process.

THE OPENING STATEMENT

In the opening statement the mediator must take temporary control of the argument, thus creating a sense of security for his clients. He or she must establish rapport, confidence, and trust with his clients. She must set the stage, detail the process agenda, and introduce the concept of mediation. Depending on what he sensed in observation during his field trip he might spend some time addressing the stress often associated with conflict resolution and feelings associated with separation or impending loss. Often the acknowledgment by the mediator of the presence of these feelings will serve to reduce the trauma being experienced. Additionally, if the mediator is perceived as being in control of the process, the stress will be minimized.

INTERVENTION

Effective Crisis Intervention consists of five major components. These are:
1. Immediacy
2. Control

3. Assessment
4. Disposition
5. Referral and Follow-up

Immediacy

Intervention must be skillfully begun at the moment that it is determined that a crisis situation is present. The mediator/intervener must attempt to relieve anxiety, prevent further disoriented and insure that the disputant/sufferer does not harm herself and/or others.

Control

Because the victim of a crisis is not totally in control of his life at the time of crisis, the mediator/intervener must assume control of the situation. The sufferer is not able to see alternatives to the present situation or to utilize personal and social resources. During this time, the intervener serves as the needed source of structure and stability which can and must provide the needed support.

Assessment

To be effective as an intervener, the mediator must make a quick and accurate assessment of the crisis and its specific causes. This must be done on the spot and will focus on the immediate history of the victim rather than on extensive information about the past. It is from this assessment that the next step can be taken most efficiently.

Disposition

Once the mediator understands something about the immediate causes of the crisis, attempts are then made to assist the sufferer to reinstate his or her own coping abilities. The mediator may accomplish this by merely providing a listening point for the victim or may find it necessary to become more active and involved. Crisis Intervention actively assists the sufferer to identify and to mobilize personal resources as well as those of family and friends. Even though immediate solutions may not be available to the person in crisis, the intervener always holds out the possibility and the hope that it is possible to manage the current situation and that the victim can do it, at first with needed help and then on her own. When effective intervention occurs and the parties can resume mediation, there is an increased receptivity to exploring options, to creativity in thinking and to problem solving.

Referral and Follow-Up

The final step of intervention involves assisting the victims of crisis to obtain additional, ongoing assistance if such care is needed. The degree to which such a referral is necessary is related to the effectiveness of the intervention. The degree to which such a referral will be accepted and acted upon by the victim is also dependent on the skill with which the initial assistance was given.

GUIDELINES FOR EFFECTIVE INTERVENTION

1. Attempt to limit the personal disorganization that the victim is expressing by calming him and relieving as much of the anxiety and stress as possible.
2. If possible, remove the victim from the crisis situation and provide a place for her to relax and compose herself.
3. Always remain confident and be firm and reasonable.
4. Do not agree or disagree with the victim. The way he perceives the world at this time in his life is real for him.
5. Encourage family members to be with the sufferer if appropriate. Some family members may be disruptive or in crisis themselves. The mediator must assess the potential helpfulness of significant others before bringing them into contact with the crisis victim.
6. Encourage the victim to relax and to tell what is troubling him.
7. Help the victim to see the crisis as temporary rather than chronic. Recovery is usually quicker when the problems are viewed in this way rather than as an unsolvable situation which may never be fully managed.
8. Allow the victim to speak freely and to ventilate his feelings.
9. In a multiple victim situation, allow each person to speak without interruption by the other parties. Establish ground rules immediately and insist that they be followed.
10. Avoid unnecessary interruptions while the sufferer is speaking.
11. Build a sense of structure to which the sufferer can relate as you talk with her. In crisis, she may see life as chaotic and out of her control. The more she understands the nature of her crisis experience and the more quickly she can secure a sense of structure for herself, the more quickly she will recover and be able to function effectively.
12. Avoid arguing with the person in crisis. There are many ways of viewing a situation. The role of the mediator/intervener is to help direct the problem-solving, not to judge or to badger.

GUIDELINES FOR HANDLING HOSTILITY AND HOSTILE GESTURES

1. Handle the problems of hostility by preventing them from happening in the first place.
2. Handle physical violence by immediate separation of the parties.
3. Learn to attend to one's own senses in determining impending crisis in a mediation session.
4. Always remain in firm control.
5. Act and remember that all actions taken must be warranted, effective, clear and knowledgeable.
6. Pay attention to the physical arrangement of the mediation room to provide the best alternatives for handling hostility.
7. Enforce all ground rules.
8. Allow the expressions of hostile feelings in a mediation session.
9. At all times, be aware of the potential for violence and hostility in a mediation session.
10. Convey control, concern, sensitivity, effectiveness, warmth and integrity in posture, verbal presentations and physical and psychological attitudes.

11. Demonstrate that the hostility of one client will be handled without intercession of the other client.
12. Terminate the mediation session at the point when it becomes clear that progress is not possible because of hostility or potential hostile actions. This is done to salvage the possibility of future negotiations.
13. Use firmness in the face of hostility.
14. Realize that hostility can be a sign of impending crisis in the life of the disputant.
15. Recognize and confront hostile body language in a disputant constructively.
16. Prevent guns, knives, and other weapons from being brought into the mediation session and causing injury.
17. Provide for security of mediation offices and agencies, and establish standing operating procedures with law enforcement and paramedical agencies.
18. Consider a "buddy system" for mediators to enable them to respond to and to assist each other when needed. This is especially important whenever mediation takes place after usual business hours or when the building is closed.
19. Provide clear explanations of security arrangements in potentially volatile situation to curtail future problems.
20. It has been said that in situations of hostility or violence that there is no such thing as a fair fight. The mediator/intervener must prepare himself with skills, protective measures, knowledge and back-up support in advance, and be prepared to use them.

MEDIATOR SAFETY GUIDELINES

1. Do not take the possibility of weapons lightly.
2. Plan in advance for your personal safety and for the safety of clients.
3. Check the arrangement of your office or mediation room. Be sure that all safety factors are accounted for before beginning a mediation session.
4. When greeting your clients, notice anything strange or unusual about their words, actions or dress. Train yourself to sense their emotional state and to learn to understand their implications.
5. Learn to read body language.
6. The mediator should avoid having her back to her clients, especially those who are suspected of having weapons or those who may erupt violently.
7. Enter the mediation room behind clients.
8. Have clients sit with their back in the direction of the door through which they will go when they leave.
9. Remove any potential weapons from the mediation room and from the table or desk used for mediation prior to bringing in the parties.
10. Seat clients so that the potentially violent person does not have to pass the other party when entering the room.
11. Use the table or desk as a barrier between mediator and client or between client and client when needed.
12. Sit in such a manner that openness and interest is conveyed and that the ability to react quickly to outbreaks of violence is not hampered.
13. Attempt to keep the parties seated during the mediation session.

14. Discuss suspected weapons with each party separately. Use direct, precise, and non-euphemistic approach.
15. Require weapons affidavit if necessary. This affidavit is a written statement by the disputants that they have no weapons, and will bring no weapons into the mediation room. (Evarts et al., 1992, p.122)
16. Require personal searches when necessary.
17. Require that all weapons either be surrendered or locked in the trunk of the client's car.
18. Unload all weapons confiscated.
19. Return weapons as requested, or turn them over to local law enforcement agency.
20. Take seriously your safety and the safety of your clients. Refuse to mediate if your concerns about safety are not satisfied.

RETURNING TO MEDIATION

Disputants seek out mediation in an attempt to settle differences without the usual hassles of the court. Because of the novelty of this approach, it is of paramount importance that the client can trust the system. Part of that trust is built by the skillful mediator assisting them in solving their own problems in an equitable way. Another part of that trust involves the mediator's ability to recognize when other problems must be handled before mediation can begin or continue. Such problems are those involving severe stress and tension often present in conjunction with the mediation issues. To that extent, the mediator must be trained to recognize and to respond to severe emotional trauma as it occurs within this context. The greater the storehouse of resources, the more effective will be the mediator/intervener. The Crisis Intervention pioneer, Dr. Edward S. Rosenbluh said it best when he reminded us that, "To be helpful, we must be effective" (Greenstone & Leviton, 1987).

REFERENCES AND READINGS

Evarts, R., Greenstone, J. L., Kirkpatrick, G., & Leviton, S. C. (1983, 1992). *Winning through accommodation: The mediator's handbook*. Kendall-Hunt.

Greenstone, J. L., & Leviton, S. C. (1979). *Crisis intervener's handbook* (Vol. 1). Crisis Management Workshops.

Greenstone, J. L., & Leviton, S. (1987, September). Crisis management for mediators in high stress, high risk, potentially violent situations. *Mediation Quarterly, 2*(1), 10–15.

Greenstone, J. L., & Leviton, S. C. (1992, 2002). *Elements of crisis intervention: Crises and how to respond to them* (2nd ed.). Brooks/Cole.

Leviton, S. C., & Greenstone, J. L. (1997). *Elements of mediation*. Brooks/Cole.

Communicating Effectively for Successful Negotiations and Crisis Intervention

Regardless of the negotiation situation or immediate need for these skills, the keys to success are the skills of the negotiator or intervener to effectively communicate. Little else matters if communications are not established, maintained, and utilized in such a way that management of the instant situation becomes possible. Most negotiators think that they are effective communicators. Some are. Many are not. Communications must be practiced repeatedly to assure proficiency. This provides the rudiments of the skills needed for success in the field.

Before a problem can be managed, the intervener must determine what the problem is. Often, more than one problem may be present in a situation. When this occurs, the following six questions may be asked to determine the priority for intervention.
1. Which problem is of most immediate concern?
2. Which problem would prove most damaging if not treated immediately?
3. Which problem can be most quickly resolved?
4. Which problem must be dealt with first before others may be handled?
5. What resources for handling problems are available?
6. What barriers and obstacles will hinder problem solving? (Rosenbluh, 1981)

Although it is necessary to answer all the preceding questions, if the intervener is to help manage the victim's crisis, the intervener must be able to acquire the needed information quickly and accurately. This means that the intervener must listen actively to the victim's total message and give the victim full concentration and undivided attention. Further, the intervener must sift through the person's words to gain information and insight into the victim's problems and views on those problems.

Every communication contains three messages: a content message, a feeling message, and a meaning message. The content message provides information about what the sender believes, thinks, or perceives the situation to be. The feeling message conveys the nature and intensity of the sender's emotion about the situation. The meaning message concerns the behavior or situation that has generated the feeling. Usually the person who sends the communication implies, rather than explicitly states, the behavior or situation that creates the feeling. The intervener must try to infer what the behavior or situation is.

Rosenbluh (1981) explained that when another person communicates with you, distortion can occur in three areas:
1. What the other person means to say
2. What the other person actually says
3. What you, as the intervener, believe you hear

The present discussion is concerned with what interveners think they hear. The key to effective listening is accurately hearing the feeling and meaning behind the content of communication. The skill discussed here is *empathy*. Empathy is one's ability to enter the other person's world and to reflect this understanding to the person. Empathy, as Rosenbluh (1981) pointed out, contains two elements:
- *Passive:* the ability to hear the facts contained in the words and the feelings contained in the other person's body language, intensity, and tone.
- *Active:* the ability to reflect this understanding to the other person in a manner that generates warmth, trust, and a willingness to be open.

CLARIFICATION

Sometimes a victim or disputant will make a statement that the intervener does not fully understand. At other times, the victim's words and nonverbal behavior may not agree. At that point the intervener focuses on the misunderstanding and tries to clarify the statement in question before continuing with the interview. Interveners must never assume that they understand what the victim means. Two people can witness the same event and describe it very differently. Conversely, two people can have very different experiences and relate these experiences similarly. Interveners must be sure they know precisely what the victim is talking about. To do so, the intervener must press the sufferer to clarify any vague or ambiguous statements. An intervener cannot work effectively with a victim unless both the intervener and the victim are talking about the same crisis.

Clarification Techniques

Interveners can use the following four techniques to help victims clarify their statements:

1. *Repeating key words.* Using this technique, the intervener repeats key words or phrases that the victim uses and that the intervener does not clearly understand. By emphasizing a certain word or phrase, the intervener focuses attention on a particular thought or feeling and encourages the victim to explain it in more detail.

   For example:
   > **Victim:** I feel helpless when I think of all these bills ... and I have no income.
   > **Intervener:** Helpless?
   > **Victim:** I just don't care anymore. I feel so isolated and depressed.
   > **Intervener:** You don't care anymore? or You feel isolated? or You feel depressed?

   Interveners should use this technique carefully. When used too frequently, repeating what the person just said can sound like a gimmick. The intervener's parroting may make the victim distrustful and uneasy. Repetition is, however, a useful tool when used cautiously.

2. *Restatement.* The intervener can rephrase the victim's statements in such a way that the person is encouraged to clarify what was said.

   For example:
   Victim: I'm behind in all my bills, and my father, who is a local banker, told me it was embarrassing him because my creditors have been calling him, too.
   Intervener: So, you're having financial problems, and you are feeling heavy family pressure to find a solution.

   When an intervener uses restatement, the victim will often respond by talking about the most pressing area of concern. Using restatement also encourages the victim to explain the situation in more detail. This additional information will help the intervener understand what the victim is thinking and feeling.

3. *Direct method.* Perhaps the most direct method of eliciting information is for interveners to admit that they are confused or puzzled about the victim's statement and to ask the victim for clarification so that better understanding will result. This technique has the added advantage of letting the victim know that the intervener is interested in what is being said. Additionally, this kind of communication helps to build trust in the intervener-victim relationship.

4. *Asking questions.* An intervener can obtain a clearer idea of the other person's meaning simply by asking questions. When interveners want more information, they can ask "open" questions. To pinpoint specific items, interveners can ask "closed" questions. A *closed question* can be answered with a simple "yes" or "no." An *open question* allows for amplification of meaning by the respondent.

   For example:
   Victim: I don't know what my husband is talking about.
   Intervener: What does he say that you don't understand? [open question]
   Victim: All I want is the best for my child. I am so miserable and feel so defeated that I want to kill myself.
   Intervener: How would killing yourself help your child? [open question] or Do you have a suicide plan in mind? [closed question]

   The closed-question technique is particularly useful when an intervener is sure of what additional information is needed.

Identifying the victim's concerns during the assessment and attempting to clarify the real issues involved help both the victim and the intervener to better understand the total situation that must be dealt with.

USING QUESTIONS EFFECTIVELY

Asking questions to obtain accurate information in an intervention is both necessary and helpful. The intervener must be careful, however, to pace the questions carefully so as not to increase the victim's stress level. Bombarding victims with a series of questions could confuse and frustrate them. Also, allow enough time for the victim to answer. Ask the questions in a nonthreatening, not accusatory tone.

DEALING WITH SILENCE

The intervener should know how to use silence during an intervention. For some interveners, silence is deadly. It may seem as if nothing is happening, and this can cause the intervener great discomfort. Interveners should handle silence by being silent themselves while observing the victim's behavior and what the victim is *not* saying.

RESPONDING EFFECTIVELY

Responding to another person's feelings is a delicate process. In gathering information from victims, the intervener must handle the victims' feelings with care and concern. If the intervener wants a victim to continue talking about facts pertinent to the problem, the intervener cannot judge, use logic, or give advice. The individual's feelings must be legitimized. The following example illustrates ineffective response to emotions:

Boy: I can't stand my father. He's been mean to me all of my life.
Intervener: That's unfair. What would you do if anything happened to him? You'd feel awful to have said things like that.

In this instance, communication has been effectively shut off. The intervener has passed judgment and shamed the boy instead of seeking the root of the hostility.

GUIDELINES FOR EFFECTIVE COMMUNICATIONS IN CRISES

1. **Listen effectively.**
   - Fully hear what the other person is saying. Maintain eye contact if possible.
   - Let the other person talk freely.
   - Try to comprehend what the other person is saying.
   - Listen for both feelings and content.
   - Paraphrase the other's statements to gain clarification.
   - Ask for clarification when necessary.
   - Don't let your own feelings get in the way of understanding what the other person is trying to say.
2. **Respond descriptively.**
   - Don't be evaluative in your response; evaluative statements tend to elicit defensiveness.
   - Keep in mind that "rightness" or "wrongness" may not be the issue.
   - Remember, effective communication is not a contest; a "win or lose" mentality is inappropriate.
   - Learn all you can about the other person's thoughts and feelings.
   - Let the other person know some things about you.
   - Use descriptive statements and reveal your reactions to the other person.
3. **Use your own feelings.**
   - Remember that feelings are important in communicating and that they are always present.
   - Practice expressing your feelings.

- Take responsibility for your feelings.
- Use "I" messages rather than "you" messages; CC113 messages reduce threat to the other person.
- Use descriptive statements that contain feelings.
- Be clear and specific about your feelings.

4. **Assess needs.**
   - Consider the needs of all involved.
   - Address issues over which the victim has actual control.
   - Avoid being judgmental and critical; avoid preaching.
5. **Make timely responses.**
   - Deliver responses at the time they are most important.
   - Deliver responses as soon as possible after the behavior that requires response.
   - Do not store up old concerns for later discussion.
     - Do not use old or saved concerns as a weapon.
     - Assess whether the other person is ready to handle your responses at this time.
     - Consider delaying responses on sensitive issues until you are in a more appropriate setting.
     - Discuss emotional issues in private.
     - Practice communication skills for greatest effectiveness.

LISTENING

During conversations with victims, keep in mind the following items about the importance of listening:
1. Listening is basic to successful communications.
2. Listening requires responsiveness.
3. Listening enables the listener to know more about the speaker.
4. Listening encourages expression.
5. Listening allows exploration of both feelings and content.
6. Listening helps establish trust between the parties.
7. Listening allows greater accuracy of communication.
8. Listening requires practice and is not always easy to learn.
9. Listening includes listening for content, feelings, and point of view.
10. Listening lets the speaker relax.
11. Attitudes and feelings may be conveyed nonverbally.

When you listen, remember to do the following:
1. Attend to verbal content.
2. Attend to nonverbal cues.
3. Hear and observe.
4. Attend to the feelings expressed by the speaker.
5. Don't think about other things when you are listening to someone.
6. Don't listen with only "half an ear."
7. Become attuned to the speaker's verbal and nonverbal messages.

8. Note any extra emphasis the speaker places on certain words.
9. Notice the speaker's speech patterns and recurring themes.

NONVERBAL COMMUNICATIONS

The following are examples of nonverbal acts a speaker may use to communicate:
- Sighing
- Flipping through papers
- Wincing
- Looking around, up, or down
- Smoking
- Chewing gum
- Yawning
- Tapping a finger or foot
- Frowning
- Displaying nervousness
- Avoiding eye contact
- Saying nothing
- Making jerky gestures
- Dressing sloppily
- Blinking rapidly
- Constantly looking at a clock or watch
- Showing favoritism
- Acting bored
- Being drunk

Certain nonverbal cues can indicate a specific attitude. Some examples follow.

Nonverbal cues that may indicate openness:
- Uncrossed legs
- Open hands
- Unbuttoned coat, or unbuttoning the coat
- Hands spread apart
- Palms up
- Leaning forward

Nonverbal cues that may indicate defensiveness:
- Fists closed
- Arms crossed in front of individual
- Legs crossed
- One leg over the chair arm

Nonverbal cues that may indicate cooperation:
- Opening coat
- Tilted head
- Sitting on the edge of a chair
- Eye contact
- Handtoface gestures
- Leaning forward

Nonverbal cues that may indicate evaluating:
- Head tilted
- Chin stroking
- Looking over glasses
- Pacing
- Pinching the bridge of the nose

Nonverbal cues that may indicate readiness:
- Hands on hips
- Leaning forward
- Confident speech
- Moving closer to the other person

Nonverbal cues that may indicate suspicion:
- Lack of eye contact
- Glancing sideways at the other person
- Body apparently pointed toward exit from area
- Touching the bridge of the nose
- Rubbing the *ears*
- Rubbing the eyes

Nonverbal cues that may indicate confidence:
- Elevating oneself by sitting on a higher chair or standing on a platform
- Finger "steepling"
- Hands clasped behind the back
- Feet on a desk or table
- Leaning on an object
- Clucking sound
- Leaning back, with both hands supporting the neck

REFERENCES

Greenstone, J. L., & Leviton, S. C. (2002). *Elements of crisis intervention: Crises and how to respond to them* (2nd ed.). Brooks/Cole.

Greenstone, J. L. (2004, October). *The elements of police hostage and crisis negotiations: Critical incidents and how to respond to them.* The Haworth Press.

Rosenbluh, E. S. (1981). *Emotional first aid: Crisis intervention and counseling.* Behavioral Health Services.

A Practical Guide for All Types of Negotiation: A Look at 150 Laws of Negotiations

"The laws of hostage and crisis negotiations?" (Greenstone, 2005). Are these really laws? Or, better put, are they significant apothegms intended to remind of vital elements or to help remember specific procedures when under the stress of negotiations? None of the Laws of Hostage and Crisis Negotiations are absolute. Neither are the "laws" intended just for police interactions. Most are universally applicable. They are the collective wisdom of many who have worked and labored in this particular vineyard. Some are as old as the hills; some are made up; some are of recent origin given the growth and complexity of our field. If the novice were to study each of the laws and gain some understanding of their roots and meanings, these novices would probably have completed an entire course in negotiations minus the practical experiences often provided. Read them. Apply them. Heed them. And, while some of the laws, or apothegms, are applicable in other areas of life, they are certainly applicable in this particular endeavor, the goal of which is to save life and to manage conflict.

THE "LAWS"

1. Reason rather than react.
2. Innovate, adapt, and prevail.
3. Contain, isolate, evaluate, negotiate; evaluate, negotiate; evaluate, negotiate.
4. Never water barren trees.
5. When you find yourself in a circle, go for the feelings.
6. If your gut says "no," don't go.
7. Develop your skills so that mistakes are what other people make.
8. Maximize the utilization of available resources.
9. Negotiate for as long as a life is worth.
10. Negotiators don't command, and commanders don't negotiate.
11. Add nothing for, "What it's worth."
12. Knowing what to stay out of is as important as knowing what to get in to.
13. Care about your other negotiators. Support each other.
14. Develop arrows for your quiver.
15. Seek to understand, then to be understood. (Covey)

16. Speak softly and carry big shtick.
17. Walk like you fight; fight like you walk.
18. If the train is not going where you want to go, get off.
19. To assume anything makes an "Ass" of "You" and "Me."
20. Don't hate your enemies. It will cloud your judgment.
21. Learn to be comfortable being uncomfortable.
22. Silence is golden. Learn to shut up and strike gold.
23. Never retreat. Just attack in a different direction.
24. The only failure is nonresolution or nonmanagement.
25. Negotiations is a team effort; not an individual event.
26. Individuals make the best team players.
27. Pass the buck regularly.
28. All things come to those who wait if they work like hell while they wait.
29. Just because they're crazy doesn't mean they're stupid.
30. Bumbling isn't always bad.
31. Acceptance does not imply agreement.
32. Shotguns scatter; precision matters.
33. Win the mind; win the day.
34. Change behavior. Attitudes will follow.
35. Most people live in their gut.
36. Never meet force head-on.
37. Negotiators have one mouth and two ears. The operational implications are obvious.
38. "It is a wise man who uses words before resorting to arms." (Terrence Publius)
39. "…men, when they receive good from whence they expect evil, feel all the more indebted to their benefactor…" (Machiavelli, "The Prince")
40. Semper Ubi Sub Ubi.
41. "I am not what I think I am. I am not what you think I am. I am what I think you think I am."(George Herbert Mead, Social Psychologist)
42. "In order to remain helpful, we must remain effective." (Dr. Edward S. Rosenbluh, 1975)
43. Negotiations is not a "wait and see" option.
44. Downtime is work-time.
45. Train as if your life and the lives of others depended on it; someday it will.
46. The more you know, the more you have.
47. Something for nothing has little value.
48. If at first you don't succeed, the hell with it.
49. Successful negotiations require some common sense and a lot of uncommon sense.
50. Needs + Wants + Needs = Success
51. Don't sell used cars.
52. Many have the time to do it over; the negotiator must do it right the first time.
53. The mark of the professional is the condition and availability of his/her tools.
54. Nothing works all the time with all people.
55. Gather intelligence intelligently.

56. Winning isn't everything; it's the only thing.
57. There is no such thing as a good loser.
58. Suicide has nothing to do with death.
59. The buck stops somewhere else.
60. Don't bullshit a bullshitter.
61. Avoid lying.
62. If you do lie, don't get caught.
63. Lie only about big things; never about little things.
64. Negotiators seldom lie. They just engage in tactical expressions.
65. Deliver what you promise.
66. Perception is in the eye of the beholder.
67. Some things are not as easy as they seem; some are.
68. Ask them to come out.
69. Speak of "suicide."
70. Words are the lifeblood of the negotiator.
71. Negotiators can ill-afford the imprecision of language.
72. Jargon is spoken by jargs.
73. Control by not controlling.
74. Courtesy costs you nothing.
75. Determine, diagnose, dispose.
76. Plan well. Then, plan again.
77. The major virtue in telling the truth is that you don't have to remember what you've said. (Personal Communications, My mother of blessed memory)
78. Negotiators are real cops, too.
79. Negotiations are like crock-pot cooking; it takes time.
80. "Good will" is illusive.
81. First of all, do no harm.
82. No matter how thin you make your pancakes, they always have two sides.
83. Persons will never be left the same as you found them.
84. Hostages deserve our concern.
85. Bad guys are people, too.
86. Crazy people are doing the best that they can.
87. "Deadlines are the sand-traps on the golf course of life." (Personal Communications, Snoopy by Schultz)
88. It is better to take your time than to take a life.
89. Slow everything down.
90. Visualize a successful resolution.
91. Have a reason.
92. Don't let your opening be your closing.
93. Make haste slowly.
94. Buck-passing is an art form.
95. Be an agent of reality.
96. Rapport unlocks the door.

97. A negotiator must be: hard of hearing; not too smart; somewhat of a bumbler; a little ignorant; unexciting; and "normal" as well.
98. Boring is good.
99. Cover your assets.
100. Demands are the basis of bargaining.
101. Sow the seeds of doubt and risk.
102. Deal only with the problems; and everything is a problem.
103. Nothing is so important as that which is trivial.
104. Think "intell."
105. Beware of the "spiral of excitement."
106. No to "No."
107. A negotiated resolution can only occur between two perceived equals.
108. Difficult negotiations take a while; miracles take a little longer.
109. Don't shoot with bullets.
110. Don't promise if you can't do it.
111. The Goldilocks rule: "It can't be too hot or too cold; it can't be too much or too little; it must be just right." (Personal Communications, George McGowan)
112. If you don't understand, don't say that you do.
113. Crystallize your objective.
114. Create social expectations.
115. Concentrate on "now," not on "next."
116. "What if" it.
117. Prove life.
118. Bank agreements.
119. Build the positive. Level the negative.
120. Hot wash up always.
121. Don't surrender to surrenders.
122. Use deaf and dumb interpreters.
123. Invest in emotions.
124. Check the time.
125. Imperturbability is boring.
126. Train to win; prepare to lose.
127. Be soft on people; hard on problems.(Personal Communications, Roger Fisher)
128. Go for interests; avoid positions.
129. Seek alternatives.
130. Use objective standards.
131. Don't call me, I'll call you.
132. Try to resolve each situation; acknowledge that you may not resolve every situation.
133. Hear what isn't being said.
134. Luck = Preparation + Opportunity.
135. You can go anywhere if you have the time.
136. Don't judge if you feel no compassion.

137. Trust in God but tie your camel tight.
138. Time will dispose of the trivial.
139. Negotiators are persons who make waves, and then convince the taker that they are the only ones who can save the ship.
140. It's not over until it's over.
141. Plan your surrender plan.
142. Hook 'em hard.
143. You can learn many good things from a bad situation.
144. You must do more than "talk the talk." You must know how to "walk the walk."
145. Keep your friends close; keep your mayo jar even closer.
146. Keep breathing.
147. Divert force.
148. Use the subject's strength against them.
149. Know when the sky is falling; and when it isn't.
150. Persistence is omnipotent.

REFERENCES

Greenstone, J. L. (2005). *The elements of police hostage and crisis negotiations: Critical incidents and how to respond to them.* The Haworth Press.

Ethical Negotiating: Negotiating Ethically

Ethical negotiating? Is this the all-time oxymoron? Ethical? Legal? Moral? Ethical v. Legal; Ethical v. Moral; Legal v. moral; moral v. ethical. Can a behavior be ethical and not legal? Legal but not ethical? Can a behavior be ethical and not moral? Moral but not ethical? Can a behavior be legal and not moral? Moral but not legal? Are these separate issues or are they really all the same? How do you know? Why might you need to know? Isn't everything fair in love, war and negotiations? Can a negotiator be ethical and still be an effective negotiator? Must a negotiator be ethical to be an effective negotiator? How do you arrive at an ethical decision? From where do morals derive? What is the role of the law in society? While here we cannot begin to answer all of these questions, we will attempt to address some of the issues of ethical behavior and ethical decision making. As well, it is hoped that the unanswered questions will foster additional thought.

REASONED DELIBERATION

Ethics may involve morality. They may even involve legalities (Evarts, Greenstone, et al., 1984). But without a doubt, ethics is about reasoned deliberation. The ethicist David Isch (2005) says, "The practice of ethics is the systematic reasoned deliberation regarding values and the appropriateness of choices that are made in the ever-changing circumstances of personal and organizational life with the goal of fostering a full, good and noble existence." He continues that, "Ethics is reasoned conversation in a spirit of engagement about values and choices that identifies and analyzes the underlying presuppositions and the features that give rise to the matters under consideration." Such deliberation may occur while facing legal and or moral concerns or as standalone considerations. Either way, while some might argue that these concepts are the same, ethical action requires that reasoned deliberation take place regardless of the other concerns or the eventual decision (Greenstone, 2009). The International Association of Chiefs of Police (IACP, 2012) defines ethics as, "…the high standards of personal conduct. It consists of attributes such as honesty, impartiality, trustworthiness, and abiding laws, regulations and procedures. It includes not abusing the system nor using the position of authority for personal gain; not bending rules or otherwise trying to beat the system by tampering with evidence, slanting reports, providing inaccurate testimony; not engaging in assaultive or violent conduct; and not engaging in illegal or immoral activities, either on or off duty." This makes ethics a matter of current concern and related to specific situations or specific issues. Such an approach to reasoned deliberation then suggests and proposes some of the following examples when approaching meaningful and effective negotiations (Hartsell & Bernstein, 2008).

SOME GUIDELINES FOR ETHICAL REASONING

1. Prepare for the instant negotiations depending on what is needed for this situation regardless of what you may have done in previous or similar situations.
2. Regard each party, opponent or adversary in the negotiations from the standpoint of what is the reasoned response regardless of other feelings or concerns. For example, a negotiator may feel that the other party has acted immorally or illegally. Regardless, the concern of the negotiator must be what is the best approach to this person rather than what might be punitive. While one might feel morally justified in punitive action, such action may not be ethically sound.
3. Be aware of one's own agenda when preparing for or when undertaking negotiations. Some agendas may be reasoned to be ethical under the circumstances, others not. Without an awareness of the presence of personal agendas, actions may be taken without due understanding and deliberations.
4. Do not short circuit negotiation attempts because you may not have the time to do it correctly. If you are not able to negotiate, let someone else who is equally or better trained take your place. To paraphrase that famous philosopher Kenny Rogers who once said, "You got to know when to hold them and know when to fold them, know when to walk away, and know when to run."
5. If you do not know how to handle a situation, ask for help and get someone involved who does know (Greenstone & Leviton, 2011).
6. Consider your actions carefully. Never put anything into the mix for, "What it's worth."
7. Ask questions cogently.
8. Listen carefully.
9. Observe keenly.
10. Think deeply (Groopman, 2008).
11. Consider truth-telling seriously. For example, it may be immoral to lie. Is a lie ever ethical? What would your reasoned deliberation dictate? As some negotiators may be trained, is it really ethical to lie about large things even though you do not lie about smaller things? (Greenstone, 2005, 2008).
12. Consider your ethical responsibility to level the negotiations playing field or to keep it unlevel, or to give the illusion of levelness. What to do is dictated by the instant situation, what might be most effective to ensure resolution, the skills of the negotiator, and by the evaluation of those involved.

13. Understand and respect relevant confidentiality.
14. Reason rather than react.
15. Care about your team members. Support them as necessary (Greenstone, 2008).
16. Acceptance does not imply agreement.
17. Deliver what you promise or do not promise it.
18. Remember that even the trivial may be important.
19. Try to resolve each situation; acknowledge that you may not be able to resolve every situation. (Greenstone, 2005).
20. Remember the Bell, the Book and the Candle: The Bell could be the bells and whistles that may go off in your mind and head suggesting that the decision you are about to make is flawed. The Book represents the attendant relevant legalities of your anticipated act. The Candle reminds us to ask whether our decision, if made, will stand scrutiny in the light of day.

CONCLUDING REMARKS

Reasoned deliberation furthers the cause of a full, good, and noble existence. This is the basis of the ethics for which all of us strive. The specifics may vary. The goal and outcomes will be closely related to how we go about evaluating them. The same specifics, goals and outcomes may be viewed differently by the parties to the deliberation. What emerges can and should be the ethical approach for which we all seek. The process is not easy, but it is essential if we are to tackle the very difficult positions in which each of us may find ourselves from time to time. Nothing here discourages or diminishes the place of morality or legality. These are part of who we are. What this does encourage is a way of handling these issues effectively.

REFERENCES AND BIBLIOGRAPHY

Evarts, W. R., Greenstone, J. L., Kirkpatrick, G., & Leviton, S. (1984). *Winning through accommodation: The mediator's handbook*. Kendall-Hunt.

Greenstone, J. L., & Leviton, S. (2011). *Elements of crisis intervention: Crises and how to respond to them* (3rd ed.). Brooks/Cole, Thomson Learning.

Greenstone, J. L. (2005). *The elements of police hostage and crisis negotiations: Critical incidents and how to respond to them*. The Haworth Press.

Greenstone, J. L. (2008). *The elements of disaster psychology: Managing psychosocial trauma—An integrated approach to force protection and acute care*. Charles C. Thomas.

Greenstone, J. L. (2009, Winter). The ethics of publishing police hostage and barricade situations: Protecting identities. *Sense or Nonsense: Peer to Peer, 1*(4), 6–7.

Groopman, J. (2008). *How doctors think*. Houghton Mifflin.

Hartsell, T. L., Jr., & Bernstein, B. E. (2008). *The portable ethicist for mental health professionals, with HIPPA update: A complete guide to responsible practice*. John Wiley.

IACP. (2012). *Ethics survey*. International Association of Chiefs of Police.

Isch, D. (2005). The role of ethics in healthcare decision-making. Harris Methodist Hospital, Ethics Department.

Leviton, S., & Greenstone, J. L. (1997). *Elements of mediation*. Brooks/Cole.

Chapter Takeaways

Personal Notes

Eating under Stress and Trauma: Its Need at Post-Stress Meetings

James L. Greenstone, Ed.D., J.D., DABECI

The Inquiry

"An off-duty suicide occurred last night. This was a recent officer assigned to East Division. He was not known well by me. What foods, if any, should we have at meetings with the affected officer's team, or class, or other groups? What kind of food should it be or not be?"(Anonymous, personal communication, January 8, 2019)

The Response

Having food and drink at meetings that are held post traumatic incidents pose several issues. At such meetings, or debriefings, it is not unusual for participants to bring or to have water available to them. The question of other types of drinks and the availability of foodstuffs needs to be carefully considered. Not to do so adds to these important meetings the risk of increasing the stress of the participants while trying to reduce it. Additionally, participants focus on food, in and of itself, may take away from the stress management process for which these meetings may be held, that is, "If I am eating, I may not be paying attention to the stress reduction process or to the needs and responses of others in the group." Unless there is an overriding need to provide food at these meetings, perhaps it would be better not to introduce this variable. Individual situations will dictate the response to this need, should it exist. (Greenstone, 2000, 2008, 2013, 2015; Greenstone & Leviton, 2010).

FOODS TO AVOID

- Candy Bars—These may aggravate stress levels due to the elevation of cortisol levels in the body.
- Coffee—A stress elevator. Use herbal tea instead.
- Red Meat—Increases dopamine in the body. Use fresh fruits and vegetables.
- French Fries—May give immediate energy but leave you without later. Don't make it a meal.
- Energy Drinks—May cause caffeine jitters and a sugar crash.
- Alcohol—Stimulates the body's natural stress response.
- Chips and Snack Crackers—These are of little nutritional value and will not reduce stress.
- High Fat Dairy—Cream, high fat milk and cheeses are harsh on the digestive system and can disrupt sleep.
- Spicy Foods—Aggravates the digestive system. Under stress we often feel gaseous, abdominal pain and bloating.
- Vegetable Oil and Margarine—If they contain trans-fats, memory may be affected and there may be an increase in stress levels. (Lockhart, 2014)

SAFER FOODS UNDER THESE CONDITIONS

- Plain water
- Fresh fruits and vegetables
- Eggs
- Foods containing Vitamin E such as avocados, Almonds
- Green tea
- Plain Greek yogurt
- Whole grain carbohydrates such as brown rice, whole wheat pasta and whole wheat bread
- Sources of fatty acids such as Omega-3, flaxseed, walnuts, salmon, anchovies, and sardines (Findlay, 2016)
- Oysters
- Oatmeal
- Dark chocolate. Do not confuse with milk chocolate
- Orange juice. Vitamin C
- Asparagus
- Pistachios (Lockhart, 2018)

See Figure 12.1, The Food Crisis Cube.

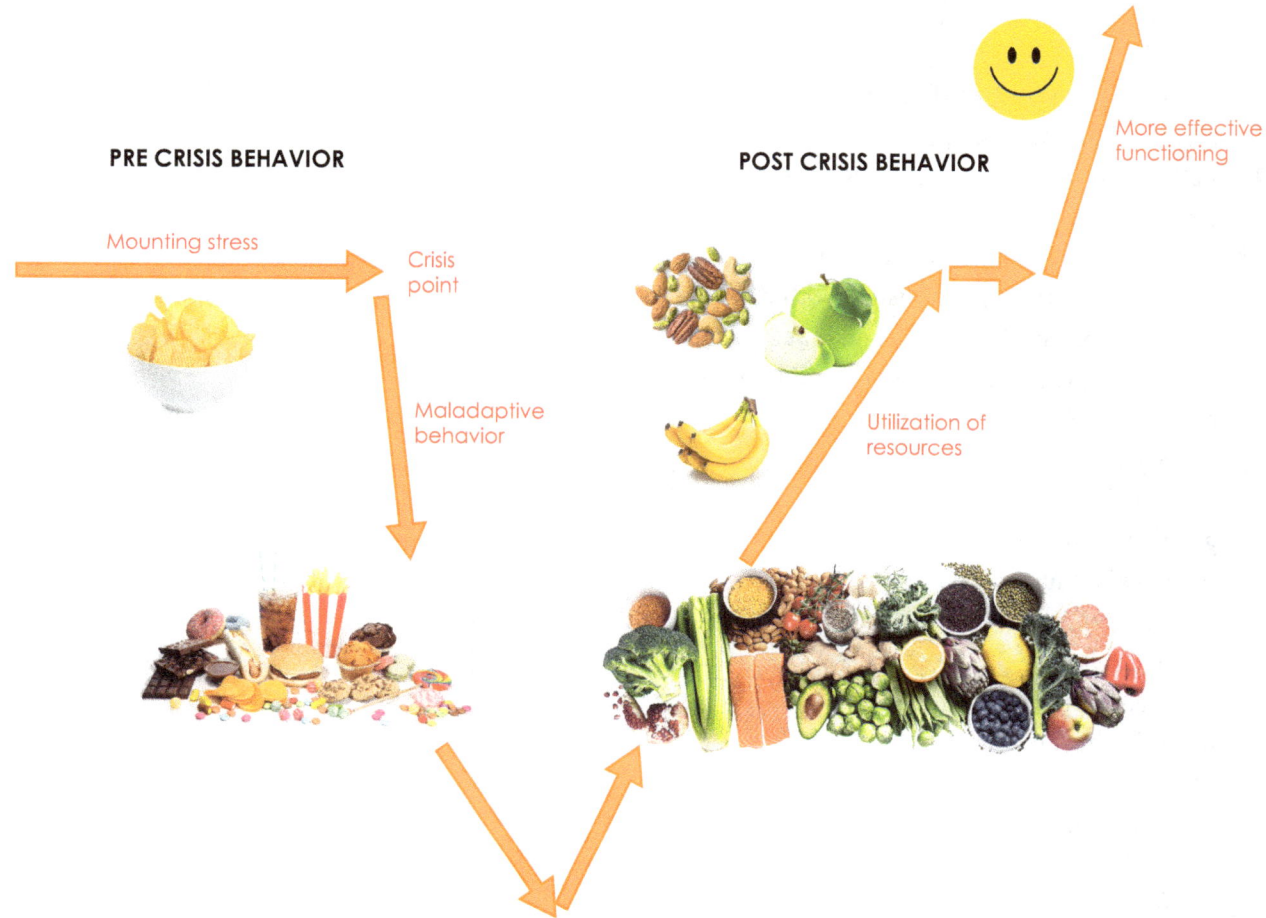

FIGURE 12.1. THE FOOD CRISIS CUBE

Diagram Source: James L. Greenstone. Images: chips © New Africa/Shutterstock.com, junk food © beats1/Shutterstock.com, healthy food © Tatjana Baibakova/Shutterstock.com, bananas © bergamont/Shutterstock.com, nuts © AmyLv/Shutterstock.com, apple © grey_and/Shutterstock.com, smiley face © Yulia Glam/Shutterstock.com.

CONSIDER

- Not serving any food during the meetings. Water may be a necessity; food is not.
- The absence of foodstuffs may allow the meeting participants to participate fully in the discussions that are held.
- The absence of food may also remove an impediment to involving oneself in the discussions. that is, "If I am eating, I don't have to say anything." Even if multitasking was possible, trying to do several activities at the same time under these conditions may prove unsuccessful and therefore not beneficial to those most needing assistance.

HIGH STRESS OR TENSE SITUATIONS

Recommendations for handling individual stress in these and other related situations should include:
1. Sleep, or at least regular periods of rest.
2. Eating regular meals even though there is no immediate hunger present. The lack of hunger is not unusual under stressful situations.
3. Physical activities that might include:
    a. Activities that are consistent with current level of fitness
    b. Usual physical exercises and other related activities (Greenstone, 1993)
    c. Moving experiences. Get up and move around even if you don't feel like it
    d. Meditation and breathing activities
    e. Pilates
    f. Tai Chi
    g. Communing with nature
    h. Kickboxing
    i. Martial Arts
    j. Team Sports
    k. Gardening
    l. Running at your level
    m. Walking at your level
    n. Dancing
    o. Qi Gong

Conclusions

Food or no food? That is the question. Of course, the answer must always be an individual one that is carefully considered in light of facts available and resources at hand. From the standpoint of this author, no food is really needed or helpful in these situations. Water is the exception; either provided to or brought by the participants. Just plain water. Other waters should be left at the door to be retrieved later by its owner.

Have a reason for providing food that is consistent with your purpose in the meetings or debriefings. Making such provisions because someone voiced the idea or opined on the usefulness of food, should not be the deciding factors. If the specific situation dictates, and it is decided that having food would serve an important purpose, limit what is provided. Fresh fruits and vegetables are usually a good plan as well as other possibilities listed earlier. Also listed earlier are those foods to avoid. If other choices are made, consider them carefully. Find out the effect of those foods that you may decide to serve.

And finally, how should the food be distributed to the participants? Let each serve themselves rather than being served by another. This is similar to the practice of making tissue paper available nearby for those who are crying. Let them get what they need when they need it. This type of individual self-help under these conditions reinforces the abilities of people to handle their own lives effectively and to do what is necessary on their own. A minor point, but an important lesson (Greenstone, 2015; Greenstone, Dunn, & Leviton, 1994).

REFERENCES

Findlay, J. (2016). Foods that melt away panic and reduce stress. *HealthPrep.* www.healthprep.com

Greenstone, J. L. (1993). *Critical incident stress debriefing and crisis management.* Texas Department of Health.

Greenstone, J. L. (2000, March/April). Peer support in a municipal police department. *The Forensic Examiner, 5*(10), 1–4.

Greenstone, J. L. (2008). *The elements of disaster psychology: Managing psychosocial trauma—An integrated approach to force protection and acute care.* Charles C. Thomas.

Greenstone, J. L. (2013, February). Negotiator resiliency. *The Negotiator Magazine, 4*(1), 5. www.negotiator-magazine.com

Greenstone, J. L. (2015). *Emotional first aid: Field guide to crisis intervention and psychological survival.* Whole Person Associates.

Greenstone, J. L., & Leviton, S. C. (2010). *Elements of crisis intervention: Crises and how to respond to them* (International edition of 3rd ed.). Broadman and Holman.

Greenstone, J. L., Dunn, J. M., & Leviton, S. C. (1994). Promotion of mental health for police: The departmental peer counselling programme. In D. R. Trent & C. A. Reed (Eds.), *Promotion of mental health* (Vol. 4, pp. 319–340). Avebury, Ashgate Publishing.

Lockhart, E. (2014). Ten worst foods to eat when you are stressed. *Activebeat.* www.activebeat.com

Lockhart, E. (2018). Seven surprising foods that fight stress. *Activebeat.* www.activebeat.com

Chapter Takeaways

_____
_____
_____
_____
_____
_____
_____

Personal Notes

_____
_____
_____
_____
_____
_____
_____

CONCLUDING REMARKS

The areas covered are broad and cover select areas. However, all are related to disaster response and the effectiveness with which we respond. Such an important response-ability requires the knowledge of multiple areas. It also requires that we understand how each of these areas are interrelated and must be studied in tandem. The response areas covered here are directly interrelated even though the topics themselves seem diverse. Knowing the intervention procedures for intervening in the personal crisis of a disaster victim is closely connected to understanding the  legal ground on which one stands when doing so effectively. It also requires an in-depth understanding of communication skills and conflict resolution modalities. It is carefully acknowledged here that the other facets of disaster understanding, and assistance are as important as the three discussed herein. It must also be understood that the three discussed here must be integrated with the other aspects that are too broad for this particular discussion.

ABOUT THE AUTHORS

Dr. Greenstone is a psychotherapist, mediator, arbitrator, negotiator, author, professor, police officer and police behavioral health specialist. He is well known as a police hostage negotiator and trainer. Formerly, he served as the director of psychological services for the Fort Worth, Texas Police Department and as the operational police behavioral health specialist for the Hostage and Crisis Negotiation Team. He is the author of *The Elements of Police Hostage and Crisis Negotiations: Critical Incidents and How to Respond to Them*, The Haworth Press, Inc., 2005 (www.HaworthPress.com), *The Elements of Disaster Psychology: Managing Psychosocial Trauma* was published in 2007 by Charles C. Thomas, Publishers (http://www.ccthomas.com/), and *The Elements of Crisis Intervention* (3rd edition) that was published in 2010. He is the editor-in-chief emeritus of the *Journal of Police Crisis Negotiations* and served on the governing council of the Committee on Publication Ethics. He was a member of the Ethics Consultation Committee, Police Psychological Services Section, International Association of Chiefs of Police, and the Ethics Consortium of the Tarrant County Medical Association and has taught ethics at Capella University. Additionally, he is a diplomate of the Society for Police and Criminal Psychology. Currently, he is professor of disaster and emergency management, The Kiran C. Patel College of Osteopathic Medicine, Nova Southeastern University.

Dr. Leviton is a crisis management specialist, mediator, and author. She was one of the first mediators and trainers for the Dispute Mediation Service of Dallas. She was an early practitioner member of the Academy of Family Mediators and served as one of the organization's training supervisors. Formerly, she served as an adjunct professor of law at the Texas Wesleyan University School of Law. She practiced as an individual and family psychotherapist. She has published books, articles, training manuals, and editorials in the fields of crisis management, dispute resolution, stress management, and crisis communications.

Weldon Walles is an honorably retired Texas Master Peace officer who served with the Fort Worth police department for 25 years. During his career, he served as a patrol officer, background investigator, and for 19 of those years as a crime scene analyst. Certifications held during his career include crime scene analyst as certified through International Association for Identification and special investigator certification through the Texas Commission on Law Enforcement. He currently consults on crime scene investigation and police procedures for criminal defense attorneys and acts as a creative consultant for writers and filmmakers.

Bethany Shaw earned her bachelor's degree in homeland security from the University of New Hampshire in 2018 and her master's degree in disaster and emergency management from Nova Southeastern University in 2020. She is a member of various organizations and honor societies and has received academic awards for her scholastic efforts. Working within Austin, Texas Independent School District Police Department as the emergency management coordinator, her work focuses on preparedness, mitigation, response, and recovery efforts throughout the community. She is passionate about those she serves and is fortunate to work in a career she enjoys! Currently residing in Austin, Texas, with her husband and dog Mr. Nibbles, she is supported by her two sons, her sister, her father and stepmother, her daughter-in-law, and extended family and friends in the Northeast. She is an avid hiker and enjoys traveling at every opportunity she gets.

Printed in the USA
CPSIA information can be obtained
at www.ICGtesting.com
JSHW060843240124
55496JS00003B/5